Black Faith
and
Public Talk

Black Faith
and
Public Talk

Critical Essays on James H. Cone's
Black Theology and Black Power

Dwight N. Hopkins

editor

ORBIS BOOKS

Maryknoll, New York 10545

Queries regarding rights and permissions should be addressed to: Orbis Books, P. O. Box 308, Maryknoll, New York 10545-0308.

Published by Orbis Books, Maryknoll, NY 10545-0308

Manufactured in the United States of America

Library of Congress Cataloging-in-Publication Data

Black faith and public talk : critical essays on James H. Cone's Black theology and
    black power / Dwight N. Hopkins, editor.
        p. cm.
    Includes bibliographical references.
    ISBN 1-57075-290-7 (pbk.)
      1. Cone, James H. Black theology and black power.   2. Race relations—
Religious aspects—Christianity.   3. Black power—Religious aspects—Christianity.
4. Black theology.   5. Black power.   I. Hopkins, Dwight N.
BT734.2.C623B57   1999
230'.089'96073—dc21   99-37871
                                                              CIP

To James H. Cone, for starting it all

Contents

Acknowledgments   ix

Introduction: Black Faith and Public Talk   1
  Dwight N. Hopkins

Part I
Black Faith and Religious Themes

1. Black Theology and Human Identity   11
  Cornel West

2. The Black Church and Religious Freedom   20
  Stephen L. Carter

3. African American Thought: The Discovery of Fragments   29
  David Tracy

Part II
Black Faith and Prophetic Faith Communities

4. Black Theology on Theological Education   41
  Dwight N. Hopkins

5. Racism and the Church:
  An Inquiry into the Contradictions between Experience, Doctrine, and
  Theological Theory   53
  Jamie T. Phelps

6. Black Leadership, Faith, and the Struggle for Freedom   77
  Manning Marable

7. Black Theology and the Parish Ministry   89
  J. Alfred Smith, Sr.

8. An Underground Theology   96
  Jeremiah A. Wright, Jr.

Part III
Black Faith and Women

9. Searching for Paradise in a World of Theme Parks   105
  Emilie M. Townes

10. Servanthood Revisited:
Womanist Explorations of Servanthood Theology   126
   Jacquelyn Grant

11. Disrupted/Disruptive Movements:
Black Theology and Black Power 1969/1999   138
   Renée Leslie Hill

12. Reimagining Public Discourse   150
   Rebecca S. Chopp

Part IV
Black Faith and the Third World

13. Liberation Theology and African Women's Theologies   167
   Rosemary Radford Ruether

14. Emancipatory Christianity   178
   Linda E. Thomas

15. Black Latin American Theology:
A New Way to Sense, to Feel, and to Speak of God   190
   Silvia Regina de Lima Silva

Part V
Black Faith, James H. Cone, and the Future of Black Theology

16. Race and Civil Society: A Democratic Conversation   205
   Jean Bethke Elshtain and Christopher Beem

17. Comparing the Public Theologies of James H. Cone
and Martin Luther King, Jr.   218
   Peter J. Paris

18. Black Theology at the Turn of the Century:
Some Unmet Needs and Challenges   232
   Gayraud S. Wilmore

19. Looking Back, Going Forward:
Black Theology as Public Theology   246
   James H. Cone

Contributors   261

Acknowledgments

The initial core of nine essays for this volume resulted from a conference called "Black Theology as Public Discourse: From Retrospect to Prospect." Held April 2-5, 1998, the national gathering anticipated the thirtieth anniversary of publication of James H. Cone's *Black Theology and Black Power*.

I would like to thank the primary conference sponsors: the University of Chicago Divinity School (especially Dean W. Clark Gilpin), the Martin E. Marty Center (at the Divinity School), the Public Religion Project (especially Martin E. Marty), and the Center for the Study of Race, Politics and Culture (especially Michael Dawson, the Center's chair at the University of Chicago). The Aims of Religion Address, delivered by James H. Cone on the third day of the conference, was sponsored by the University of Chicago Campus Ministries and the University of Chicago Rockefeller Memorial Chapel (Dean Alison Boden and Associate Dean Samuel Speers). I also extend recognition and thanks to Tim Child (the former Associate Dean, External Relations at the Divinity School), Sandra Peppers (Senior Administrator to the Dean of the Divinity School), my research assistants, Kazi Joshua and Kurt Buhring, and Marsha Peeler, secretary. My wife, Professor Linda E. Thomas, aided in ongoing conversations and conceptualizations with me. From the very beginning, Robert Ellsberg (editor-in-chief, Orbis Books) was very eager and supportive of this project for publication; and Susan Perry was patient, persistent, professional, and productive in her editing.

Introduction
Black Faith and Public Talk

DWIGHT N. HOPKINS

The black community has a long tradition of practicing faith as a total way of life. It has shown that faith is not limited to certain areas of being human and then absent in others. In fact, faith covers all of reality, secular and sacred. Such a way of living includes a belief that each individual and the community have a vocation and a responsibility to fulfill the maximum potential possible. Within the context of the community, specifically the black church, faith touches on every aspect of living. This has been the case in indigenous African societies before white Christians arrived from Europe. And this has been the case since the days of slavery in America when the secret, underground churches of enslaved Africans and African Americans developed a belief in Christianity that sustained them in all that they did. Today, likewise, we find black churches and related forms of faith institutions operating on the spiritual, economic, political, and cultural levels. In a word, black faith is public talk; it covers the inner individual pains and rejoicing as well as the challenges and victories of the broader society.

The black church, as a public faith institution, has developed rituals of survival and liberation which enhance the individual's drive toward attaining maximum potential. Within worship, especially, the church is noted for its uplifting preaching, singing, shouting, dancing, and recognition of individual achievements and pain. But this healing of the individual soul has more and wider implications than the mere maintenance of a person's vision on life after death. Only a superficial understanding would prioritize a compensatory role as the primary purpose of the church. What has to be grasped is that the rituals of individual healing and celebration serve to recharge the worshipers' energy to deal with the rigors and racism of "a cruel, cruel world" from Monday through Saturday. Thus the church offers an armor of endurance, perseverance, self-esteem, and hope to allow people "to get over" with soulful dignity and psychic survival "for another day's journey."

Yet the church does not stop at enabling personal maximization of individual potential. In addition, it has functioned as the practical organizing center of all major aspects of group life. The church constructs housing; provides ministries

1

for single adults and married couples; treats addictions (e.g., alcoholism, substance abuse, and domestic violence); implements female and male youth programs (e.g., scouts and rite of passage programs); combats drugs and perverse sex industries in the community; wages campaigns against police brutality; supplies lawyers, doctors, and accountants; calls political candidates and office-holders to stand before the congregation for accountability; organizes voter education and voter registration efforts; takes high school students on national black college tours; develops summer camp facilities; brings remedial education and computer technology to students; provides jobs and connects people to industries and corporations; facilitates reconciliation among black folk, other people of color, and the white community; offers justice and forgiveness for wrong-doers regardless of race or community; extends its hand and time to work with diverse communities of faith; participates in national electoral politics; wages economic boycotts against racist corporations and businesses; leads local and national demonstrations, marches, and protests; trains and provides leaders for the broader civic society; establishes firm links between countries in Africa and the Caribbean; builds health and family life centers; and engages in public policy formation and implementation. Truly, black faith is public talk about God and the human struggle for a holistic salvation, liberation, and the practice of freedom.

This volume of *Black Faith and Public Talk* celebrates such accomplishments and analyzes critically what this public faith believes, says, and does. It draws on a diverse spectrum of views contributed by experts in their own fields of study and practice. Within this vast array of challenging voices, we find the theme of black faith and public talk questioned and examined from a variety of perspectives. Among others, the following queries are brought to bear on the central theme: what is the relation between black faith and public talk to— issues of human identity; religion and the law; fragmentation of oppressive, dominating belief systems; white feminist God-talk; women in Africa, Asia, and Latin America; the practical prophetic and pastoral concerns of the black church; black Catholic life; self-critical reflection and current challenges of the black church and black theology; political economy and radical social transformation; new paradigms for theological education; black gay/lesbian rights in relation to black theology; the connection between black theology and Martin Luther King, Jr.; womanist theology and ethics as public thought and practice; black women's theology in the United States and South Africa; and the idea of Christian "servanthood" from a womanist perspective.

However, every text has a context. That is to say, what prompts this engaging and comprehensive volume on *Black Faith and Public Talk* was a conference held at the University of Chicago, the Divinity School.[1] In April 1998, the Divinity School took the lead in hosting a three-day meeting entitled "Black Theology as Public Discourse." Sponsored by the Martin E. Marty Center (of the University of Chicago Divinity School) and cosponsored by the Public Religion Project, the Center for the Study of Race, Politics, and Culture (at the University of Chicago), the University of Chicago Campus Ministries, and the Rockefeller Memorial Chapel at the University of Chicago, the conference took place in anticipation of the thirtieth anniversary of James H. Cone's *Black Theology and Black Power,* published in 1969.[2] After a successful and well-attended gathering, James H. Cone concluded the conference by delivering the prestigious Aims of Religion address in the Rockefeller Memorial Chapel on April 4th, the thirtieth anniversary of Martin Luther King, Jr.'s assassination. Indeed, Cone's provocative remarks provided a capstone to the theme of black faith as public talk. Drawing on his experience as distinguished professor of systematic theology, a member of a historic black church, and his insightful reading of the contemporary "signs of the times" (and standing within the black church tradition of faith as public discourse and practice), Cone spoke to various publics. He offered a critical and challenging word to all churches, disparate educational institutions, and the broader American civil society.

Indeed, Cone's talk encompassed the interdisciplinary and multiple publics of society, church, and academy which undergirded the flow of the entire conference. For instance, both the conference preparations and the event itself reflected a way of doing black theology or engaging black faith and public talk. In preparation for the conference, a planning group of diverse disciplines, faculty, administrators, students, and community people worked together on this major project. Moreover, a group of fifty African American high school students (along with their teachers) read various works of black theology for three months prior to the conference. Similarly, various graduate study groups and public forums were held at the University of Chicago and at different graduate schools in the surrounding area in anticipation of the gathering. Consequently, the close reading of divergent voices in black theology, prior to the conference, served as a process of building toward the conference. Another significant development was the gathering (one day before the conference) of national black pastors and black leaders from various Protestant denominations and the Roman Catholic Church. Sponsored by the Public Religion Project, this meeting covered a wide range of issues facing not only the black church and the black community, but the larger American nation and, in fact, the world. This historic meeting positioned the theme of black faith and public talk in the crises and opportunities of today's global affairs.

Furthermore, those who attended the three-day conference testified to the public impact and nature of black theology and black faith. Women and men of different professions, faiths, and ideological persuasions gathered. In attendance were judges, pastors, professors, public school teachers, lay persons, administrators, the media (including a taping by CSPAN), high school and graduate students, community activists, a wide mixture of church denominations, professors who brought students from local campuses as well as those who had come from out of state, elected public officials, chaplains, nurses, representatives of the Nation of Islam, women's groups, clinical pastoral leaders, psychologists, political economists, writers, publishers, secretarial staff, and University of Chicago alumni.

The planning, process, and the conference event itself testified to the importance and ongoing significance of *Black Theology and Black Power.* In 1969, James H. Cone published this ground-breaking book, inaugurating black faith as public talk. Cone established the public nature of the black church's and black community's faith as not simply a political, cultural, economic, or sociological belief system and ritual practice. Quite the contrary, Cone put forth a critical and comprehensive argument that the public nature of black faith was primarily and essentially a theological vocation of liberation given by God. With the arrival of *Black Theology and Black Power,* black theology situated the African American faith tradition as a challenge to at least three publics: the church, the broader society, and the academy.

It was as if Cone had entered a dark bell tower, stumbled, accidentally pulled a bell rope, and awakened the entire village population. The reverberation of the bell, inadvertently pulled, not only changed the course of theology and our perception and belief in God, it also impacted the global process of doing theology. Therefore, on two accounts, Cone's first published effort created echoes both in its depth and its breadth. First, *Black Theology and Black Power* was the first book in the history of the United States to perceive and position liberation as the heart and theological center of the Christian gospel. Second, *Black Theology and Black Power* was the first book in the world written on liberation theology. In fact, Cone's first two books (e.g., *Black Theology and Black Power* and *A Black Theology of Liberation,*[3] 1970) as companion volumes preceded any other books on liberation theology from Africa, Asia, or Latin America.

When he sat down to write his book in 1968, Cone was acutely concerned with speaking truth to power in the public realm. That is why he addressed the black and white churches, the media, and those concerned with public policy making. However, he chose not to write a sociology of the black church or to offer an economic or cultural analysis. He, instead, sought a theological approach. Theology deals with what one believes and whether or not what one believes is the same as what God has called one to believe and do. To this end, he engaged the following questions: What does the gospel of Jesus Christ have to do with the struggle against white supremacy and for the liberation of black poor folk? What was the relation of Christianity to black power or the lack of it? What did it mean to be black and Christian? And, what was the linkage between the particular faith of black people and universal humanity?

During the period in which Cone was writing, America had the rare experience of confronting directly the current and future status of African Americans. Civil rights, human rights, and black power agendas were national topics of debate and decision making. Drawing on the role of the Hebrew scripture prophets and the Christian scripture role of Jesus as standing for those at the bottom of society, Cone aimed his theological undressing at both liberal and conservative Christians. The liberal white Christians, in Cone's eyes, wanted to talk about integration, nonviolence, and universal love for all of humankind. But, for Cone, this group failed to take seriously the gospel call of liberation of the oppressed; thus, what white liberals truly wanted was to maintain the structures in which they lived, which Cone characterized as monopolized white power over black life and death. Conservative white Christians openly linked the gospel with keeping black folk "in their place."

As for the black church, Cone chided it for its conservative interpretation (and, hence, misreading) of the Bible and the faith. The black church failed to take on the principalities and powers of this earth; it failed to risk all for the gospel by standing "in the gap" for the black poor and the least in society. Moreover, the black church too often imitated the white church. Consequently, the African American faith community did not draw enough on the rich sources from black history, including Africa. White theology (for example, the interpretation of Christianity as the theological support for capitalism) deeply permeated the black church.

In addition, the pioneering position of *Black Theology and Black Power* was how Cone linked black power and religion. For many at that time, it was not possible to be black and Christian. Black power advocates in the larger American society derided Christianity as "the white man's religion"; therefore, to be black was to be a non-Christian, and to be Christian was, for black power activists, to be an "Uncle Tom." For white conservatives, Christianity was a white man's religion. For white liberals, "Negroes" (using the language of that time) could be Christian as long as they modeled themselves after whites and did not challenge the structural relations between the races where whites had a monopoly on power and wealth. The Nation of Islam, given the prominent legacy of Malcolm X, offered a clear alternative to Christianity and showed what faith and blackness could mean, only if one did not become a Christian. And the mainstream black church leadership dismissed the possibility of being "black" and Christian. Because they were integrationists and considered themselves "Negroes," they felt it was impossible to be black and Christian because of their definition of "black." For them, "black" meant violence, revolution, radical changes in the status quo, criminal and uncivilized elements within the Negro community, anti-U.S. government, and secular, nonreligious people. A Negro was one who believed in Jesus Christ as a turn-the-other-cheek figure, who suffered innocently as other people beat and killed him. A "Negro" was one who upheld the U.S. Constitution and the Declaration of Independence.

Thus Cone concluded a whole new way of viewing the black freedom struggle and interpreting the good news of Jesus Christ. He embraced several sources from which he gathered his argument and drew his conclusions. He looked at the progressive parts of the black church tradition, where he found the Bible calling on enslaved African Americans to use any means necessary to fight for freedom. Similarly, he applied the thought of various black church leaders such as Henry McNeal Turner who said God was a black, and Marcus Garvey who set up his own black denomination and also perceived God as black. Cone adopted the black folk tradition of survival and resistance heard in Br'er Rabbit tales and in the blues. On the global stage, he observed the movements for national liberation in Africa and Asia. Closer to home, Cone looked at contemporary events taking place throughout the nation. From the Civil Rights and Black Power movements, he redefined the church as one that struggles in the streets against unjust laws and systems aimed at the weak in society. From these same movements, he understood black power as black poor people having the right of self-identity in their culture and self-determination in politics and redistribution of wealth. Even whites presented an obvious contradiction for Cone; he saw how white scholars and churches had always utilized religion and politics but now argued against black churches involving themselves in the politics of black power.

But most importantly and most decisively, Cone felt called by God, through his encounter with the Bible and his own personal faith experience, to see the liberation of the oppressed and the poor as the heartbeat of the biblical message and the sole definition of what it meant to be a Christian. In addition to other biblical stories, Cone saw this message in the Exodus, in the Hebrew prophets, in Mary's Magnificat, in Luke chapter four, and in Matthew chapter twenty-five. Thus the message of liberation in the Bible was the same message of liberation advanced by poor blacks in their struggle to practice total freedom. And if the white community as well as middle-class-minded churches wanted to find Jesus, then they would all have to base their ministry and their humanity on the complete spiritual, cultural, material, and political freedom of poor blacks in America. Anything short of that, for Cone, was the work of the Anti-Christ and its agents.

Cone felt called by God to redefine revelation and the presence of the Spirit among and within humanity. For him, spiritual revelation was an event within creation. It was not a hocus-pocus invisible mystery. God offered liberation and love and came to earth in the material and visible reality of humanity and creation; and, there, God took sides with the oppressed and the poor, who are the majority population. Therefore, this revelation sided with the least in society in their efforts for liberation into a new reality of communal life and control of all of God's wealth and other resources. More specifically, Jesus was God becoming human for the poor, the marginalized, and the broken-hearted. The Incarnation was concrete and not mystifying. For Cone, the poor and the marginalized were the black poor and marginalized. Because the gospel of Jesus was liberation for the poor and the disadvantaged and because poor blacks were oppressed and marginalized and desired liberation, there was therefore a need for a black theology of liberation.

At the same time, Cone opened up the connection between the particular situation of the black poor (and other poor people) on the one hand, and the vocation of black middle-class-minded Christians and whites on the other. If they all sided with Jesus in Jesus' presence in the freedom movement of the poor, then that liberation called for by the Spirit would eventually change structures and individuals. Once individuals and structures changed, then there would not be white power over black life and other poor people. Without the oppressive white power structures, and with all sharing equally in the ownership and use of God's wealth on earth (including cultural, political, and emotional power), then oppressors would no longer have the systems to oppress others. And the least in society, along with everyone else in society, could express their full potential as human beings.

It is because of *Black Theology and Black Power*, what it has meant, continues to mean, and will mean, that we offer these critical essays about black faith and public talk. As long as there remain poor black folk and a system of monopolized wealth by the extreme minority in society, there will be the need for this ground-breaking book. As long as white supremacy (even in its mutated forms), male dominance, heterosexual privilege, and other asymmetrical arrangements are the norm in society, we will need this book. As Cone wrote in his 1969 text, America belongs to all, especially the majority of the population who are not the creators or the beneficiaries of oppression. It is this note of hope, faith, inclusivity, intellectual rigor, and prophetic passion which characterizes *Black Theology and Black Power*. We hope that you will find the same here in *Black Faith and Public Talk*.

Notes

1. A couple of years before the conference, I approached W. Clark Gilpin, dean of the Divinity School, about the idea of the school hosting the conference. Special thanks are due to Dean Gilpin for his enthusiasm, vision, and practical role, along with Tim Childs (then associate dean for external relations for the Divinity School), in helping to bring an idea into reality.

2. James H. Cone, *Black Theology and Black Power* (New York: Harper & Row, 1969; Maryknoll, N.Y.: Orbis Books, 1997).

3. James H. Cone, *A Black Theology of Liberation* (Philadelphia: J.B. Lippincott Co., 1970; Maryknoll, N.Y.: Orbis Books, 1990).

Part I

Black Faith
and
Religious Themes

1

Black Theology and Human Identity

CORNEL WEST

In this essay, I intend to reflect on James H. Cone's classic of 1969, *Black Theology and Black Power*. This text changed the lives of thousands and thousands of young brothers and sisters of all colors who were wrestling with the question: what does it mean to be Christian in a turbulent time in which the vicious legacy of white supremacy was being contested, pushed back as it were? For me, this particular text in the history of American civilization raises the most fundamental question of what it means to be human. When Professor Cone raised the question of how we relate our Christian faith to the challenge of the Black Power movement, he raised a question that each and every American, each and every human, has had to come to terms with: namely, how do we conceive of ourselves as featherless, two-legged, linguistically conscious creatures? How do we conceive of ourselves who are in search of a little meaning, a little care, and a little love in the face of unavoidable and inescapable extinction of some sort?

This is very much like one of the first towering texts of modernity to wrestle with the question of what it means to be human in the face of death. I am thinking of Voltaire's *Candide* of 1759[1] which responded to the thousands of corpses (on All Saint's Day, November 1, 1755, in the city of Lisbon) that would fracture and shatter any optimistic conception of there somehow being a providence that could serve as a basis for explaining those corpses. Voltaire wrote of the second earthquake of December 21, 1755, that would shake the foundations, not just of Lisbon, but of any thin, impoverished, and truncated Enlightenment conception of progress. No, we have to look the terrors of nature in the face; we have to look the horrors of history in the face; we have to look the cruelties of fate and the furies of destiny in the face and still somehow find a way of going through and keeping on. Voltaire was wrestling with death not only as a particular event but also as process. He was wrestling with the death of any optimism in his own philosophical project. Professor Cone in *Black Theology and Black Power*, as I shall attempt to show, is wrestling with how death and

11

existential crises relate to his own particular life in terms of what it means to be a particular black man from Bearden, Arkansas, then at Adrian College (Adrian, Michigan) and, finally, wrestling with the death of Martin Luther King, Jr., on April 4, 1968.

But before we move to Cone, let us move to the second moment in modernity just to serve as some kind of historical backdrop and context. And I am thinking of none other than the work, *Of Human Freedom*[2], 1809, by the great Schelling, which presents his philosophical investigations on the essence of human freedom. This is probably the grandest text of nineteenth-century Europe, one that fundamentally confronts the palpability and reality of evil. This evil shatters any German idealistic system that thinks that somehow all that is needed is to probe into the internal dynamics of consciousness and thereby conclude that the rationality of the world can be shown and displayed. The great Heidegger said in his Freiberg[3] lectures that Schelling had shattered Hegel's logic before it was written. Why? Because of the reality of evil in the ineradicability of the nonrational, the intractability of the unfathomable, and the recalcitrance of reality, maybe even the accursedness of being, as he wrote in that frightening and poetic text. Let us recall those powerful and potent moments in Schelling's text where he said that maybe, in fact, the unruly that sits at the very center of the origins of things, the difference between existence and the ground of existence, is such that a veil of sadness pervades all nature. Deep unappeasable melancholy is shot through all of life. He was to live forty-five more years and not publish another major text. It is a small pamphlet attacking Jacoby. But he also responded to the death of his wife, Caroline. This particular event and process would overwhelm him and push him to the edge of life's abyss.

One should consider *Black Theology and Black Power* in the context of the corpses of young black folk in Newark of 1967, in Detroit of 1967, and the 329 uprisings in 257 cities between 1964 and 1969. We can imagine the young James Hal Cone saying, "I'm overwhelmed by this. What do I have to say? I either write this book or I'll go crazy." That is the kind of theology I like. Outcry. Like Aretha Franklin singing her song; she either sings it or the rocks are going to cry out. We need more intellectual work like this: work that comes from the heart and the soul and mind, the type of intellectual work that the academy does not know what to do with it.

But I would like to pause one more moment before we move to Professor Cone's work, and that, of course, is at *The Grand Inquisitor*[4] written by the great Dostoyevsky in 1879 in the face of the death of his three-year-old son, Alexi. In that section of *The Brothers Karamozov* is the prose poem that is probably the high moment of wrestling with the reality of evil in European literature. Dostoyevsky wrote of the ways elites dangle miracle and mystery and authority in the faces of the masses to pacify them, assuming that they do not have the capacity to actually bear the burden and responsibility of freedom, as terrifying and horrifying as freedom actually is. There is an indescribable moment when the Inquisitor is waiting for an answer from Jesus. Jesus approaches in silence and softly kisses the bloodless and aged lips of the Grand Inquisitor, the old man who manipulates, who represents the institutions that believe that we have neither the courage and vision to actually take on freedom nor the capacity to choose between good and evil. And what does that old man do, what does the Grand Inquisitor do? He shudders the cosmic shudder, the existential quiver, the tragic qualm.[5] This is ontological vertigo in the face of what seems to be an inexplicable reality of such darkness, the night side, the underside.

James H. Cone spoke to America and said: I know that you are an exemplary death-dodging and death-ducking culture, sentimental and melodramatic. You come up with ingenious modes of denying and evading and avoiding the underside of things. But there is some suffering here; there is some sadness and sorrow and heartache and heartbreak. There is some grief here, there are some doings and some actions here with which you must come to terms because 1968 has reached the point now where the foundation of America civilization has begun to shake.

After 212 uprisings on the night that the bullets went through the precious body of Martin Luther King, Jr., America can no longer deny the fact that either it comes to terms with the vicious legacy of white supremacy, or the curtain will fall on the precious experiment in democracy called America, just like the Civil War one hundred years earlier. In this volatile context of white supremacy silencing the Dreamer and the resulting reaction of the black community, Cone wrote: "This work . . . is written with a definite attitude, the attitude of an angry black man, disgusted with the oppression of black people in America and with the scholarly demand to be 'objective' about it. Too many people have died, and too many are on the edge of death. . . . Is it not time for theologians to get upset?"[6] What does it take to unsettle some of these paradigms that generate these fascinating and subtle formulations about God and society while there are people dying in your very midst and you do not have a word to say about it?

But in this text, Cone is dealing with not just the death of Martin, nor just the death of so many freedom fighters of all colors, though disproportionately black. He is also dealing with the death of something in him; it is the death of the "Negro" and the birth of "blackness." It is the death of a certain kind of deferential disposition to white supremacy in the hearts and minds and souls of black people themselves and the birth of a certain kind of self assertiveness—a courage to be.

There is a fascinating section in Professor Cone's book called "Black Power and Existential Absurdity."[7] It is one of my favorite treatments, and it is rarely talked about in this text. Professor Cone alludes to an essay entitled, "Beckett's Last Long Saturday: To Wait or Not To Wait?"[8] The essay is not about Good Friday or Easter, but Saturday, when God, even for Christians, is dead. I am not talking about any postresurrection Christ. I am talking about the Jesus who is dead and Easter is not yet here. I am talking about the *Waiting for Godot*,[9] the waiting for God, and how black folk have been locked into this space between a rock and a hard place. Professor Cone began his book saying, "The rebellion in the cities, far from being an expression of the inhumanity of blacks, is an affirmation of their being despite the ever-present possibility of death."[10] He continued by writing: "Black power . . . is hope in the humanity of black people."[11] For Cone, that particular affirmation of black humanity is predicated on the death in black folk of a certain conception of themselves.

What I find so fascinating about this particular text is that it is not interdisciplinary, it is dedisciplinizing. It is a frenetic and frantic text, which means it is thoroughly unconcerned about what particular discipline it fits into or how it connects one discipline to another. Professor Cone was simply trying to get out from the bowels of his existence some conception of what it means to be human so that the death he is wrestling does not have the last say. He puts it so well when he wrote: "This is a word to the oppressor, . . . not in hope that he will listen (after King's death who can hope?) but in the expectation that my own existence will be clarified."[12]

That is powerful, to me. It is existential crisis, self-examination, self-interrogation, self-clarification and, most importantly, self-justification. And I believe that it is a question all of us, including young people today, ought to ask a number of times in our lives. It is not just questioning one's self in terms of what one is doing; not just examining one's self in terms of trying to connect one's own profession or vocation to a cause, a set of principles bigger than all of us. Rather, it is one's self-justification. Why is one doing what one is doing in the face of such unjustified suffering, unnecessary social misery, and unmerited pain in the world? How do you respond to that question?

We can imagine Professor Cone teaching in Adrian College in 1968 and looking around him in America and saying, "Why am I doing what I'm doing? I tell people I'm a systematic theologian. And they say, well what does that have to do with these people out here being shot down like dogs?" And in his vision and in his courage he says, "I can find some intellectual resources, though fragmented, that allow me to still respond to the call of being a theologian and a Christian in the face of what seems to be so overwhelming."

Now granted, Professor Cone recognizes that his education had been problematic and, therefore, it had not provided him with as much support as he would like. He characterized American theological and seminary studies in the following manner:

> [M]ost American theologians are too closely tied to the American structure to respond creatively to the life situation. . . . Instead of seeking to respond to the problems which are unique to this country, most Americans look to Europe for the newest word worth theologizing about. Most graduate students in theology feel they must go to Germany or somewhere else in Europe because that is where things are happening in the area of theology. Little wonder that American theology is predominantly "footnotes on the Germans." Theology [in America] is largely an intellectual game unrelated to the issues of life and death. It is impossible to respond creatively and prophetically to the life-situational problems of society without identifying with the problems of the disinherited and

unwanted in society. Few American theologians have made that identification with poor blacks in America but have themselves contributed to the system which enslaves black people. The seminaries in America are probably the most obvious sign of the irrelevance of theology to life. Their initiative in responding to the crisis of black people in America is virtually unnoticeable.[13]

Around 1969, Professor Cone's training was such that he learned much from Barth, Brunner, and the grand Niebuhr brothers, H. Richard and Reinhold. Yet these profound thinkers still had not wrestled in any serious, sophisticated, or substantive way with the multidimensional character of the legacy of white supremacy. Hence, Professor Cone oftentimes felt himself, at that young age, disarmed, having to do his own intellectual work, his own reading, and his own dialogues with others.

There is no doubt about the impact of Professor Cone's work and also that of a whole host of other intellectuals of all colors whose works focus on the doings and sufferings not just of people of African descent, but of the vast majority of humankind: of women of all colors, sisters of all colors, of working peoples, of Africans, Asians, Arabs, Jews, and all those who have been viewed as degraded others. Things have changed since 1969, and yet we still have so far to go; hence the continuing relevance of *Black Theology and Black Power*.

At that particular time, of course, there was a fascinating dialogue going on among the so-called theothanatologists about the death of God. Cone had some fascinating formulations about that particular discipline because, of course, it is a very serious school of thought. One must take quite seriously the ways in which grand claims of the death of God in section 125 of Nietzsche's *The Gay Science*[14] and in Thomas Hardy's grand poem of 1912, "On God's Funeral"[15] force us to rethink our conception of ourselves. Professor Cone goes much further here. He says, "There's something ironical about affirming God's death in view of one's identity with a cultural structure which enslaves."[16] If the affirmation of God's death grows out of one's identity with suffering, then it is understandable, perhaps necessary. However, if it arises out of one's identity with an advancing technological secular society which ignores the reality of God and the humanity of individuals, then it appears to be the height of human pride. This is the most disturbing fact in relation to recent developments in American white theology.

Professor Cone raised a fundamental question that has pervaded the entire black freedom struggle: namely, whether there actually are enough intellectual, political, and cultural resources in American life to fully undermine the vicious legacy of white supremacy in America. I discern in this text a death of faith in the promise of American democracy. I think that this particular sensibility is one that millions of people of African descent experienced after the death of Martin Luther King, Jr. It is the question of the Honorable Elijah Muhammad, it is the question of Marcus Garvey, it is the question of Minister Louis Farrakhan. What makes us think that America has the capacity to produce a full-fledged multiracial democracy in which people of African descent are treated as kindly and equally as anybody else in every sphere of our lives? What evidence do we have? Historically speaking, we have two hundred forty-four years of enslavement, seventy-one years of Jim and Jane Crow, fifty-one years of every two and a half days with some black child or woman or man hanging on some tree like the strange fruit that Billie Holiday sang about. What makes us think that just within these last twenty-five or thirty years, the significant progress and break-throughs made can cut deep enough so that these white supremacist sensibilities, be they subtly or not so subtly expressed, would not come back in the way they did after Reconstruction? What evidence do we have? Professor Cone wrote,

> Whether the American system is beyond redemption we will have to wait and see, but we can be certain that black patience has run out, and unless white America responds positively to the theory and activity of Black Power, then a bloody, protracted civil war is inevitable. There have occa-sionally been revolutions—massive redistributions of power—without warfare. It is passionately hoped that this can be one of them. The deci-sion lies with white America and not least with white Americans who speak the name of Christ.[17]

When we look back over the years since the 1969 publication of *Black Theology and Black Power*, we hear from our dear and blessed conservative and neoconservative friends and brothers and sisters: "Brother West, why not start with all the great progress? We've got a middle class now." We do have a black middle class (or what E. Franklin Frazier called a black lumpen bour-geoisie; that is, a middle class with less wealth beneath the American middle class).[18] And it is true that progress is real. Since Martin Luther King, Jr.'s death, progress has been made, and we must not deny that. But Malcolm X reminds us that "Four hundred years the white man has had his foot-long knife in the black man's back—and now the white man starts to *wiggle* the knife out, maybe six inches! The black man's supposed to be *grateful*? Why, if the white man jerked the knife *out*, it's still going to leave a *scar!*"[19] There is a long way to go.

Professor Cone's text begins with death, it is calling for us to die daily. It reminds me a bit of what Farrakhan said at the Million Man March.[20] The *New York Times* and *Washington Post* did not print this. But he said white supremacy must die in order for America to truly live. Most Americans are not used to agreeing with Farrakhan, but I think all of us would agree; it must die. We could add that male supremacy must die, anti-Arab racism must die, anti-Semitism must die, vast economic inequality must die, homophobia must die, ecological abuse must die. But, again, it is a process not an event. It dies in part when we look deep, deep down within our hearts and souls and minds and rec-ognize that the white supremacy, male supremacy, and homophobia are in me the individual as well as in our institutions.

This is how Professor Cone ended his text. He wrote, "To be black means that your heart, your soul, your mind, and your body are where the dispossessed are. We all know that a racist structure will reject and threaten a black man in white skin as quickly as a black man in black skin. It accepts and rewards whites in black skins nearly as well as whites in white skins."[21] Now he is really moving at this point, becoming symbolic and metaphorical.

> Therefore, being reconciled to God does not mean that one's skin is phys-
> ically black. It essentially depends on the color of your heart, soul, and
> mind. Some may want to argue that persons with skins physically black
> will have a running start on others; but there seems to be enough evidence
> that though one's skin is black, the heart may be lily white. The real ques-
> tions are: Where is your identity? Where is your being? Does it lie with the
> oppressed blacks or with the white oppressors? Let us hope there are
> enough to answer this question correctly so that America will not be com-
> pelled to acknowledge a common humanity only by seeing that blood is
> always one color.[22]

This is a powerful ending to the text that goes far beyond mere polemic and jere-miad. This is the notion of wrestling with what it means to be human.

I want to end by acknowledging what I discerned to be a "blues sensibility" in Professor Cone's text. In his essay in this volume, Gayraud Wilmore suggests that *Black Theology and Black Power*, published in 1969, was immediately fol-lowed by *A Black Theology of Liberation*[23] as a companion text. That is a plau-sible point. But I would want to read this particular text of Professor Cone's over against his 1972 text, *The Spirituals and the Blues*.[24] I make this move because what I see Professor Cone attempting to do is to inject a tragic sen-sibility into American theological discourse, one that not only focuses on the sufferings of people of African descent, but also tries to get us to see the various ways in which heroic energy can be enacted despite limits, constraints, and boundaries.

In fact, that tragic sensibility will force us to shatter any sentimental or melo-dramatic conceptions of an American past or present. It will force what Henry James called this "hotel civilization" to recognize that the lights are not on all the time, and that sunshine is unintelligible without the night. Do we have a deep enough sense of history with a tragic sensibility? Do we have enough com-passion out there that builds on this sense of history with tragic sensibility? Do we have enough courage and vision to confront our mortality so that we are willing to live and die for something bigger than we are?

I end with one example. In January 1998, President Bill Clinton informed the nation that it was good times for America. In light of what he has written, Professor Cone would respond, "Good times for whom?" In fact, today we face a new moment of triumphalism with new idols like markets and privatizing forces, accompanied by new forms of mendacity, such as using stock market records and balanced budgets as benchmarks of good times rather than the quality of lives lived for the least in society. Perhaps good times should be gauged by the depth of spirituality needed to keep keeping on in the midst of material poverty, *and also* in the spiritual poverty of brothers and sisters disproportionately white in disproportionately vanilla suburbs. These sisters and brothers are dealing with existential emptiness and spiritual malnutrition, because they have not received enough care and nurture and love along with all their money and prosperity.

Furthermore, what kind of good times can this be when suicide rates are increasing among young people? Twenty-one percent of all children live in poverty; 52 percent of young brown brothers and sisters live in poverty; and 51 percent of black children live in utter poverty in the richest nation in the history of the world; and we hear talk about good times! I suggest that the prophetic voice of Professor Cone would say to his fellow citizen Bill Clinton: "With 1 percent of the population owning 30 percent of the wealth and 80 percent of fellow citizens wrestling with long-term tendencies of wage stagnation since 1973, what good times do you have in mind?" Though no longer legalized, *de facto* segregation in American life is still more radically prevalent today in terms of where we live, with whom we socialize, and to which churches and mosques and synagogues we go.

Have we come a long way? Indeed yes. Yet the same sugar-coated language that accents the superfluities and superficialities of our day must be pierced to deal with the harsh realities. It is not just globalization as the context, but it is globalization with choices being made, such as managerial greed at the workplace, so that downsizing goes hand in hand not only with higher profits but also with higher salaries and benefits for management. That is not a natural process; that is an intentional political choice being made.

Today, we need to continue to listen to Professor Cone's prophetic voice that links these issues of race to those of class and gender. And this is not politically correct chit-chat. It has everything to do with the future of American democracy. It has everything to do with the calling of a particular kind of thinker — a thinker who loves enough to attempt to tell the truth about himself as he tells the truth about others. Professor Cone ends *Black Theology and Black Power* on a note of hope, within the best of the black freedom struggle tradition. It is a blood-drenched hope. It is no sunshine optimism, but a blood-drenched hope. We look in prisons today, dilapidated housing, decrepit school systems in cities, not enough jobs with a living wage, inadequate health care, unavailable child care, and we see blood-drenched hope.

And yet, in the midst of it all, Jesus opens His arms and says, "Whosoever will, let him or her come," if one is willing to be metaphorically blackenized. This has nothing to do solely with skin pigmentation. Very much like Keats's conception of identity, Professor Cone has asked us to dip our intelligence into the world of pain and trouble in order to emerge with a response to the fundamental question: energy or despair, courage or complacency, love or might? Professor Cone says quite explicitly that it is all about energy, it is all about courage and, in the end, it is all about love and justice.

I thank you Professor Cone and all of humanity thanks you for the work that you have done, the life that you have lived, and the example that you have set for young brothers and sisters of all colors. We are all trying to wrestle with how one responds intellectually, existentially, and politically to unjustified suffering as we are trapped in space and time. Yet, at the same time, we have the wonderful gift of grace that allows us to attempt to be free in our hearts and minds and souls to engage in the truth telling and soul searching and witness bearing that represent the highest heights of the human spirit. James Hal Cone, like me, remains part of the Christian tradition, in all of our audacity, in all of our humility. Why? Because we are still convinced that Jesus of Nazareth has something to do with that courage to be and the courage to love and the courage to fight for justice in the midst of such intolerable and overwhelming circumstances and conditions.

Notes

1. *Candide: A Bilingual Edition*, trans. Peter Gay (New York: St. Martin's Press, 1963).

2. Trans. Joan Stambaugh (Athens: Ohio University Press, 1985).

3. *"Heidegger uber Logik als Frage nach der Sprache"* (Summer semester 1934).

4. In *The Brothers Karamazov*, trans. Constance Garnett (London: Penguin Books, first printing 1958, 41st edition 1999), 239-57.

5. Ibid., 255.

6. *Black Theology and Black Power: Twentieth Anniversary Edition* (New York: Harper and Row, 1989; reprint of the 1969 original), 2-3.

7. Ibid., 8-12.

8. By W. R. Mueller and Josephine Jacobsen, in *Man in Modern Theatre*, ed. Nathan Scott, Jr. (Richmond: John Knox Press, 1965), 77.

9. Samuel Beckett (New York: Grove Press, 1956).

10. Cone, *Black Theology and Black Power*, 7.

11. Ibid., 28-29.

12. Cone, *Black Theology and Black Power*, 3.

13. Ibid., 85.

14. Trans. Walter Kaufmann (New York: Random House, 1974), 181-82.

15. In *The Complete Poetical Works of Thomas Hardy, Volume II*, ed. Samuel Hynes (Oxford: Clarendon Press, 1984), 34-37.

16. Cone, *Black Theology and Black Power*, 98-99.

17. Ibid., 143.

18. E. Franklin Frazier, *Black Bourgeoisie* (New York: Free Press, 1965).

19. *The Autobiography of Malcolm X: As Told to Alex Haley* (New York: Ballantine Books, 1992), 311.

20. October 16, 1995, in Washington, D.C.

21. Cone, *Black Theology and Black Power*, 151.

22. Ibid., 151-52.

23. James H. Cone, *A Black Theology of Liberation* (Maryknoll, N.Y.: Orbis Books, 1990; reprint of the original 1970 edition).

24. James H. Cone, *The Spirituals and the Blues* (Maryknoll, N.Y.: Orbis Books, 1991; reprint of the original 1972 edition).

2

The Black Church and Religious Freedom

STEPHEN L. CARTER

For all of the importance of black theology, both as constitutive in the black community and also as an influential factor in the construction of the larger society, it can lose its meaning if not accompanied by a robust understanding of and protection for religious freedom. What is interesting is that, of course, the black community in America really was born in the absence of religious freedom. First there was the concerted, although not completely successful, effort to destroy the African religious traditions that the slaves tried to preserve. Then there were the prohibitions, which were adopted across the South, on preaching even the Christian gospel to slaves. However, negative proscriptions did not prevent blacks from grasping the power of the biblical message. Indeed, such potential in the gospel was made manifest in the rebellions led by Denmark Vesey and Nat Turner, both ministers of the gospel. Therefore, when we think about the problem of religious freedom, we tend not to think about it as a problem with a special connection to the black community and the black church. However, I think the connection is very close and, in fact, of crucial importance.

One of the understandings I share with many liberation theologians is the understanding of the tremendous importance of preserving religious communities not only as centers of difference, that is, places where one grasps the meaning of the world as different from what you find in the dominant culture, but even more so as centers of resistance. That is, not simply places which proclaim "we don't believe what the rest of you believe," but places that proclaim "we are willing and ready to sacrifice, to lose something material for the sake of that difference in which we believe." One of the tragedies of American history has been that whatever particular part of the culture has been dominant has always worked hard to domesticate or to destroy whatever religions seem to be turning into genuine communities of resistance. This, indeed, is a problem that the black churches always faced and face today. Even though sometimes the destruction is through inadvertence or ignorance, it is also sometimes a matter of will.

For instance, a few years ago I was on a panel with a gentleman who had been the pastor for many years of one of the largest inner-city black churches in the state of Connecticut. He described to me a meeting of ministers of several large inner-city black churches at which they discussed the continuous litigation attempting to strip the Roman Catholic bishops of their tax-exempt status. The plaintiffs in the suit claimed that the bishops were violating the tax code by engaging in either lobbying or, more importantly, in favoring or opposing political candidates. Most people do not even know such litigation is taking place. Furthermore, no one seriously believes that any court will try to take away the tax-exempt status of the Roman Catholic bishops. But that is not the real point of the story. The reason the ministers had this meeting was because they were terrified. They voiced the following concern: if, because of their political advocacy, the Roman Catholic bishops were to lose their tax-exempt status, what ramifications would this have for the various black denominations and their political involvement?

These black ministers' concern was that the people who were suing the Roman Catholic bishops did not appreciate a crucial difference between political activity in black communities and political activity in white communities. Moreover, these black clergy believed white people have a model of how civil society works where many diverse institutions coexist with different functions. Consequently, it is not that important if one says, churches cannot engage in politics, because many other institutions perform such activity in civil society. The problem, argued the ministers, is that in the inner city, one does not discover that model. On the contrary, the only institution of civil society able to facilitate political activity is the church. There, if one does not do political organizing in the churches, one does not do political organizing at all.

This anecdote illustrating the contrasting roles of political organizing in distinct communities indicates the larger concern regarding the law of religious freedom. The law of religious freedom, in America, often falls on the religions not only of the black community, but also of people of color generally, with a harshness, with a force, and with an edge which often does not strike communities of other kinds. This is important to us because of the need to preserve our religious traditions and because of the need to preserve the idea of religion as a center of resistance. The following example will serve to make the point concerning the weight of religious freedom or, rather, of the failure to protect religious freedom.

In 1988, the U.S. Supreme Court decided a legal matter called the Lyng case (Lyng v. Northwest Indian Cemetery Protective Association; Case 485U.S.439). In this instance, the U.S. Forest Service, in its wisdom, decided to allow someone to cut down a national forest. The party granted this permission planned to cut down the forest and, in addition, to build a road through the area in order to transport the trees down to a mill. This would have been fine I suppose, depending on how one feels about trees, except for the fact that there were three Indian tribes for whom this was sacred ground. When I say sacred ground, I do not mean sacred in the sense in which Christians tend to think of sacred spaces; that is, something that has been consecrated and, if destroyed, something else can be consecrated in its place. What I mean by sacred is that the Indians' religious traditions were tied to the keeping of this land in its pristine form. Indeed, as some of them claimed in their later lawsuit, their religious traditions *were* the land, in the sense that if the trees were cut and the road were built, their religion would cease to exist.

Therefore, the tribes had the quaint idea that the Federal government could not cause a religion to cease to exist. So they challenged the Forest Service's decision. And when they failed to get relief, they, in the great American tradition, brought a lawsuit, claiming their first-amendment rights were being violated. In due course, the lawsuit reached the Supreme Court and, in due course, they lost. The court informed the tribes that this decision by the Forest Service had to be challenged, if at all, through the democratic process and not through the judicial process. Of course, the tribes' whole point was that they had tried the democratic process and it did not work. Furthermore, the court went on to say, in a version of language it would repeat again and again in other cases, how the government simply could not exist if it had to meet the religious needs of all of its citizens. Now this, of course, had the tribes' argument backwards.

The tribes, in the great conservative tradition, wanted government to get out of their way and let them meet their own religious needs. But the court almost willfully misunderstood this. The court's point, I think, pursued the following logic: it is perfectly all right for the government to make it hard or impossible for you to practice your religion as long as you cannot prove that they did it because of hostility to your religion. As long as government officials can rationalize their actions based on inadvertence, carelessness, ignorance, or a just studied indifference, they can proceed and do it. Most interestingly, there are a vast number of similar cases. In most of them, the plaintiff loses; and disproportionately in those cases, the plaintiffs, like the Indian tribes, are members of "outsider" religions. Their religions are not part of the American mainstream.

Indeed, one of the most frequent places you discover these lawsuits is in prison where inmates have converted to Islam while incarcerated and are petitioning the prison authorities to allow them to practice their religion. And they almost always lose, and the prison almost always wins. Even though the cases involve such simple things as the desire of an inmate to attend his required religious services, held on the prison grounds but in a different building from his own, the prison authorities say no. And the court concurs. Moreover, as long as the government is free, through indifference or ignorance, to destroy the religions that do not fit its model, it becomes harder for the people who adhere to the outsider religion to create and sustain the community of resistance that a religion, at its best, helps an outsider people create. And yet, one sees court case after court case in which this is the outcome.

In fairness, one has to acknowledge Congress's 1993 adoption of a statute called the Religious Freedom Restoration Act. There was much debate and controversy over whether this act would actually change the course of these cases. Interestingly enough, the Lyng case, about the Indian tribes and deforestation, was expressly mentioned by Congress as one of the cases it did not want to overturn. Nevertheless, the act was adopted with great to-do and was heralded as the fixer of problems involving controversy over religious freedom. But in 1997 the Supreme Court, in its wisdom, held that statute unconstitutional.

The point of the example is not about a statute, it is about an attitude. The attitude says that if your way of being religious is recognizably like the way in which the larger culture views religion, you can have a robust religious freedom. If, however, your way of practicing your religion is very different and especially very threatening to the way in which the larger culture practices religion, you will encounter a much harder time.

Religious freedom is important to our community because of our need to constitute ourselves as a community of resistance. One of the great powers of black theology is precisely that it calls on us as a people to understand the connection between the actual day-to-day experience of our lives and the history of our people on the one hand, and the work God wants to do in the world on the other. That is a powerful connection; a connection that is different for different people; different for different groups of people; and even different for different groups of black people. But the power of that connection is what is important. The power of that connection and the power of religion working in the human imagination provide the potential resister, the member of this community of resistance, with the strength to stand up and be different. It is quite easy to stand up and be different when nothing is at stake. Anyone can do that. But the power of resistance is what is on display when one has to stand up and be different when something is at stake.

One of the wonderful things about the ministry of the Rev. Dr. Martin Luther King, Jr., was precisely the ability to articulate, with some force, a vision that would lead people to say: "All right, I'm going to stand up as an act of resistance, grounded in my religious understanding of the world and stand up against the police dogs, against the bombs, against the assassins' bullets." The resistance is the power of the faith, but the faith is interpreted through the concrete experience of the people. Faith provides strength to stand up for something which is at stake. It is the power of the faith and resistance dynamic which fosters the inspiration that can sometimes move a nation, even when the nation neither shares nor understands the underlying theology. But one can only do that if religious freedom is robustly protected.

One of the places it was not robustly protected, interestingly enough, was in Birmingham, Alabama. When Martin Luther King, Jr., wrote "Letter From Birmingham City Jail,"[1] he was not in jail for violating a city ordinance which banned parading without a permit, as the popular histories recall. That is false. He was in the Birmingham city jail for contempt of court. More specifically, the Southern Christian Leadership Conference (SCLC) had applied for a permit to march in Birmingham on Good Friday and Easter Sunday. Already from the choice of dates and the name of the organization, there was a hint that there might be a religious aspect to these date selections. But the permit was denied. The SCLC held a meeting to decide whether to march anyway. When the city authorities learned of the meeting, they obtained an order from a judge prohibiting the march. Once Martin Luther King, Jr., was in the Birmingham city jail, the SCLC broke the ordinance twice. They defied the court order twice—once by marching on Good Friday and once by marching on Easter Sunday. On Monday morning, they were hauled into court for contempt and were sentenced to a specified number of days in jail.

As a legal matter, there is a difference between the charges of parading without a permit and violating a specific court order and then being in contempt of court. The difference is that if you think that an unconstitutional law is being applied to you, you can violate the law and then claim that the law is unconstitutional once you are in court. However, if it is a court order, you cannot do this. If it is a court order, you have to obey it and then claim it is unconstitutional. But the SCLC could not obey it if they wanted to march on Good Friday. They could not obey it because they received the order on Thursday night. When they were held in contempt of court, they claimed the unconstitutionality of the order. The court rejected this notion. As a result, the case went all the way to the U.S. Supreme Court where Martin Luther King, Jr., lost. He did not win because the Court claimed that one cannot violate a court order, no matter what one's cause is. The Court made no mention of the religious dimension of the need to march on Good Friday. The Court's position was: "You can march next week. If you want to challenge it, you can march some other weekend. What is so important about this weekend?"

This is the willful overlooking of the religious dimension of activism. When one overlooks that, one loses a comprehension of the profound relationship between daily life and the sacred understanding of that life. One of the remarkable things today is how many otherwise very smart scholars or politicians or journalistic commentators believe that it is possible to make sense of the black community in America while giving no thought to its religiosity.

Let us examine another instance of African American religious sensibilities. Most Americans, in surveys, support organized classroom prayer. I happen not to support it, but most Americans do. The data of these surveys reveal the following. If one segregates the data and looks separately at white Americans and black Americans, what one finds is that white America is just about split over the issue of support or nonsupport. However for black Americans, one discovers overwhelming support for classroom prayer. When one talks about this to scholars, generally they will say, "Oh well, that's because of despair in the community, and people are searching desperately for answers." The stance of black people in these surveys is never credited to a genuine evangelical fervor in the community. Scholars and the like always offer some other reason that is driving this phenomenon.

I offer one additional example of black people's religiosity. A few years ago, I was asked to appear on a Sunday morning television talk show to discuss school prayer. I declined the producer's offer because I was unable to participate. The show aired on Easter Sunday, and I had previous commitments for that Sunday morning. Though I opposed organized school prayer, I, nevertheless, would have participated. As my replacement, the producer suggested Pat Robertson. In response to her soliciting my opinion, I suggested, instead of Pat Robertson, one of the three democratic candidates from the mayoral primary which was about to occur in Washington, D.C. All three were African Americans, all liberal democrats, and all supporters of classroom prayer. I told the producer about the support for classroom prayer in the black community. Moreover, I said that one could not enter an inner-city black church or talk to parents of kids in the inner city without classroom prayer surfacing in the conversation. The producer thought it over for a second or two, and then she said, "Well, you know, maybe if it were a show about urban crises, you know, I could have them on. But classroom prayer, you know, it is not a black issue."

America has a long way to go before it can claim a closeness to racial justice. We have made important strides in the past, yet these strides have occurred in a discontinuous fashion. In the history of American race relationships, we discover long periods of inactivity and then a great upswing of energy, followed by a long period of lethargy. In fact, one can realistically say there have only been two important periods of progress. One encompassed the abolitionist movement, the Civil War, and the end of legalized slavery. The other took place during the Civil Rights movement and the Second Reconstruction.[2] What these periods held in common was the display of enormous religious activity sparking people to action. Yet very often, one can read in history books about each of these movements without receiving a clear sense of how deeply religious they were. Both the abolitionist preachers and the Southern Christian Leadership Conference clergy who led massive protests exemplify the idea of a community of resistance. These clear examples indicate people trying to develop and build a community of resistance in part through helping the community to a greater self-understanding and furthermore to an understanding of the community's place and the world's place in God's plan.

One of the things I really value about Dr. Cone's book, *Black Theology and Black Power*, is his emphasis on the way that God, in black theology, is present in the world. God's presence is something that has been drained out of so much of American religion. The idea of God as someone, something, an entity or a being who is there, who is present, and who is here among us, has always been an important part of the black churches' thought, belief, and experience of the world.

This matters to the community of resistance because one behaves differently if one believes God to be before you and within you and around you. You behave differently if you believe in the presence of God. That idea of behaving differently is one of the gifts that ought to be something that the church is able to spread. We must spread it because we cannot wait a hundred years for the next great upsurge of activity or the next great radical transformation of society. We need one now. And the churches must, once more, envision themselves as being in the vanguard of that movement. I am not talking about preaching on Sunday or volunteering in the soup kitchen once a week, though these are important. I am thinking of genuine sacrifice, about letting something be at stake.

At this juncture, I think about the issue of radical transformation. In a sense, liberals and conservatives both have correct ideas. The liberal idea is correct in that the radical transformation is going to cost money. Part of the radical transformation that we need, if we are not going to overthrow our present economic system, requires some people to be willing to spend what is needed to alter the deleterious situation. This necessitates a great deal of spending to improve dramatically the conditions in which many poor Americans, black and white, find themselves. Such an awful lot of money challenges citizens because they do not wish to pay more taxes. Here, liberals have a correct idea—money needs to be spent.

But, in a radical transformation, the spending of monies requires great sacrifice. Such a fundamental effort flows from the idea that love of neighbor actually demands that one give up something, rather than simply saying, "I will give up what I can afford to give up. I will give up what I feel comfortable giving up. I will give up what leaves me what I need for my own personal comfort." Unfortunately, we live in a world today in which it is a scary thing to ask people to sacrifice. It is sad how much fun is poked at John F. Kennedy's line in his inaugural address: "Ask not what your country can do for you, ask what you can do for your country." That line today has become almost a joke. And no politician today would run for office on a platform challenging American citizens with, "I'm going to ask you to do hard things. I'm going to ask you to sacrifice for your fellow human beings whom you are instructed by your God to love." Nobody would argue such a principle today, and that is a great loss. In this sense, we are worse off than we were just thirty or forty years ago.

Indeed, radical transformation will obligate us, which means it will demand a sacrifice. But a fundamental demand for sacrifice will not arise in politics. Such a vital demand will have to arise from the church, which is really the only contemporary, genuine source of resistance to the existing order that there is. There is nobody else that can do it. Nobody ever was persuaded to go out and risk life and limb because they read a smart article on philosophy and public affairs. No one ever said they were going to organize a march and be beaten by the police because of something they read in the *New York Times* op-ed page. It is only religion that still has the power, at its best, to encourage sacrifice and resistance.

Yet, one should have no illusions. All too many pastors today, black and white, are so worried about filling the seats. Clergy deliver brilliant sermons which preach up to the edge of asking people to do something, and then they will pull back in their messages. Some pastors display a prophetic leadership and call for sacrifice, but their numbers are small.

In contrast to the liberal idea of spending money as a sacrifice to better the conditions of the poor in America, conservatives also have a correct idea which demands a change in behavior. Unfortunately the conservative position remains too limited because it always instructs the poor to change their behavior. Of course, the conservatives are partly right at this point. For instance, we cannot have kids shooting each other over a pair of $150 sneakers. But the only reason that poor kids kill each other over a pair of $150 sneakers is because there exists a market for such a commodity. Most of the people buying those sneakers are neither poor nor black. When a well-to-do white parent is willing to send his or her child to school wearing $500 or $600 worth of clothes, which does happen, you are laying the groundwork, you are modeling the behavior for all children in the society.

As a further example, we all talk correctly about the crisis of illegitimacy. Most people know that the strongest predictor of whether a child is going to be poor or not is whether the child has one parent at home or two. Everyone agrees: we have to intervene in the cycle of babies having babies. That is exactly right, of course. But such intergenerational repetition is, also in part, a learned behavior. When one lives in a society sanctioning illegitimacy, more and more, why should black kids have less access to that "privilege," if you will, than other kids? People could undertake a different path and state: "I will change my behavior by not pursuing all the desires I may have, because I have a concern about how I am going to model behavior. I have a concern for what kind of moral world kids, all kids, grow up in." These two sacrifices of economics and behavior represent two enormous sacrifices in a world valuing the material and the satisfaction of desire; and more and more we value those things.

One of the great contributions of black theology, at its best, is the ability to point beyond those things. Any theology pointing beyond the material world to the spirit can be of service in this effort to transform. But a transforming effort is only going to succeed if one lives in a world which honors religiousness enough to perceive communities of resistance as embodying value to the larger society rather than manifesting a threat to it. I fear we are so caught up in worries about the threat this or that religious group seems to pose to our society that we are destroying the ability of communities to build themselves around their religious understanding. If we continue down such a path of destruction, we will make the black community, the community with which I am most greatly and immediately concerned, worse off. The denial of religious freedom takes away the black community's ability to form a community of resistance and to act on that resistance, even in the realm of politics.

Widespread sentiment exists today condemning religious activism in politics because, from this perspective, somehow, we would suffer from the lack of separation of church and state. As one who believes deeply in the ideas of the communities of resistance and particularly in my own black community, I find this a terrifying notion. As one who is a legal scholar, I think it is a misunderstanding of the separation of church and state. The separation of church and state, properly understood, comes from the work not of Thomas Jefferson, as is widely perceived, but from the insights of Roger Williams.

Specifically, Williams developed the metaphor of the garden and the wilderness. The garden was the place where the people of faith would gather to struggle to understand God's word. The wilderness was the rest of the world; the world where the light had not yet been received. In between the garden and the wilderness stood a wall. The wall existed for one purpose and one purpose only. It was not there to protect the wilderness from the garden; it was there to protect the garden from the wilderness. The wall of separation between church and state is not there to protect the state from the church; rather it is there to protect the church from the state. It stands as a divide to preserve religious freedom. And one needs to protect the church from the state because the latter will utilize its enormous powers to go through each religion and do what the state has always done, either subvert the religion or destroy it. If we continue our slide in the direction toward a state that breaches the wall of separation whenever it is convenient, then I worry about the great risk to religious freedom. And, in the end, such a breach could destroy our ability to form the communities of resistance which are crucial if we are going to have a chance to transform the nation.

Notes

1. Martin Luther King, Jr., "Letter from Birmingham Jail," in *A Testament of Hope: The Essential Writings of Martin Luther King, Jr.*, ed. James M. Washington (San Francisco, California: Harper and Row, 1986), 289-302.

2. The abolitionist movement against the enslavement of black people covers the period before the American Civil War of 1860-1865. Though, in general terms, it signifies the effort of individuals and groups to abolish slavery, the abolitionist movement, however, intensified during the nineteenth century.

The Civil Rights movement (i.e., to extend civil rights to black Americans) unfolded during the 1950s and 1960s. This period is also called the Second Reconstruction because it paralleled some of the progressive legislation passed and progressive coalitions built during the First Reconstruction (1866 to 1877).

3

African American Thought

The Discovery of Fragments

DAVID TRACY

Introduction

I have been trying to develop the category of "fragments" for contemporary reflection on philosophy and theology. I have been reading African American thought for many years starting with, of course, James Cone, and have been driven back to "fragments" which, as far as I can see, were first discovered and employed in African American culture and thought. That at least is my hypothesis. I believe that it is not only significant to acknowledge the importance and meaning of black theology, it is also important for white theologians to acknowledge the profound ambiguity of the cultural category "whiteness," which is present in philosophy and theology where it is too often thought not to be.

Postmodernities

If postmodernity is to avoid essentialism, its great enemy that it hopes to rout, a necessary first step is to admit that there is no such phenomenon as postmodernity. There are only postmodernities. And if modernity is ever to free itself from the trap of totalizing that it has unconsciously set for itself, its first step is not only to continue the great modern experiment, the political democratic pluralism experiment, the still unfinished project of modernity (as Habermas correctly calls it), but also to admit, at the very same time, that there are, in fact, modernities. The shift to the plural for both postmodernity and modernity does not mean only the obvious differences everyone is now aware of between the forms of Western modernity and the forms of modernization taking place in Asian and African cultures. But I mean, more importantly for our own American culture, the shift means the need to rethink the category of modernity and postmodernity in relationship to the many traditions, especially the African American tradition, that really demand a reformulation of the category.

To expand the cultural, philosophical, and religious horizons of the discussion, so prominent across the disciplines today, between modernity and postmodernity is also to let go of a category that was once my own favorite, namely pluralism. Pluralism still seems to assume that there is a center with margins. In fact, anyone who is aware of the contemporary discussion now knows that there is no such center any longer. Pluralism is no longer adequate to describe our situation. Perhaps we need a word like polycentrism—a word that tries to articulate the reality of the many centers that are now present in our culture. Most forms of postmodernity are, indeed, exposing once-forgotten, marginalized, repressed, and oppressed realities and traditions, including their presence in Enlightenment modernity, which did not seem to know how much its successes depended upon colonization, as Paul Gilroy, in his brilliant book *The Black Atlantic*,[1] shows. It is no surprise that the initial categories employed by postmodern thought, the "other" and the "different," became very quickly a recognition that all of us are now "other" in a polycentric world.

Hence the category "fragments." Fragments show the need to shatter any reigning totality system, such as the "white" understanding of modernity and culture. And at the very same time, fragments embody a quite positive meaning: a break out of totality into infinity by discovering one's own routes and one's own traditions. In this process, one discovers all the others and the different, in the very same way, as possible disclosures of infinity. Perhaps these elements of the modern Enlightenment were far less repressed in early modernity, that is, the sixteenth and early seventeenth centuries. Indeed, early modernity is now far more significant for understanding the achievements and the ambiguity of modernity than the classical Enlightenment modernity, that is, the late seventeenth and eighteenth centuries.

The key cultural phenomenon needing new study by both philosophers and theologians is the phenomenon of religion, especially religion in what William James called its "intense forms"; for example, the intense religion of the black church traditions. It may well be, as several contemporary philosophers claim, that religion is the most nonreductive ("saturated" is their favorite word) phenomenon of all. Indeed, I have come to believe that to be the case. And yet, even before that contemporary case can be made, it may be necessary to clear the decks of some further cultural debris.

Religion has always been the unassimilatable other (as distinct from conquered or colonized) in many versions of Enlightenment modernity. And just as one can see this reality (thanks to feminist critique of how Freud's critique of religion is curiously and troublingly similar to his critique of woman), so too I believe one can see in American intellectual life how the critique of religion was often linked to the ignorance of, even indifference toward, the black religious traditions of this country. Any form of the religious phenomenon as saturated seems suspicious for Enlightenment modernity: from romantic symbols to the recovery of African rituals; from the discovery in the nineteenth century of the Hindu excessive forms for the sacred to the twentieth-century Western interest in Buddhism and formlessness.

Consider, for example, Judaism and the amazing rediscovery of the kabbalistic and mystical traditions in Judaism by Sholem and Edel and so many other great scholars of our century. These readings now provide a much richer and complex reading of Judaism than the classical modern reading of Mendelson and even Herman Cohen, for whom modern Judaism was an ethical monotheism and the kabbalistic traditions, merely secondary or even marginal realities. In the kabbalistic traditions, the notion of fragments, fragments of God going out of God and coming back to Godself by human struggle, became a central thought in understanding religion.

But, above all, it is African American thought (especially in the academy these days, in philosophy, theology, cultural studies, history, and social science) that has clearly led the way to recover these repressed, intense, saturated, and fragmentary religious forms. This can be seen in the recovery of the slave narratives, as in Dwight Hopkins's[2] work and that of so many others, through the understanding of the amazing theology of the gospel songs, and the distinct theologies of the spirituals and the blues. Above all we can witness, in James Cone's work, the intensity of the religious experience of the black churches and the accuracy of demanding liberation, justice, and struggle as the heart of prophetic Christianity. The God of black religion is a fragmentary, liberating God.

All of these clearly religious, intense, fragmentary phenomena that are presently being rediscovered are clearly outside the demands for intellectual closure in what will be allowed to count as rational. Why does one otherwise observe the bizarre parade in classical modernity (I mean the eighteenth century) of the invention of modern "isms" for naming God? This is the case whether it be, as it first was, "deism," or even modern "theism," or "atheism" in its modern form, or "pantheism," or the greatest discovery and development of modern thought in the twentieth century, "panentheism."

Can the question of God, when now asked when retrieving traditions that refuse to engage in this Enlightenment discussion on what is the correct "ism" for naming God, really be controlled as a question by any of these modern "isms," or even in their greatest achievements? Even before the categories the "other" and the "different" became such central philosophical, cultural, ethical, religious, and theological categories in contemporary thought, African American thought never gave in to the dominant temptation to reduce all (as Foucault honestly states about Western modern thought) to more of the same, or, at best, to the similar (too often calling on modernity to serve as an ever-more-tattered covering for the same in a new totalizing form).

The German romantics sensed this difficulty but could not do much with it even with their development and privileging of the metaphor "fragments" over any category of wholeness. Unfortunately, Romantic thoughts on fragments, as Derrida and others correctly argue, never quite broke out of the modern totality, because the metaphor "fragments" always suggested a kind of nostalgia for a lost totality rather than breaking through into infinity and thereby calling into question all notions of totality itself. Rather, fragment does become, in African American thought, exactly what the Romantics wanted but could not achieve: a shattering of any totality system and the possibility of positive rediscovery of the intense presence of infinity in religious forms.

African American thought, better than any thought even in the last century, succeeded at exposing the pretensions of any modern system of totality and at exposing the contingent and deeply ambiguous cultural character of all claims to universality, including "whiteness." Christianity as a totality becomes merely christendom. Christendom could not and cannot survive any true experiment with authentic Christianity. This was not just Kierkegaard's insight in his brilliant attack upon all totality systems. It was clearly the insight that one can find in the African American thinkers without exception, even those who were not particularly favorable toward or inclined toward religion, at least in its Christian form.

One witnesses this especially with Frederick Douglass in the three extraordinary narratives of his life,[3] and, above all, in the pathbreaking social scientific work of W. E. B. Du Bois. Both Douglass and Du Bois, unlike many other thinkers of their period, did indeed demand a study of the most intense forms of religious experience in the black churches in order to understand American culture. Each of them (Douglass more than Du Bois) was, in fact, also very much involved in the modern Enlightenment intellectual project and in attempts to understand God and religion from that point of view.

But unlike many other white thinkers of their periods, Douglass and Du Bois never ignored the phenomenon of religion. They were never naive enough to think that a thinker could possibly understand this culture or any culture without attending (as Du Bois's colleague William James also insisted) to the intense saturated, fragmentary cases of religion, especially as they are described in Du Bois's classic work on religion and on religious spirituals, *The Souls of Black Folk*.[4] It is surprising that Douglass and Du Bois, however modern they were in their basic philosophical positions as they were in their distinct ways, nevertheless (unlike so many other intellectuals) still could not let go of this phenomenon of religion in its most intense forms, for example the slave songs, the spirituals, and the blues.

Douglass and Du Bois never made such totality claims. It is not surprising therefore, to find Du Bois drawn not to try and develop a system, but to try ever new experiments in thought, both social scientific thought and philosophical thought, to comprehend how fragments might relate to a whole but never to a totality. Likewise, it is not surprising that Zora Neale Hurston did the same, both in her social scientific work and in her literary work.[5]

Fragments: Three Approaches

There are three kinds of contemporary thinkers for whom the category "fragments" tends to be crucial. The first are radical conservatives who, often with brilliance, witness fragments with regret and nostalgia as all that is left of what they view as a once-unified Western culture. This is perhaps best expressed in T. S. Eliot's famous words that all we now have are "fragments to shore up against our ruin." But fragments need not have merely that nostalgic meaning either of the romantics or the great conservative thinkers of our day, including such African American thinkers as the great literary and theological critic Nathan Scott.

The second group appealing to fragments are the postmoderns, almost all of whom see fragments not as an occasion for nostalgia but as emancipatory from the deadening hand of all reigning modern totality systems, especially those systems that have tried to hide their own complicity in how the totality works against the victims.

The third group of thinkers (explicitly philosophical and theological) see fragments even more positively than the postmoderns as bearers of hope for some form of redemption in our own time, if we would but attend to them. This is especially the case in contemporary intellectual history, from such Jewish thinkers as Franz Rosenzweig and Walter Benjamin, and in such Jewish Christian thinkers as Simone Weil and, above all, in African American thought after W. E. B. Du Bois. Fragments first entered the postmodern sensibility through the love of fragments in so many forms of modernist culture. These fragments intended to undo the domesticating power of modern rationality's claim to universality and totality and to provide something that was finally excessive toward or transgressive of the modern totality systems.

However, contemporary thought has moved on, whether under the explicit banner of some version of postmodernity or some other rubric hardly matters. For the love of excess and transgression in practically every postmodern thinker can be clearly seen. They tend to be nervous, like Derrida, of the explicit category "fragments" since they fear that an appeal to fragments could be trapped in a nostalgia for a lost totality or could be trapped in the romantic or the conservative modes. But if one follows the recoveries that are being made in contemporary thought of traditions which were once not, in fact, considered major traditions by most white thinkers for their own reflection, one can observe what happened. Think, for example, of the recoveries I cited earlier in James Cone's work from his earlier influential book, *Black Theology and Black Power*, to his theologies of the spirituals and the blues. Likewise so many other African American theologians, philosophers, and cultural theorists are recovering the traditions of the slave narratives, the spirituals, the blues, the gospel songs, and the preaching, rituals, and customs of so many black churches with their fragmentary, liberating Christianity.

Perhaps, like the Jesuits of Voltaire's wonderful imagination, religion must always quietly enter the rooms of modernity without warmth and leave without regret. But that, alas, is not religion. For religion is vibrant—usually in its most transgressive and excessive forms, such as one can find in the great gospel songs, or in the love mystics of all the traditions, in the kabbalists, in the sufis, and in the marginalized, repressed, and ignored traditions like the radical apophatic traditions of the West or the traditions like African American thought that always had an apophatism on the incomprehensibility and hiddenness of God in history.

Such fragmentary, saturated religious phenomena could often be ignored as not bearing intellectual weight. That is exactly what is now clearly seen as a deep and devastating error. There are many ways to dismiss such phenomena. We all know how great a religious figure Sojourner Truth was. But we all also know that she too easily is described as something like a saint (which too often implies that the rest of us do not have to take her too seriously). Dorothy Day was right when someone called her a saint in her own lifetime and she replied, "Do not trivialize me." We all sense why religion has become so central a phenomenon to be described and analyzed in so much of African American thought and why in postmodern thought religion has become a central topic.

For religion could never really be contained. It could only be conquered or colonized, as, indeed, it was; or rendered a once-necessary form on the route to absolute knowledge as in Hegel and his great modern idealist successors; or made into pleasant narratives and symbols that may help moderns feel again, as best they can, their own way to some ethical position; or thought of as really some other phenomenon than religion itself. Perhaps it is really ethics, or bad science, or disguised metaphysics. Perhaps religion was once real, even fierce, but it now has become just one more captive of the universalist strains of ontology. There was no major thinker at the beginning of this century, that I can recall, that predicted either the catastrophes of the century or that religion would be anything other than something that would quietly and nicely die away by century's end.

The many strategies of modern thought toward religion are always like those that often refuse to admit "whiteness" and any other rubric of universality or totality: strategies of benign neglect, strategies of indifference, and strategies like Schleiermacher's nonaggression pact. These strategies seemed unable or unwilling to describe either the phenomenon of religion or even to try to seriously think about it. The phenomenon seemingly most other to and different from what counted as real and reasonable was, in fact, religion. The phenomenon that was, in fact, the one most ignored and, more exactly, repressed was race. Both of these phenomena—religion and race—have returned and returned together to force any serious thinker in our period to rethink his or her position.

But it is not just the postmodern love of extremes of transgression or excess that are now needed to study religion. It has, of course, almost become a truism by now that literary modernism, whatever else it was, preferred the unfinished, the syntactically unstable, the semantically malformed. Literary modernism produced and savored discrepancy and what it shows and how it shows it, since the highest wisdom is often knowing that things and pictures do not add up. Modernism itself (literary modernism) had also been rethought by great thinkers and writers of the Harlem Renaissance. This occurred at the very time in 1922 when Ezra Pound and Gertrude Stein were, in fact, trying to break out of the bounds of the language once approved as standard English by trying to destabilize it, attempting to use dialects from the black peoples and the black writers of the period. This took place at the very same time Zora Neale Hurston and others in the Harlem Renaissance were rethinking the possibilities of such dialect and such syntactic breaks for thinking and writing itself.

What African American thought principally adds to this familiar portrait of modernist writers on fragments is something like a theological and philosophical theory of the modernist image. The contemporary image, after all, is a fragment, as information technology makes even clearer. History does not yield to the continuity of a grand narrative as once envisaged by philosophers and theologians. Nor does it yield even, perhaps, to the intellectual hope of either a dialectical or analogical imagination. History, including intellectual history, breaks up into images. Such images can be found in all the major African American theologians, particularly the womanist theologians[6] who seem to have an exceptional ability to deal with and make clear the need for a constellation of messianic Jesuanic, apocalyptic images. In African American thought, images seem to become fragments that not only destroy all claims of totality, but also yield to fragments of hope, suggestions, even redemption. The image African American thinkers seek to blast from past experiences of suffering and joy even puts dialectic at a standstill, as Walter Benjamin hoped.

Above all, one must avoid modernity's (and not only Hegel's) central temptation: the drive to totality, the drive to try to eliminate differences in order to produce once again a totality system that can claim universality as it levels all difference. To attempt any totality system is inevitably to try to efface every fragment from every culture, to try to deny the singularity of each culture, to try to eliminate those discrete and potentially explosive images that one finds in such works as the slave narratives and in the great gospel songs. If one carries out this modern temptation, one ends up in favor of some larger conceptual architectonic of which the fragment would be made a mere part. Even the category of historical context (i.e., the favored category of the great modern nineteenth-century discovery of history) is too often conceived itself as a kind of totality to disallow the present from experiencing the historical event as a unique fragment of time. Thus read, the fragments of marginal, forgotten, repressed traditions always knew and were often forced to live the lie of a reigning totality system.

In Christian terms, this would suggest an odd privileging of a gospel like Mark's: that fragmentary, discontinuous, non-closing gospel centered on the suffering of this strange prophet, Jesus, who never seems to be understood by his own followers, although he is understood by such marginal characters as the oppressed, the deeply psychologically troubled, those at the limit, or demons. Luke's Acts can lend itself so much more readily to continuous history like realistic narrative. Mark cannot; there, history itself is fragmentary.

In the African American theological terms of James Cone, a radically eschatological, indeed, messianic and apocalyptic understanding of history is constituted by a series of fragments blasted from a repressed past as resources for some of the present.

This third meaning of fragments is also to be found in many African American writers. Why is it that, for many of us, Toni Morrison is not only the best American living writer, but is also the most experimental in her forms—

forms that always seem to be willing to try almost any image to see how such fragments may also yield new light? Consider this famous passage from *Beloved.*

> I am Beloved and she is mine. Sethe is the one that picked flowers, yellow flowers in the place before the crouching. Took them away from their green leaves. They are on the quilt now where we sleep. She was about to smile at me when the men without skin came and took us up into the sunlight with the dead and shoved them into the sea. Sethe went into the sea. She went there. They did not push her. She went there. She was getting ready to smile at me and when she saw the dead people pushed into the sea she went also and left me there with no face or hers. Sethe is the face I found and lost in the water under the bridge. When I went in, I saw her face coming to me and it was my face too. I wanted to join. I tried to join, but she went up into the pieces of light at the top of the water. I lost her again, but I found the house she whispered to me and there she was, smiling at last. It's good, but I cannot lose her again. All I want to know is why did she go in the water in the place where we crouched? Why did she do that when she was just about to smile at me? I wanted to join her in the sea but I could not move; I wanted to help her when she was picking the flowers, but the clouds of gunsmoke blinded me and I lost her. Three times I lost her: once with the flowers because of the noisy clouds of smoke; once when she went into the sea instead of smiling at me; once under the bridge when I went in to join her and she came toward me but did not smile. She whispered to me, chewed me, and swam away. Now I have found her in this house. She smiles at me and it is my own face smiling. I will not lose her again. She is mine.[7]

After his first two more traditionally written theological books, James Cone's theological essays have also adopted a similar use of fragments and fragmentary forms. Thus we see his brilliant forays into fragments that speak for themselves in their singularity, that generate new meaning and new tensions as they work with and against all the other fragments in an ever-new constellation or even into something like the Toni Morrison passage, a phantasmagoric collage of brilliant theological fragments from the African American past.

The now-familiar academic debate of modernity versus postmodernity needs to question itself; at least it needs to take two crucial new moves. I do not hesitate to call these moves theological or spiritual. First, we need to shift the contemporary debate from an eighteenth-century version of modernity, and from a late-twentieth-century dominant cultures' version of postmodernity, which can often seem too relaxed and too unaware that the fragments they pick up include ethical demands for justice. Too many postmodern thinkers fail to develop an ethics of justice; Derrida happily now does under the very Jewish rubric of a messianic ethic.

Second, we must shift our attention away from any false hope for any total-ity system and focus instead upon the actuality of the explosive, marginal, liber-ating fragments of our many heritages. I do not mean in the conservative fashion so familiar today, which seeks to shore up some perceived past unity against our present ruin. On the contrary, sometimes this spiritual search must demand a destructive moment. We must be willing to fragment whatever the reigning totality system is: economic, cultural, religious, social, or gendered. We need more moments not only of critique but of deep suspicion of all totalities and of all claims to innocence like the hidden claims of "whiteness."

We can do so by finding the spiritual fragment that can expose the pretense that lies lurking in our untroubled claims to universality. Thinkers such as Cornel West[8] accomplish this feat through an amazing ability to produce a con-stellation of fragments. Who else could put fragments like tragedy, prophecy, and pragmatism together into a new, believable constellation? There is also the opportunity to rethink other thinkers of our culture in terms of the fragments that they either try to deny or could not release themselves from. Think of the one fragment that Kant's classical modern three critiques could not and did not contain—radical evil. Notice how Kant, in his later essays (his, to me, very seri-ous essays on history and the singularities of history and religion), rethinks the fragments that will not fit his critical system.

Why did Hegel, that greatest and most confident of the moderns even at the end of his life, after not only the *Phenomenology of Spirit* but *The Logic*,[9] find it necessary to rethink again and again (as the different editions we now have of his lectures on philosophy of religion show) the fragments that kept rendering his system not a totality, not a whole. Those fragments were religious ones. Regarding Judaism, Hegel could not contain it except by the lie that after the biblical period Judaism became a dead religion; or the Buddhism which Hegel himself kept trying over and over again to understand in its formlessness as he kept changing his philosophy; or African traditions which Hegel kept repressing because they did not and could not seem to fit the system.

And surely, it is time for all of us to face the fragments that lurk as land mines in all the classical modern systems; for example, the great flexibility and mod-esty of the speculative fragmentary power of such extraordinary modern thinkers as Douglass and Du Bois who, driven by their reflections on black reli-gion, turned against their own modern understanding. For me, as I suspect for most people, it is Douglass's first autobiography that is the truly powerful one. Douglass, of course, became and was a great man, just like many great Victorian men who had written a second and then a third biography. But it is the first autobiography, that fragmentary, disturbing, unnerving narrative, that lurks in the imagination of anyone who has ever read it, or has even read all three. No major African American thinker, long before the rest of us, ever attempted or wanted a system. They have left us, all of them (especially James Cone in his theology, Cornel West in his philosophy, and Toni Morrison in her literature) with something far more valuable than a system. They have left to us fragments that break and undo such pretense to totality, and that describe hints and guesses of hope. And, finally, they have left to us fragmentary glimpses of light and redemption. These are the crucial resources which African-American thought, if heeded, can provide for our desiccated public realm.

Notes

1. Paul Gilroy, *The Black Atlantic: Modernity and Double Consciousness* (Cambridge, Mass.: Harvard University Press, 1993).

2. See his article in this volume and his *Shoes That Fit Our Feet: Sources for a Constructive Black Theology* (Maryknoll, N.Y.: Orbis Books, 1993).

3. Douglass wrote three autobiographical narratives: *Narrative* (1845), *My Bondage and My Freedom* (1855), and he presented the finalized version of these autobiographical accounts in *The Life and Times of Frederick Douglass, written by himself* (1881, 1892) introduction by Rayford W. Logan (New York: Collier Books, 1962 reprint of the 1892 edition).

4. Boston: Bedford Books, 1997.

5. Zora Neale Hurston, *The Sanctified Church* (Berkeley, CA.: Turtle Island, 1983); *Their Eyes Were Watching God* (Urbana, Illinois: University of Illinois Press, 1978); and *Mules and Men* (Bloomington, Indiana: Indiana University Press, 1978).

6. In this volume, see the articles by Jacquelyn Grant, Linda E. Thomas, and Emilie M. Townes.

7. Toni Morrison, *Beloved* (New York: A Plume Book, New American Library, 1988), 214.

8. See Cornel West's article in this volume and his *Prophetic Fragments* (Grand Rapids, Michigan: William B. Eerdmans Publishing Company, 1988).

9. *Phenomenology of Spirit* (Oxford: Clarendon Press, 1977); and *The Logic of Hegel,* second edition (Oxford: Clarendon Press, 1892).

Part II

Black Faith
and
Prophetic Faith
Communities

4

Black Theology on Theological Education

DWIGHT N. HOPKINS

James H. Cone's classic text *Black Theology and Black Power* initiated an irre-versible dynamic within theological education. With the publication of his Christian manifesto about the life-and-death meanings concerning the human-ity of the oppressed, seminaries and divinity schools had to begin to deal with the reality of black Americans. No longer could they continue to look to Europe (particularly Germany) for the latest word in theology when these cloistered religious academics could see the smoke from black folk rebelling and burning in urban areas. No longer could they simply take trips to other countries throughout the world without doing a theological self-test about the nature of their God-talk and God-walk right in their own country, the United States. Cone's *Black Theology and Black Power* dropped a bombshell that shook the intellectual stools of the academy then; even today we still feel the reverbera-tions of that book throughout theological education.

Introduction

This essay[1] investigates theological education from a black theology viewpoint. It argues for an analytical understanding of how theological education engages the dynamic between critical faith and the equalization of God's gifts for all humanity. This view cuts across denominational allegiances, privileging of aca-demic disciplines, and both an abstract belief and a utilitarian witness. The cen-tral claim focuses on a theological pedagogy that recognizes that something fundamental is at stake. That is to say, God has called creation to fulfill a mis-sion of liberation: the process of seeking full spiritual and material freedom starting with the least of society, but encompassing all of creation. To pursue this line of argument, this essay frames its conclusions around the issues of the-ological stand, method, and viewpoint. With this foundational scaffolding, all people of good faith and Christians in particular can play their roles in the God-human *telos*—the struggle for liberation and the practice of freedom

From the perspective of a black theology of liberation, theological education

41

pertains to how people of faith change the world for a communal sharing of resources given to humanity by God. In this sense, the starting point of discourses on theological education is neither the important debate over the nature of theological education and religious studies, nor does one commence the interrogation of the contours of theological education by seeking, discovering, and proclaiming a universal, static meta-means of interpretation. One does not, furthermore, undertake such a religious pedagogy by situating oneself within the confines of any one particular ecclesial tradition. And finally, but not in any completely exhaustive sense, the endeavors to define theological education do not lie in a privatized epistemological faith or in individualistic acquisition of profit—that is, a capitalist prosperity gospel.

Theological education looks beyond the walls of the academy, historically truncated faith genealogies, contemporary institutional communities of believers, and the centering of the self as the ultimate lenses of adjudicating reality. In other words, the aim, structure, and criteria of theological education arise from an analysis and experience of the movement for full humanity in the anthropological and ecological interactions in the world.

Theological education, therefore, is the practice of a holistic liberation constituted as a front of struggle and by a creative dynamic toward psychological, social, cultural, economic, political, and linguistic full humanity. If theological education involves reality in the world, then the notion of power occupies a central location and is a highly contested site within theological education itself. Power—who has it, who does not—becomes key because God has created all of humanity to share power equally in a holistically balanced self, community, and world. Again such a totalness denotes and connotes full humanity—the communal sharing of all resources at every conceivable level among social relations, with the ecology, and within the self-other particularity.

Theological education looks at the God-human effort in the world wherever Christians and others attempt a strategic effort to reveal and sustain a movement of liberation—a struggle to balance a communal connection of self, society, and creation. For theological education to pursue such a telos requires the detection, analysis, and transformation of knowledge regarding power. Theological education means starting with a practice of liberation faith in the world: that is, the striving of humanity to own and share communally the divine gift of resources. Theological education, then, is a pedagogy of equal distribution at every level of life. And, from the perspective of black theology, it signifies a conscientious stand, method, and viewpoint with the least in society.

Theological Stand

Theological education does not have a stand that is neutral; the story of God's revelation of divine intent in both the Bible and human social relations indicates and substantiates this claim. Put differently, theological education stands with the interests of the majority of the United States and the world: poor and working-class people and, through them, all humanity. Black theology of liberation derives this notion of "stand" from both scriptural witness and the ordinary experience of black people: that is to say, divine revelation in scriptural witness as well as in black vernacular modes and styles of life. The issue of stand in theological education is constituted by an epistemology grounded in a nexus between ultimate concerns and the pain-resistance dynamic of the least in society. For black theology this nexus is located in the Bible and black vernacular experiences.

We perceive an engaged theological education from black theology's reading of the Christian narrative. In the biblical story the primal hope act of God is the exodus story. It signifies the paradigmatic expression of covenantal partnership of divine-human coconstitution of the oppressed self into a new liberated self. Divine intent works with marginalized humanity through liberation to exit out of the physical restraints of Egyptian bondage (wherever it exists today) and into material free space undergirded by a spiritual belief in the power of Yahweh and the human community. The spirit of total liberation or holistic freedom of Yahweh is never in itself, but is always an empowering *ruach* (breath) for poor humanity. The finger of God is for us, and the divine spirit breathes on us for us. Thus the decisive nature of a noncolonizing exodus story in the Hebrew scriptures and a decisive mission of Jesus' proclamation and vocation for the poor in the Christian scriptures reveal the concretization of holy *ruach* and *pneuma* among broken and struggling humanity.

In other words, to encounter the identity of God's liberating spirit—the divine face of freedom—we look for what God is doing in the ongoing process of embedded transcendent ethics of holistic spiritual and material humanity. Divine ethics (i.e., the doing of God) does not escape us in an ephemeral invisibility or in a distant space acting on us absent from us. The work of God is actively present for us in the poor's attempt to construct themselves anew. God for us is always socially situated with the poor communities on this earth. To believe otherwise is to deny and fracture the original covenant of the spirit's presence for broken humanity. God does wherever and whenever marginalized humanity cries out in the pain and pleasure of forging a new self. Divine activity is the voice of the voiceless fighting to make a way out of no way. There is the action of Yahweh and Jesus.

The acts and ethics of God are also in direct response to the monopolizers of powers and resources of society who project their fears upon the other (in the instance of black theology, the other is the African American oppressed community in solidarity with other groups in struggle). Somewhat similar to the Israelites of old, black people today embody the otherness of skewed social relations, skewed not in their favor. For instance in the book of Exodus, the new king who came to power in Egypt stated:

> "These Israelites are so numerous and strong that they are a threat to us. In case of war they might join our enemies in order to fight against us, and might escape from the country. We must find some way to keep them from becoming even more numerous." So the Egyptians put slave-drivers over them to crush their spirits with hard labor. (Ex. 1:9-11, *Good News Bible*)

In today's society, race remains a negative indicator of black evil and untrustworthiness. It serves, for those with resources to propagate such a vision, as a thesaurus for criminality, slovenliness, sexuality, and nonintellectual labor. The social location of racial formation is either outstanding or standing out. The black self is perceived to excel beyond the norm (therefore an outstanding exception) or expected to fail (hence a palpable disaster which, in commonsense understanding, is the African American norm); either an unbelievable herculean success or a predictable collapse beneath the pressures of life. Race matters in Christianity and American culture as demonic presence and as the two options of standing out or outstanding. As the new king stated in the book of Exodus: "They are a threat to us."

The projected threat of a defined community marked by color pigmentation then operates at many levels. The monopolizers of power in society define a mission to "crush their spirit with hard labor." The oppression of African Americans (particularly the poor) is spiritual and material. Material oppression is to extract profit, either by a disproportionate presence of the black poor in the unemployed ranks or by a general asymmetrical income and wealth scale detrimental to African American workers. On the spiritual plane, the attempt is to crush the memory, vision, and desire to struggle for freedom. Marginalized African American communities are thereby anesthetized into a blurred perception of who has the monopolized power over resources to create a threat from them as the other, and to implement a systematic locking out of the majority of the black humanity from the earth's gifts created by God. In contrast and in response, God works with the oppressed black community to coconstitute a new liberated, spiritual, and material humanity. God is a spirit of freedom for us.

The fundamental act of God, the doing and ethics of the divinity of liberation for us, is earthly emancipation for those in bondage, both spiritual and material; and this act operates in a coconstitutive fashion. The poor and broken-hearted are co-agents with divine intent, resulting in the fashioning of a new emancipated human self. In a word, God works with us through the act of freedom as we constitute ourselves from oppression to full humanity with the highest potential. God liberates us totally and holistically. The basis of the new self is found in the ethics of divine freeing on earth. As one former African American slave asserted in faith:

> Indeed I, with others, was often told by the minister how good God was in bringing us over to this country from dark and benighted Africa, and permitting us to listen to the sound of the gospel. To me, God also granted temporal freedom, which man without God's consent, had stolen away.[2]

Though sacred power pervades the spiritual dimension as well, the giving of full humanity—the Spirit of liberation for us—is all the time manifest in the temporal realm. For the earth's dispossessed, "the sound of the gospel" is temporal freedom. We cannot encounter the language of the gospel, the work of Yahweh and Jesus, without it being embedded or embodied in the tangible. The temporality of freedom might manifest in miniature acts of God or in obvious major fractures of the restraints that enchain oppressed humanity. Regardless, God's ethics and doing come to us or are granted to us as a sign of divine grace. The gift of the spirit of total liberation is the manifest presence of a holy, omnipotent God whose constancy of being for us is eternal and whose glory appears in mercy, whose patience of working with and for us (despite our frail limitations) reflects the fullness of divine wisdom. The power of God to work on behalf of and with the oppressed never ceases.

God offers a liberating presence. We are not alone, for the covenantal engagement between Yahweh and the oppressed (both on the spiritual and material plane) arises out of the haunting testimony of the enslaved African American poor and the cries of the biblical witness. In the exodus drama, Yahweh proclaims to those in bondage:

> I have seen how cruelly my people are being treated in Egypt; I have heard them cry out to be rescued from their slave-drivers. I know all about their sufferings, and so I have come down to rescue them from the Egyptians and to bring them out of Egypt to a spacious land. (Ex. 3:7-8, *Good News Bible*)

The power of God to work for the oppressed is eternal. In the divine time of patience and knowing all about the plight of the poor, Yahweh's demonstrative glory comes as the harnessing of divine might for the "little ones" of this earth. For the marginalized believer, God's acts are real.

In this believing of those without access to resources for living their full humanity, we discover a faith to act on the covenantal promise of Yahweh. The doctrine of God is liberation for those who believe and act on this faith. For instance, having departed from the system of slavery in the old South, Etna Elizabeth Dauphus confessed the following to an interviewer:

> In setting forth her reasons for escaping she asserted that she was tired of slavery and an unbeliever in the doctrine that God made colored people simply to be slaves for white people; besides, she had a strong desire to "see her friends in Canada." [3]

Etna Dauphus exemplifies the coconstitution of the self, the divine and human agreement of transformation from the old to the new humanity. God provides the faith in liberation (as the divine intent for us) upon which the sufferer is freed with an emancipating belief to act (in response to and in accord with that which is offered by Yahweh) on the word or doctrine of the freedom spirit for us.

The divine gift of God, therefore, is both the active presence of the spirit for us (i.e., Yahweh acts on hearing the cries of the oppressed) and the granting of free agency as liberating common sense to the oppressed. The doing of the spirit for us is the manifest might of God and the gift to us to act freely with divine purpose. As another fugitive ex-slave penned in his autobiography: "In no situation, with no flowery disguises, can the revolting institution [of bondage] be made consistent with the free-agency of [humanity] which we all believe to be the Divine gift." The intertwining of divine act, human faith, divine gift, and human agency is the empowering covenant for a God-human coconstitution of oppressed humanity into a free humanity.

Moreover black theology's perception of theological education as an enterprise which is not neutral but one which takes a clear stand with the least in society is, in addition to the biblical witness, argued from the fact of black folk's everyday wisdom sayings. Thus liberating biblical stories and poor and working-class folk's everyday common sense experiences are resources for theological education as a practice of freedom.

Common Sense Experiences

The common sense experiences of poor and working-class black folks consist of sayings pregnant with folk theological wisdom. In the black vernacular tradition, one hears the following: "God may not come when you call him, but he's right on time." In this tradition the divinity is a time-God who operates on God's own time. From the human perspective, one could neither instruct nor always understand the mysterious ways of the all powerful. But somehow and some way, in the vernacular of black faith, God appears "on time" to ease one's "troubled mind, lift your burdens, prop you up on every leaning side, and help you climb the rough side of the mountain." It is this time-God, who "makes a way out of no way."

Similarly, the expression that "God sits high but looks low" images a majestic Being whose providence and ability encompass all of reality. Though this all-powerful One holds the whole world in divine hands, still God knows the individual hairs on each of the heads of society's weak and downtrodden. Our arms might be too short to box with God (paraphrasing a slave saying), but this God is never positioned too high to pour the divine spirit into the human predicament. Indeed, the appearance of God's Word in the form of the human Jesus symbolizes precisely the divine spirit becoming poor in order to ensure the liberation of suffering humanity. Referring to the metaphor of death to sin/slavery and resurrection to life/liberation, one former black slave witnessed to his new Christian freedom brought to earth by the Spirit. He stated the following:

> Whenever a man has been killed dead and made alive in Christ Jesus he no longer feels like he did when he was a servant of the devil. Sin kills dead but the spirit of God makes alive.[4]

"God don't like ugly," another popular faith statement in African American vernacular, implies the eschatological certainty that trouble does not always last for the voiceless of society. For example, commenting on God's ultimacy in defeating slavery by bringing on the Civil War, ex-slave J. W. Lindsay proclaimed: "No res' fer niggers 'till God he step in an' put a stop to de white folks meanness."[5]

Though evil might reign in the immediate realm, in the end God's will would be done on earth for the sufferers of pain and abuse. Such an expectation of the finality of justice gives poor and working-class black Christians hope in a future that would be theirs. Hope engenders the power to keep on struggling—to survive and persist—because their divinity will take care of them through trials and tribulations. The ugliness of life has no dominion and will be defeated someday because the desire of the oppressed for full humanity coincides with the divinity's disdain of evil.

The everyday life experiences of the black folk teaches them that though God is on time, looks low, and detests ugliness, oppressed humanity is, nevertheless, a colaborer with God. We find this belief in another saying: "God helps those who help themselves." As divine creations, the nature of human beings compels them to defend themselves and struggle for full humanity in the course of achieving their fullest creative possibilities. This indicates for the oppressed a fight against material manifestations of evil so that the least in society can help forge their own new humanity. To wait idly on God while evil forces crushed down one's spirit, body, and mind exemplified a slow suicide. To the contrary, God summons society's victims to co-labor with God and each other in life's dangerous vineyards in order to produce life's fullest fruit.

Theological Method

In addition to an engaged stand with compassion for the least in society, theological education has to attend to method. For black theology, theological method should be integrative or holistic on several levels.

First, there needs to be an integration between various types of experiences, specifically practical and cognitive. Students bring to the classroom various types of practical experiences of ministry or vocation. Theological education, therefore, should take as its starting point (within the context of our previous discussion of stand in theological education) the multifarious life experiences of students. Whether students are coming directly from completing a previous degree or are emerging from homeless organizing, explicit women's movements, antiracist work, lesbian and gay activities, travel abroad, or church ministry, the aim is to begin with the reality of the gifts brought by a diverse student body. Moreover, given the growing number of second career students who are older, theological education has the creative opportunity to speak more directly to other disciplines and walks of life in the public arena symbolized by these students. In a certain sense the classroom becomes a laboratory of multiple experiences, each grappling with and critiquing its own notion of authority, credibility, and verifiability.

The diversity of the student population, dictated by its varied experiences, allows the professor of theological education to offer a multidisciplinary curriculum. This type of teaching or syllabus will require the professor to risk integrating into her or his explicit theological knowledge pedagogical theories arising from such corners as political science, economics, anthropology, psychology, cultural studies, and the like. Here the task is two-fold. One path provides intellectual insights and theoretical frameworks appropriate for the direct experiences of the student body. The other calls for theological studies to be really public, by which I mean that theology is not primarily a private or a denominational affair. It should gear students to the public civic realm; and this realm, at least as lived by everyday people, does not distinguish between faith and secular activities, a distinction often clung to in the cloistered knowledge of the academy.

This is not to say that all citizens are Christians or even religious. It is simply to claim that religion in America, indeed in the world, involves and presents a major presence and factor of life — whether the press reports on diverse cults, the denominational voting on major issues, or the nature of civic religion in American culture. Religion and faith issues matter in the public realm.

The integration of experiences with theories is an epistemology comprised of direct knowledge of the classroom laboratory participants and the indirect insights of accumulated human scholarly constructs. A further integration is between oneself and the other; indeed, knowledge can only arise with the interchange between and among diverse voices. This implies that everyone in the classroom has vital contributions to make and they must speak and share their voices, however those voices choose to express themselves in self-affirming and constructive ways. This method of integration of self and other is particularly required when a certain political voice consistently dominates conversation. In more conservative intellectual environments, progressive voices should be allowed to elaborate their truth and knowledge claims. Likewise, even in progressive classes, liberal students need to hear or at least be able to articulate accurately (and not simply in a stereotyped fashion) conservative positions. In the world outside of the academy, all voices are battling for hegemony, that is to say, what they perceive is in the best interests of the public good; and for progressive Christians this, of course, pertains directly to the least in society.

Each student's voice emerges in her or his capacity to come to terms with the arguments of the other; that other could be someone with a similar or a different theological framework. The integration of self and other enables the student to sharpen the ability to hear and reformulate a different position, so as to better distinguish the clarity and uniqueness of the student's own voice, with its claims, evidence, warrants, criteria, and norms. Of course, the other voice includes the voice of the assigned and outside reading texts and the texts of the professor's own arguments, claims, and methods.

Again, this self-and-other dynamic entails the ability to both listen attentively (such that the self is able to articulate the assertions of the other in such a way that the other can at least say she or he has been heard) and to clearly and accurately advance the position of the self (even though the self's own perspective might be at an inchoate stage). Therefore to engage the other is really the advancement of one's own voice in the arena of competing assertions of truths and particularities. In the best scenario, argumentation for the advancement of the least of society will prevail. However, ultimately, the changing of reality and the impacting of theological views flow from the theologian's interaction with people struggling to cocreate full humanity and to realize the practice of freedom with God. God dwells in the midst of the majority, who are poor or marginalized. And it is there that witness for liberation occurs.

In addition to the integration of practice and theory and self and other, a third integration speaks to the balance or even sometimes tension between criticism and self-criticism. The self-and-other interplay is not a passive or static interchange. On the contrary, the voice of the other has to be challenged for its intellectual clarity and practical implications. The classroom is neither an abstract irrelevant space of disengagement nor is it an appropriate place for the resolution of deep-seated therapeutic issues necessitating professional intervention. The mix of voices is an active, challenging, and critical interchange which converses with classroom participants on the nature of each person's claims.

Appropriate questions for this discussion are: Why does one have a certain position? And what is the basis of one's beliefs? Criticism does not mean a purposeless deconstruction, where one is caught up in the rhythm of one's own argument or the wittiness of listening to one's own voice. Criticism is to assist the other in exploring further and to clarify even more clearly one's role in the conversation. And as indicated above, theological pedagogy has a vocational stand with the poor. This implies that at an important level, criticism helps to challenge another person's voice in relation to the outcast.

The other part of the dynamic is self-criticism—the willingness, ability, and art of offering a critique of self-growth. Each person's viewpoint is not stagnant, nor does it reflect ultimate truth. Therefore when one risks a voice in the communal discussion, one is subject, inevitably, to mistakes in judgment, interpretation of experiences, or misuse of theory, or simply fuzziness in presentation. All of these possibilities, and more, give rise to a breakdown in communication. Errors of growth can be pointed out, but the person responsible for the errors does not always perceive self-criticism as a way to enhance the search for a common vision for the public good—that is, framed by the interests of the least in society. Refusal to participate in self-criticism as a form of creative growth tends to produce calcification of thought, retrograde practice, and individualistic self-aggrandizement.

A final integration necessary for theological education is that between compassion and intellect. Since theological education grounds itself in the well being or full humanity of society's marginalized (and through them all peoples), a passionate intellect and an intellectual passion are needed. Black theology seeks a most rigorous attempt at academic and intellectual clarity and purpose, because learning as it pertains to faith and witness is a life-and-death situation if it is in the interest of the margins: the homeless, battered wives, the unemployed, the hungry, the diseased, the physically challenged, the sexually abused, the illiterate, the psychotic, and similar sectors shunned and discarded by the norm of a community. The best minds and the best of our minds should be put to the service of pulling together the foremost knowledge that the ages have produced. The mind and the highest development of the mind are gifts from God not to be wasted, but utilized for the common good.

And since the common good comprises the overwhelming majority who are without resources, intellectual work has to commence at the bottom of the social pyramid in the United States, indeed the world. Academic work, in this regard, entails focused knowledge production that will be attentive to particular social relations, both skewed relationships and visions for healthy community interaction. This, however, does not exclude pursuing exploratory academic concerns which, at first glance, might not appear germane to the common good. Indeed, intellectual undertakings allow for speculative exercises, even at times when these exercises appear seemingly irrelevant or cerebral. Yet the touchstone for such pedagogical endeavors is ultimately how the life of the mind sustains and enhances individual and collective full humanity.

Nonetheless, all intellectual work should have a degree of compassion for the oppressed other. Compassionate pedagogy is to be in solidarity with the best of the individual self, as well as to have passion or pathos with the other who does not have the same privileges as oneself. Compassionate pedagogy is to see and experience, at least vicariously, the other. It is to know and to feel that one's own humanity is at stake in the well-being of the other. This contrasts radically with the bourgeois liberal notion that change occurs by doling out reforms to the poor or indigent. On the contrary, a compassionate theological education pursues the course of structural change, both of the individual and of the community. Otherwise, one's own humanity remains trapped in an asymmetrical configuration of power and privilege.

The leading principle for compassionate pedagogy is that our own humanity cannot be healed, made whole, and free until the other's humanity reaches its fullest potential in the creation offered to us by God. For example, in certain indigenous South African languages, the formal greetings one gives to another is, "I see you and I see your family." This suggests compassionate social interaction. The other becomes a human being in the full sense of the word, making impossible nonrecognition of the human being that is before one's eyes. Similarly, this South African greeting indicates that the recognition of the other comprises saluting and affirming the well-being of the other in connection to the well-being of communal relationships. It is the old adage, found in certain African cosmologies, which states that I am because you are, and the community's existence is for the well-being of each individual.

Theological Viewpoint

The third and final overarching component of theological education, in addition to stand and method, is viewpoint. What is the long-term vision sought by theological education? What are we preparing ourselves for in theological institutions of knowledge production? In brief, theological education exists to work toward and continually re-envision full humanity—a new heaven and a new earth.

On a personal level, full humanity means a healing of personal wounds. Psychotherapy teaches us that we are all suffering as adults due to fundamental scars and unresolved issues from our negative childhood experiences. This covers the range—sexual abuse of children, children of adult alcoholics, low self-esteem, and many different forms of codependency. The individual cannot attain his or her own full potentialized self in relation to community if psychological fractures and ghosts remain to keep us broken and haunted.

If attention is not paid to these particulars, then we simply re-enact our projections and insecurities onto our children, our wives and husbands, our significant others, our students, our coworkers, and our colleagues. Moreover, for those with the power to do so, the lesions of childhood are projected onto society and the world. It is the wounded children within us who take over our adult bodies; and when these adult bodies have power and privilege (e.g., racial, gender, sexual, class), the wounded children within ourselves (which some term the old brain or parts of the unconscious) can be deadly as they seek to make the world pay for the crimes committed against ourselves when we were children. If the full humanity of the individual is not attended to, then these abusive modes of being become intergenerational, passed on to our progeny.

Furthermore, full humanity, which we strive to realize with divine spirituality, speaks also to the wounds brought against those sectors of society collectively set aside as scapegoats. Full humanity, therefore, entails providing the conditions for the unleashing of the fullest creativity of blacks, poor and working-class people, other people of color, women, lesbians and gays, the physically challenged, and others; full humanity also entails providing conditions for the natural growth of a healthy ecology. The full humanity of black Americans would necessarily mean an appreciation of black culture and heritage. This latter reality would not be seen as mere contributions to an already existing white norm. On the contrary, black Americans would enter the essential core of the very structure of the curriculum and American culture. Black people are not simply additions to America; they are constitutive of what it means to be an American.

Ultimately, the viewpoint of theological education struggles for an integrated vision where the resources of the earth are shared by all of humanity. The ultimate viewpoint, then, is a communal one based on an equality of capital ownership, of participation in space and time, of full expression of linguistic difference, of political representation with power, and of complete affirmation of unique cultures and identities. A healthy spirituality, economics, culture, language, everyday ways of being, politics, and faith demarcate the realization of a robust theological viewpoint. And when we reach that balanced full humanity for all, then black theology as a Christian perspective announces the second coming of Jesus with the familiar congratulatory words, "Well done, my faithful brother and sister. Because you have contributed to the full humanity of the least of these, then you have been faithful and accountable to God's vocational imperatives of full humanity itself." For black theology, the stand, method, and viewpoint of theological education is one of liberation and the practice of freedom.

Notes

1. This essay is a modified version of an essay which first appeared in *Theological Education: New Perspectives on Theological Education*, vol. 34, no. 2 (Spring 1998). *Theological Education* is the journal of the Association of Theological Schools in Pittsburgh, Pennsylvania.

2. William Loren Katz, ed., *Five Slave Narratives* (New York: Arno Press, 1968), 20.

3. William Still, *Underground* (Chicago: Johnson Publications, 1970), 458.

4. Quoted in George P. Rawick, ed., *The American Slave: A Composite Autobiography, God Struck Me Dead*, vol. 19 (Westport, Conn.: Greenwood Publishing Company, 1977), 124-25.

5. Quoted in Charles L. Perdue, Jr., ed., *Weevils in the Wheat: Interviews with Virginia Ex-Slaves* (Bloomington, Indiana: Indiana University Press, 1980), 126.

5

Racism and the Church

An Inquiry into the Contradictions between Experience, Doctrine, and Theological Theory[1]

JAMIE T. PHELPS

Introduction: The Challenge of the Sixties

In the late 1960s, I and many black Catholics of the period had begun the struggle to make sense of our participation in a church which, in the popular perspective, was considered by many to be "a white racist institution."[2] Black Catholics found themselves influenced by two major events, the Civil Rights movement and the Second Vatican Council. Initiated by southern black Christians, the Civil Rights movement had steadily captured national attention by focusing on the racial divide which characterized our nation both in the South and in the North. Martin Luther King, Jr.'s Civil Rights movement and Malcolm X's Black Nationalist movement offered alternate solutions to the patterns of racial relationships which viewed Blacks as intellectually and morally inferior to other members of the human race. King, a Christian, advocated integration; Malcolm X, a Black Muslim, advocated constructive separatism.[3] The call for social unity which found a central place in the speeches and writings of Dr. King was echoed by the calls for religious unity in the early writings that followed Pope John XXIII's announcement of his intention to convene an ecumenical council.[4] This double call to transformation caused many black Catholics to examine simultaneously what it meant to be black and Catholic in a racially divided church society.[5]

What does it mean to live as a person who is marginalized because of one's cultural and religious identification? For me and many of my colleagues who had come together to search for black Catholic authenticity, James Cone's book *Black Theology and Black Power* was a liberating text. His interpretation of black power and the need for a black theology, "a theology whose sole purpose is to apply the freeing power of the gospel to black peoples under white oppression,"[6] resonated with our experience of the oppressive dynamics in our ecclesial world.

The earliest position paper of the National Black Sisters' Conference, an association of black Catholic women religious, resonated with the call for the liberation of black people in general and black women in particular as an essential aspect of Christian mission in response to the "signs of the times" evident in 1969.

> We the members of the National Black Sisters' Conference, pledge ourselves to work unceasingly for the liberation of black people. We black religious women see ourselves as gifted with the choicest of God's blessings. The gift of our womanhood, that channel through which the Son of God Himself chose to come into the human race, endows us with those qualities and prerogatives which are designed for the deliverance of humanity. The gift of our blackness gives us our mandate for the deliverance of a special people, our own black folk. And the gift of our religious vocation makes accessible to us that union with Christ which guides us to the task, strengthens our determination, and sustains our efforts to free ourselves and our black brethren from the intolerable burden forced upon us as the victims of white racisms.[7]

The intellectually stimulating and nurturing environment of the National Black Sisters' Conference and subsequent joint meetings with the National Black Catholic Clergy Caucus provided the milieu which motivated some of us first generation of Black Catholic theological scholars to read extensively in the areas of African American thought as well as the Catholic theological traditions. *Black Theology and Black Power* articulated a new creative synthesis of the two worlds of thought—our own research and critical reflection upon black history and culture and academic theology—as these impacted our own journey of faith and that of those among whom we ministered in the context of our Christian service and ministry within the Catholic church.[8] Black Catholic theological and ecclesial scholars in other disciplines, along with other black theological scholars, acknowledge with gratitude Cone's contribution. It initiated, for many of us, the paradigm shift to the social historical and contextual approaches spawned by this manifestation of a formal academic liberation theology in the context of the United States.

James Cone's Ecclesiological Challenge

The third and fourth chapters of Cone's *Black Theology and Black Power* focused on the church. Cone accused both white and the post–Civil War black Christian churches of straying from the authentic mission of the Christian church. Both black and white churches failed to be an instrument of liberation for blacks and other oppressed people in the sixties. The notable exceptions were those churches and ministers who allied with Dr. Martin Luther King, Jr., in the Civil Rights movement. This movement sought to concretize King's prophetic dream of a people united for justice and liberation against the oppression and barriers of race and nationality. King's dream, Cone notes, was "grounded in God, not man."

> If the real church is the people of God, whose primary task is that of being Christ to the world by proclaiming the message of the gospel (*kerygma*), by rendering services of liberation (*diakonia*) and by being itself a manifestation of the nature of the new society (*koinonia*), then the empirical institutionalized white church has failed on all accounts. . . .[9]
>
> We may conclude that except in rare instances, the black churches in the post–Civil War period have been no more Christian than their white counterparts. . . . Black Power advocates are men who were inspired by his [King's] zeal for freedom, and Black Power is their attempt to make his dream a reality. . . . If the black church organizations want to remain faithful to the New Testament Gospel and to the great tradition of the pre–Civil War black church, they must relinquish their stake in the status quo and the values in white society by identifying exclusively with Black Power.[10]

Purpose of This Essay

This exploratory essay will examine the problematic raised by this early work of Cone. What accounts for the failure of many Christian churches to act as liberating agents in combatting the social sin of racism in its interpersonal and systemic forms? Two factors seem to contribute to this failure: first, the assumption of the separation of the sacred and the social-political spheres of reality; and second, the failure of dominant culture scholars to self-critically transcend their own racial-cultural biases because of the pervasiveness of a white supremacist cultural and intellectual ideology. To examine this thesis I will first discuss the social-historical phenomenon of racism in society and church, past and present. Second, I will identify some *select contemporary and past teachings of the Roman Catholic church* relative to race, racism, and slavery. And third, I will explore the religious, social scientific, and philosophical legitimation of race and racism views as the internalized assumptive world of church missionaries, pastoral agents, theologians, and Christians.

The Social-Historical Phenomenon of Racism in Society and Church Past and Present

It is evident that at the beginning of the new millennium, the dynamics of oppression have a Hydra-like quality (i.e., it is a monster with many heads). Such oppression requires a multidimensional and multidirectional approach to human liberation. The overt manifestation of racism has changed considerably since the middle of the twentieth century because the influx of large numbers of Latino/Latina, Asian, African, and Caribbean immigrants has expanded the cultural dimension of the oppressive dynamics of racism. In addition, people are denied the acknowledgment of their full humanity and access to and participation in the mainstreams of social and ecclesial power and responsibility not only because of a racist, white supremacist ideology, but also because of biased ideological thinking regarding gender (patriarchy), class, culture, ethnic or national origin (ethnocentrism), religion, physical ability, sexual orientation, etc. While it is valid and essential to be attentive to these diverse forms of oppression in the pursuit of the liberation of peoples from oppression, such attention must not mask, ignore, or deny the global reality of racism in our contemporary world. Church and social institutions committed to the liberation of oppressed peoples must continue to struggle on behalf of those who are victimized by the racist, white supremacist ideology that undergirds the patterns of interpersonal and institutionalized oppression predicated on racial difference.

In the wake of the highly publicized racist beatings of Rodney King in California and Leonard Clark in Chicago; and the overt racist killings of Amadou Diallo, an African immigrant in New York, Stephen Lawrence in London, and James Byrd, Jr., in Texas, no one should doubt that racism is as alive and well in 1999 as it was in 1969. Some may argue that these are the acts of isolated individuals. However, the evidence of racism's pernicious presence is documented further in the prevailing attempts to reverse the affirmative action laws (legislated during the Civil Rights movement) to overcome the impact of previous patterns of systemic discrimination and the anti-immigrant practices and laws emerging in the United States. These laws focus on limiting the presence and participation or on the expulsion of African, Latino, Caribbean, and Asian immigrants. A similar pattern is manifest in the "ethnic cleansing" occurring in European nations and the "ethnic wars" in Europe, the Middle East, Africa, Asia, and Latin America.

Attitudes of racial and cultural superiority which ground these and other oppressive patterns of relationships are supported by the miseducation of the masses about the contributions of African Americans, Hispanics, Asian Americans, and Native Americans in the history of our nation and the contributions of African, Asian American, Latin American, Caribbean, and Native Peoples to our world culture and society. The prevailing white supremacist ideology and cultural hegemony continue to benefit from the organizational arrangements and relationships which characterize many places of employment and our housing patterns.[11]

Many black Americans and other oppressed groups, who are explicit targets of racism, testify to its persistence and pernicious destructiveness.[12] The overt racist acts which contribute to the physical injury and death of black men and women in the United States are only a small manifestation of the negative human consequences of racism. More pernicious is the covert impact of racism. Racism contributes to mental, social, physical, economic, and moral anxiety for those who attempt to engage as equal and active participants and coworkers in institutions whose leadership is insensitive or indifferent to the impact of the exclusive focus on the concerns and needs of the members of the dominant culture. The continual denial of the significant contributions (of the skills, insights, and world view of persons from nondominant diverse ethnic-cultural and class backgrounds) to the whole community contributes to those institutions' inability to function on behalf of the common good of all their constituents.

Moreover, marginalization of blacks, Hispanics, Asian Americans, and Native Americans in such institutions lead to the inadequate addressing of the issues of primary concern for the social and spiritual well-being of women and men from these diverse cultural groups. Racism also threatens the spiritual, moral, and physical well-being of both the oppressor and the oppressed, the dominator and the dominated. Both fail to realize their full humanity and human potential as constructive contributors to a common good which embraces all. Only the creation of alternative culturally specific social institutions, programs, and organizations has allowed blacks and other oppressed peoples to develop and use their talents and insights in a manner which is beneficial to themselves and ultimately to the whole society. (The black church itself is perhaps the largest and most consistent evidence that culturally specific institutions can be the nurturing ground to assist oppressed and marginalized people to develop their talent, genius, and positive self-esteem and to exercise their human freedom in culturally diverse social and ecclesial arenas.)

The tragic history of racism within the Catholic church of the urban North in the mid-twentieth century is documented in John T. McGreevey's recent book *Parish Boundaries: The Catholic Encounter with Race in the Twentieth-Century Urban North*. This text documents the concrete history of misguided ethnocentrism which became the springboard for overt racist rejection of blacks and other nonwhite people from northern Catholic parishes, and the efforts of select white Catholic leaders to struggle against racism within the church.[13] Misled by their pastors' affirmation and insistence that segregation was not wrong, many ethnic Catholics in Chicago resisted the admission of African American Catholics to their parishes and schools.[14] The movement of one single family into an ethnic Catholic neighborhood or parish was often cause for protest. In such a crowd, one Catholic man was heard to say, "I don't want those jigs sitting in the same pew with me!"; while a seventeen-year-old quickly responded that "those niggers don't join the church anyhow."[15] The phenomena of "changing parishes" and the migration of ethnic Catholics to the suburbs was fueled by ethnocentrism, economic prosperity, and racism. Some clergy and religious courageously went against the tide and condemned the "middle-class materialism" which attempted to "justify segregation by saying that it produces peace and harmony by keeping separate people who would otherwise be in conflict."[16]

Made blind and deaf by fear, historical and theological ignorance, and the desire for economic material security and cultural inclusion themselves, many ethnic Catholics, during the major part of the twentieth century, failed to hear the cries of their black brothers and sisters who were Catholic. Many failed to welcome potential converts who were unchurched or journeying from one denomination to another to find a church home. Many turned a deaf ear of indifference or ignorance to the emerging voice of Catholic social teachings which gradually condemned segregation and racism. Such indifference robs the church of the gift of black spirituality and genius and thwarts its effort to preach the gospel effectively within the African American community.

However, the historical picture was not completely negative. While many Catholics remained hostile or indifferent to the presence of blacks in their social and ecclesial communities, some black and white Catholics joined together to mobilize against racism. The earliest nationally organized effort in the twentieth century was in the form of black self-help initiated by Thomas Wyatt Turner who founded the Federated Colored Catholics in 1925.[17] Turner's organization was succeeded by two distinct Catholic approaches to the problem of racism in the church. One focused on black Catholic self-help and development, the other focused on the moral conversion of whites and integration.

The conventions of Federated Colored Catholics, like the nineteenth-century congresses before them, focused on developing black Catholic initiative and leadership in the Catholic church on behalf of African Americans. Its true legacy was reactivated in the mid-twentieth century with the emergence of the National Black Catholic Clergy Caucus, the National Black Sisters' Conference, the National Office of Black Catholics, the National Black Catholic Seminarians' Association, the National Association of Black Catholic Administrators, and finally the National Black Catholic Congress.

The direct offspring of the Federated Colored Catholics was the Catholic Interracial Council which was born at the expense of the demise of Thomas Wyatt Turner's leadership and vision. This organization, like Friendship House, the Young Christian Students, and similar Catholic organizations, attempted to combat the negative impact of racism on both whites and blacks by focusing their efforts on bringing together blacks and whites to study and to establish programs to change the social patterns of segregation. Together the black self-help organization and the integrationist organizations became an Abrahamic minority valiantly struggling to overcome the moral and social challenges rooted in racism. But their efforts were insufficient to impact the consciences of the vast majority of ethnic Catholics.

During the sixties and seventies, in the same areas where predominantly white Christian congregations floundered and saw drastic reduction in the membership of their urban churches because of white flight, some predominantly black congregations began to flourish under the leadership of creative black and white pastors and pastoral staffs who were attuned to social experiences and the cultural renaissance emerging in the African American community. These pastoral ministers were able, and continue, to address the liberating gospel of Jesus Christ in such a way that it empowers black men and women to overcome their internalized racism and act as agents of social transformation.[18] Men and women who have transcended the debilitating aspects of racial and cultural patterns within dominant culture institutions in their communities have been empowered to call their black and nonblack brothers and sisters to conversion. They call their nonblack sisters and brothers to a wholeness and holiness by forsaking their racist, white supremacist attitudes and practices which foster the oppressive dynamics and unjust patterns of relationship within these institutions. They call their black sisters and brothers and other oppressed groups to embrace their human equality, freedom, and creative intelligence with the confidence of their own cultural gifts, insights, and world views as gifts given for the benefit of the whole community.

The presence of two-and-a-half to three million black Catholics (including recent immigrants from Africa and the Caribbean) within the U.S. Catholic church is a clear sign of the historic presence and action of the Holy Spirit mediated by those African American, Hispanic, Asian, Native American, and European American Catholic women and men who refused to capitulate to the racist practices which continue to haunt our church and society. Many are currently participating in the dynamics of inculturation, which enable blacks and other oppressed groups to explore the meaning and significance of the God of Jesus Christ for their particular cultural or social location. The process of inculturation has allowed African Americans within the Catholic church to reap the benefit of their dual heritage as a Catholic and African cultural people.[19]

The Racist Problematic at the End of the Twentieth Century

At the beginning of the new millennium, we are faced with an ambiguous situation within our nation. On the one hand, the nation celebrates the gifts and talents of the few highly publicized "black stars" in politics, sports, literature, science, and the corporate world who have transcended the race barrier. On the other hand, the majority of blacks are perceived as expendable for the economic and social infrastructure of our country. These poor masses continue to struggle at low levels of social and economic survival. For them and many middle- and upper-class African Americans, the barriers to full and equal participation continue.

> Barriers and disadvantages persist in blocking black advancement. Three such barriers to full opportunity for black Americans are residential segregation, continuance of diffuse and often indirect discrimination, and exclusion from the social networks essential for full access to economic and educational opportunities.[20]

A similar dynamic seems to be at work within the church. While a few local or national black "ecclesial stars" are able to transcend the cultural barriers, the skills, talents, and spiritual gifts of the majority of the black Catholic women and men are unacknowledged. Racism makes the presence of black Catholics invisible to the vast majority of Catholics. Their concerns and needs are seldom the targeted priority of the church planning offices; and they continue to exist in the peripheral view of many of our ecclesial and pastoral leaders and theologians because of their "perceived statistical insignificance"!

Yet many black Catholic women and men, with a spirit of "invisible dignity, quiet grace, and unshouted courage," continue to collaborate with their ecclesial leaders in the ministries and Christian services implemented by local congregations within and beyond the members of their civic and ecclesial communities.[21] Others, tired of the struggle and debilitating drain of constant personal negation, are abandoning the Catholic community to join black Christian denominations or Christian denominations which, to them, seem to embody more fully the unifying power of a spiritually focused life. Still others abandon Christian belief altogether or embrace noninstitutionalized religious or secular approaches to life. Systemic racism frustrates the church's mission to be a universal sacrament of salvation and the mediator of God's call to communion. The community-building (*koinonia*), service (*diakonia*), and proclamation (*kerygma*) aspects of the churches' evangelizing and social justice mission, which continues the mission and ministry of Jesus Christ, is still being compromised

Select Teachings of the Roman Catholic Church

Catholic insensitivity and silence regarding institutionalized racism contribute to the immoral, inhuman devaluation and marginalization of the life issues of Blacks, Hispanics, Asian Americans, and Native Americans within our church assemblies and institutions. In 1979, the U.S. Catholic bishops acknowledged the persistence of racism within the U.S. Catholic church. Regarding institutionalized racism, they noted that the decisions which impact the lives of Black, Hispanic, Asian American, and Native American members of the church were made by many who have little or no primary knowledge or experience of our history, culture, presence, or contributions to the church.

> All too often in the very places where blacks, Hispanics, Native Americans and Asians are numerous, the Church's officials and representatives, both clerical and lay, are predominantly white. Efforts to achieve racial balance in government, the media, the armed services, and other crucial areas of secular life should not only be supported but surpassed in the institutions and programs of the Catholic Church.[22]

This acknowledgment is just one instance of our institutional journey in which episcopal, theological, and pastoral leaders in the Roman Catholic church have continually emphasized the socially inclusive nature of the gospel. The Second Vatican Council's teachings regarding human life provide some fundamental principles central to its identification of racism as a social sin which requires a radical conversion to overcome.

Respect for life, particularly human life, has always been and continues to be a centerpiece of the Catholic moral tradition. This reality was re-emphasized in *Gaudium et Spes*, the Second Vatican Council's *Pastoral Constitution on the Church in the Modern World*.[23]

> [E]veryone must consider his every neighbor *without exception* as another self, taking into account first of all his [the person's] life and the means necessary to living it with dignity . . . *whatever is opposed to life itself . . . whatever violates the integrity of the human person . . . whatever insults human dignity . . . are infamies . . . they poison human society . . .* Do (ing) more harm to those who practice them than to those who suffer from the injury. *They are a supreme dishonor to the creator.* (GS, 27, emphasis mine)

While racism is not explicitly mentioned in the passage above, it does explicitly mention "*slavery and genocide*" as two realities which oppose life, insult human dignity, and treat humans as tools of profit rather than as free responsible persons. Acknowledging the distinctions based on "*sex, race, color, social condition, language or religion,*" *Gaudium et Spes* insists that these differences should not be the basis for denying the basic equality, rights, and responsibilities of all human beings (GS, 29). *Gaudium et Spes* renders a clear, universal, and unequivocal condemnation of slavery and racial discrimination.[24]

However, the strongest condemnation of racism was in the 1979 U.S. bishops' pastoral letter on racism, *Brothers and Sisters to Us*. The Bishops' Conference had issued four pastoral letters on racial discrimination and racism between 1959 and 1979; however, none of them had uttered such a clear and unequivocal statement on the nature of racism as a social sin.[25]

> Racism is a sin; a sin that divides the human family, blots out the image of God among specific members of that family, and violates the fundamental human dignity of those called to be children of the same Father. Racism is the sin that says some human beings are inherently superior and others essentially inferior because of race. It is the sin that make racial characteristics the determining factor for the exercise of human rights. It mocks the words of Jesus, "Treat others the way you would have them treat you."[26] Racism is more than a disregard for the words of Jesus; it is a denial of the truth of the dignity of each human being revealed by the mystery of the Incarnation. . . . Racism is not merely one sin among many, it is a radical evil that divides the human family and denies the new creation of a redeemed world. To struggle against it demands an equally radical transformation, in our own minds and hearts as well as in the structure of society. Conversion is the ever present task of each Christian.[27]

Some nine years later, the Pontifical Commission for Justice and Peace's 1988 document entitled *The Church and Racism* noted that the U.S. bishops' pastoral cited above was "the most important document of the last decade." The Roman document speaks of the long-standing racist ideologies, behaviors, and biologically determined racial prejudices which predicate a superiority of one race or ethnic group with respect to others.[28] It further describes the social historical dynamics of racial injustice and identifies the many diverse faces of institutionalized racism manifested throughout the world.

> Racial injustice, i.e. racism, is manifest "by segregation based on racial theories . . . expressed phenomena of exclusion or aggressivity" perpetrated by one group of persons against another whose physical appearance or ethnic, cultural or religious characteristics are different from those of the dominant group, and are interpreted by the latter as being signs of an innate and definite inferiority, thereby justifying discriminatory practices in this regard . . . racist prejudice, which dictates racist behavior, can be applied by extension, with equally negative effects, to all persons whose

ethnic origin, language, religion or customs make them appear different."[29] ... Racial injustice manifests itself differently throughout the
world, some examples will have to suffice:

1. *Constitutional Injustice:* The constitution and laws of a country. It is
   justified by an ideology of the superiority of persons from European
   stock over those of African or Indigenous origin or "coloured" ...
   [and] supported by erroneous interpretation of the Bible. [30]
2. *Aboriginal Devaluation:* Discrimination against and segregation of
   aboriginal peoples.[31]
3. *Racial/Ethnic Exclusion from Full Citizenship:* Traces of discriminatory legislation which limit to one degree or another the civil and religious rights of those belonging to religious minorities ... of different
   ethnic groups from those of the majority of citizens.[32]
4. *Ethnocentricity:* The denigration of persons whose identity and culture
   differ from one's own and the refusal to recognize their full human
   equality.... A rejection of differences in values, beliefs, and customs
   which can lead to "cultural annihilation which sociologists have called
   'ethnocide' and which does not tolerate the presence of others except
   to the extent that they allow themselves to be assimilated into the dominant culture."[33]
5. *Social Racism:* Citizens from the same nation are "treated without any
   regard for their dignity and their rights, driven from their lands,
   exploited and kept in a situation of economic and social inferiority by
   all-powerful landowners who benefit from the indifferent or active
   complicity of the authorities."[34]
6. *Spontaneous Racism:* Discrimination against recent "immigrants or
   foreigners of ethnic or religious origins" different from the dominant
   group.[35]
7. *Anti-Semitism:* Groups and individuals who keep alive the anti-Semitic
   racist myth and attitudes by speech, publications or terrorist acts
   "which have Jewish persons or symbols as their target."[36]

A critical reading and detailed reading of the entire text of these two major
official statements issued by the Roman Catholic church in the twentieth century form the doctrinal foundation for the Roman Catholics engaging in the
ministry of liberating our church and nation from the interpersonal and institutionalized sins of racism and white supremacist ideology. These documents
make it clear that such ministry is an essential aspect of the church's evangelizing and social justice mission.[37]

Racism and the Roman Catholic Doctrinal and Theological Tradition[38]

While both documents are clear condemnations of racism as a social sin evident
throughout the world, the Roman document, *The Church and Racism,* argues
more extensively that racism violates the teachings of the Magisterium (i.e.,

Catholic church doctrine). The fundamental error of white racism is the denial of the full humanity, intelligence, and equality of Africans and other dark-skinned peoples and cultures, thereby justifying the limitation of black and other oppressed peoples. Oppressed people are prohibited by law or social convention from exercising their human power and responsibility to participate in the construction of social and ecclesial institutions necessary to protect the common good of all their members.

The church's notion of human nature (its theological anthropology) is rooted in the biblical teaching that human beings were made in "the image of God." This notion of human nature asserts the basic goodness and the social nature of humanity.[39] Accordingly, all human persons have an inherent dignity based on their common essential identity (as children of God), their common nature and origin (graced nature and divine origin), their common means of redemption (Jesus Christ), their common calling and destiny (full union with one another and God), and their basic equality (human beings on a journey to full humanity and communion with God).

> All men [and women] are endowed with a rational soul and are created in God's image; they have the same nature and origin, and being redeemed by Christ, they enjoy the same divine calling and destiny; there is here a basic equality between all men [and women] and it must be given ever greater recognition.[40]

The philosophical ground of contemporary Roman Catholic doctrine and theology focuses on the understanding of *human persons* as rational human beings who have the right to exercise their free will in accord with their conscience in a manner which demonstrates responsible participation in processes of self-actualization and social responsibility. The latter is directed toward true happiness and fulfillment of the individual as a member of a community. The church's very existence assumes that human persons are by nature social creatures who can only develop their full humanity in the context of community.[41]

The central understandings of the church regarding the significance of history, and ordinary human experience as the medium of God's salvation and revelation, are compromised and violated by the social sin of racism.[42] While the limitation of this text prevents a full exposition of these various Catholic doctrines, their essential perspective on the meaning of life from a Christian perspective may be summarized. All human persons are divinely created "in the image of God" and are ultimately destined for reunion with the Triune God for all eternity. As Christians we find in Jesus Christ the embodied reality of our origin and destiny. Jesus reveals to us God's universal salvific love. In response to God's love, and empowered by the risen Christ and the Holy Spirit, human persons are invited to freely choose to live in harmonious community (communion) under the reign of God. We are invited to form a community of love and justice which images the Triune God "as community of three persons," having distinct personal identities and roles which they share in their identity as the divine one.[43]

The kingdom of God inaugurated and mediated the life, preaching, teaching, death, resurrection, and ascension into heaven of Jesus. But it will not be fully realized until the eschaton. We, who form the community of church committed to God as revealed through Jesus Christ, are charged to prepare for the full realization of God's reign in the kingdom. We act as mediators of God's love and liberating power and universal sacrament when our words and actions reveal to others their identity as people of God called to the fullness of life (Jn 10:10). Through these words and actions, people experience the presence of God's saving love and liberation which enable them to mediate God's love and liberating power. Salvation, in this perspective, is understood as an ongoing process and journey, in which our tendency toward evil and domination is overcome by the power of God's love and liberation, as manifested in a paradigmatic and unique way in the redemptive life, death, and resurrection of Jesus Christ.

Jesus entered into human history (Incarnation) to teach us how to live as full human beings as we journey toward full and right relationships with one another, all creation, and God. As such, human persons are called to live in harmonious community (communion). Such a communion images the Triune God (i.e., a single divine "community of three persons"[44]).

Those who say "yes" to God's invitation to life in community live under the power of God's self-gift of grace. Those who say "no" to God's invitation to community live in social and divisive alienation under the power of sin. Racism is a sin that negates everything for which Jesus lived, preached, and died. It negates his liberation of us from sin and all that oppresses, and it delays the full realization of communion in the kingdom of God. As *Brothers and Sisters to Us* reminds us, "Racism is not merely one sin among many, it is a radical evil that divides the human family and denies the new creation of a redeemed world."[45]

Structural or Institutional Racism

The most comprehensive and descriptive sociopolitical definition of racism that I have found in all my research on the topic is that of James Boggs. While Boggs's work predates the issuance of *The Church and Racism* by the Roman Catholic Peace and Justice Commission by approximately eighteen years, its comprehensive view of racism anticipates the global view articulated in that document. Boggs defines racism as a systemic or structural evil which permeates all the dynamics and patterns of human interaction.

> Racism is the systemized oppression of one race [group] by another, in other words, the various forms of oppression within every sphere of social relations—economic exploitation, military subjugation, political subordination, cultural devaluation, psychological violation, sexual degradation, verbal abuse, etc., together make up a whole interacting and developing process which operates so normally and naturally and is so much a part of the existing institutions of the society, that the individuals involved are rarely conscious of their operation. As Fanon says, "The racist in a culture of racism is therefore normal."[46]

Clearly Boggs is describing the local and global phenomenon of institutional-ized racism in its communal and interpersonal dynamic and in its embeddedness in the human and social psyche of the human community. Even today, these fac-tors make it difficult for members of the dominant culture to acknowledge the presence of racism, while members of racially oppressed groups are constantly confronted by its all pervasive nature.

Understanding community as world-wide or global reality, Pope Paul VI's encyclical, *Populorum Progressio* (The Progress of Peoples), written in 1967, expressed grave concern about class divisions within the world. While the fun-damental relationships between rich and poor nations and the rich and poor within nations were the major foci of this document, Paul VI clearly acknowl-edges racism as one aspect that militated against the progress of peoples.

> There are other obstacles to creation of a more just social order and to the development of world solidarity: nationalism and racism. . . .
>
> *Racism* is not the exclusive attribute of young nations, where some-times it hides beneath the rivalries of clans and political parties. . . . During the colonial period it often flared up between the colonists and the indigenous population, and stood in the way of mutually profitable understanding, often giving rise to bitterness in the wake of genuine injus-tices. It is still an obstacle to collaboration among disadvantaged nations and a cause of division and hatred within countries whenever individuals and families see the inviolable rights of the human person held in scorn, as they themselves are unjustly subjected to a regime of discrimination because of their race or their color.[47]

The Religious Legitimation of Slavery

The recognition of the immorality of slavery and underlying racist ideology was a gradual process for Roman Catholicism. The nineteenth-century separation of the world into social and spiritual spheres, to allow for the rightful autonomy of the monarch and subsequent forms of government, led to the false bifurcation of reality into two realms, the secular and sacred. The groundwork for the church's contemporary teachings on racism evolved as the church realized that slavery was not a social-political and economic issue but a moral one.

From the sixth to the twentieth century, the common Catholic teaching held that the *social, economic, and legal institution* of slavery was morally legitimate provided the slave was properly looked after and cared for both materially and spiritually.[48] Although the nineteenth-century letters of Pope Gregory XVI and Pope Leo XIII condemned the slave trade and slavery, the church's official recognition of the immorality of slavery and its contradiction of the funda-mental teachings of the church were hampered in the U.S. Catholic church by the pervasive adaptation of the moral interpretation of slavery of Francis Patrick Kenrick, a leading Catholic moral theologian during the nineteenth century. His major work *Theologia Moralis,* argued that slavery was not contrary to the natural law or church tradition.[49] His text, used in most of the Catholic seminaries before the Civil War, gave theological legitimacy to the general acceptance of slavery by most Catholic bishops, priests, and laity at that time.

As a consequence, some bishops themselves held slaves and were officially and publicly silent about slavery before and during the Civil War. Slavery was considered primarily as a political rather than moral issue, but some were privately proslavery because it was a legally sanctioned institution, and they cautioned against the abolitionist movement because such activity contradicted the sovereignty of the state in political matters.[50] After the war, some bishops evidenced a shift in their proslavery and anti-abolitionist attitudes, manifesting some degree of intellectual and moral conversion.[51] A variety of views were held relative to the slaves' souls, their spiritual state and potential, and the masters' role and duties in response to these religious theories.

The "Scientific" and Philosophical Legitimation of the Myth of Race

The religious legitimation of slavery was compounded by the scientific and philosophical legitimation of racial theories which arose in the context of the European "Enlightenment." Race theory was born as a result of a complex fusion of historical choices, white supremacist ideology, and social, "scientific," philosophical, and psychological theories which were used to justify the economic system of slavery in America.[52] I must underscore the fact that race is a socially constructed myth predicated on a false theoretical base, which, when perpetuated by continued racial thinking and classifications, can and has led to disastrous results for people's lives.[53] Human beings, on the basis of race, have been and continue to be treated as less than human because of their biological phenotypes or national origins. Human beings (such as African and other First Peoples of various continents) have been enslaved, colonized, and conquered on the basis of race. The "Enlightenment" racial theories, which asserted the superiority of white-skinned Europeans, worked in combination with economic greed and the religious legitimation of a "manifest destiny" to fuel the Middle Passage and the conquest and the extermination of Native Americans (in North and South America) and Native Africans (throughout the African continent). Similar motivations fueled the Holocaust in Germany.

Cornel West argues that "white supremacy" (a.k.a. racism) was an integral part of the development of modernity.

> The creative fusion of scientific investigation, Cartesian epistemology, and classical ideals produced forms of rationality, scientificity and objectivity which, though efficacious in the quest of truth and knowledge, prohibited the intelligibility and legitimacy of the idea of black equality, beauty, culture, and intellectual capacity. In fact, to "think" such an idea was to be deemed irrational, barbaric, or mad.[54]

West goes on to outline how the white supremacist *a priori* of Western philosophical epistemology precluded any positive evaluation of black humanity.

The inductive and deductive methods of scientific investigation, with their characteristic use of observation and evidence, were supported by the philosophical validations of Francis Bacon's search for some "general laws to facilitate" philosophy's aim to give humankind mastery over nature. In addition, Descartes's focus on the "primacy of the subject and the pre-eminence of representation" in philosophy's task of interpreting ("picturing and representing") the world incorporated his notions of duality as an integral aspect of scientific and aesthetic valuations.[55]

The supremacist evaluation of European culture, intellect, and morality (i.e., white supremacist ideology) was embedded in the classifications, descriptions, representations, and order-imposing aims of natural history.[56] Combined with the reappropriation of the Greek classical ideals of beauty, proportion, and moderation, white supremacy places African peoples beyond what Cornel West terms the "normative gaze" of the Enlightenment world view.

The notion of race was constructed on the negative evaluation accorded the other, who did not conform to these aesthetic and cultural ideals. Skin color would become the first observable clue toward such racial identification and devaluation. The comparative work of the naturalist Carolus Linnaeus typifies the work of the period. According to West, Linnaeus's racial classifications contrasted the character and disposition of Europeans and Africans. Europeans are white, sanguine, brawny beings having abundant flowing hair and blue eyes. They are gentle, acute, and inventive in disposition. They govern themselves according to customs among which is the wearing of close vestments (clothes). By contrast, Africans are black, phlegmatic, and relaxed beings having black frizzy hair, flat noses, and tumid lips. They are crafty, indolent, and negligent. Habitually anointing themselves with grease, they govern themselves by caprice.[57]

The primary research of Emmanuel Chukwudi Exe, Theo David Goldberg, and West is in agreement about the role of the European Enlightenment in the scientific legitimation of race theory. According to Exe, a perusal of the anthropological understandings of some of the leading Enlightenment philosophers reveals their negative evaluation of non-European persons and cultures. For example, Kant's anthropological writings suggest a natural emotional and intellectual inferiority of the "Negroes of Africa."

The Negroes of Africa have by nature no feeling that rises above the trifling. Mr. Hume challenges anyone to cite a single example in which a Negro has shown talents, and asserts that among the hundreds of thousands of blacks who are transported elsewhere from their countries, although many of them have been set free, still not a single one was ever found who presented anything great in art or science or any other praiseworthy quality, even though among whites some continually rise aloft from the lowest rabble, and through superior gifts earn the respect of the world. So fundamental is the difference between the two races, and it appears to be as great in regard mental capacities as in color.[58]

Theo David Goldberg's work argues that the development of modern race theory focuses on the Enlightenment concern for order as manifested in the social realm in terms of bureaucracy, in the political realm in terms of law, and in the economic realm in terms of the market.[59] Accompanying modernity's concern for order was its concern for material, moral, philosophical, and political progress expressed in terms of the development of civilization. Within this context of law, order, and progress, modernity introduced the notion of a Subject, abstracted from the particularities of history, and understood as an ideal person ruled solely by reason. This Subject was endowed by his (the ideal, of course, was male) impartiality, objectivity, ability, and power to mediate the difference and tension confronted within the diverse realms of reality. The concept of race emerged as a notion which "pretends to universality in undertaking to draw otherwise disparate social subjects together into a cohesive unit in terms of which common interests are either found or fabricated."[60]

Philosophical traditions of liberalism, though diverse, share a core of general ideas: the search for universal principles applicable to all human beings or rational agents by virtue of their humanity or rationality; the belief that each individual has the capacity to be moved by reason; and a commitment to the principle of equality.[61] Ironically, Goldberg notes,

> The more explicitly universal modernity's commitments, the more open it is to and the more determined it is by the likes of racial specificity and racist exclusivity. . . . As modernity committed itself progressively to idealized principles of liberty, equality, and fraternity, as it increasingly insisted upon the moral irrelevance of race, there was a multiplication of racial identities and the sets of exclusions they prompted and rationalized, enabled and sustained.[62]

The search for universality led to the identification of particularity and difference in human beings, which relegated some to be identified as less human or nonhuman.

It is clear, from the above, that the nineteenth-century religious justification of slavery and its false anthropological view of the slave, combined with the pseudoscientific developments within the fields of social and natural sciences and liberal philosophy, have collectively supported and legitimized the construction of the pseudoscientific myth of race. This myth has permeated our collective unconscious and is manifest in what Goldberg terms a racialist culture, spawning institutions which are racist.

Race and Culture

Being attentive to the notion of racist ideology, one must make a distinction between race, racism, and culture. The theory and history of slavery and racism are distinct from culture theory. Race is, as we have suggested earlier, a complex, socially constructed myth of racial categories or classifications created to establish the superiority of white-skinned peoples over dark-skinned peoples. Through the use of pseudoscience, these racial theories predicate certain moral or behavioral and historical developments as a consequence of race.[63]

Despite the failure of nineteenth- and twentieth-century biologists, geneticists, and social scientists to validate consistent attributes to distinguish races (skin color, hair type, facial form, stature, skull shape, eye structure, language, religion, and customs), racial theory is perpetuated by constant reference to racial classification as a cause for certain moral or behavioral characteristics.[64]

Culture needs to be distinguished from race. The former can be defined as the customs, norms, values, and world view a particular group constructs to nurture and sustain the life of its members.[65] Black culture refers to a wide variety of cultures on the African continent, and in the Diaspora of the United States, Latin America, the Caribbean, Europe, and Asia. Such a depiction of culture acknowledges that African peoples throughout the world have developed distinct ways of living and distinct value systems and world views to nurture and sustain their lives. Culture is a dynamic, ongoing process and is a product of people acting as subjects in human history; it represents the creation of material expressions, ways of organizing life and the creation of an interpretive intellectual lens or world view.

The writings of W. E. B. Du Bois, a black classical scholar in the field of sociology, provide a model example of how the adoption of race theory can confuse "cultural" realities with "racial" ones. In my opinion, Du Bois's classical notion of "double consciousness" is more accurately interpreted as a reflection of his *bicultural identity,* rather then an assertion of race identity.

A peculiar sensation, this double consciousness, this sense of always looking at one's self through the eyes of others, of measuring one's soul by the tape of a world that looks on in amused contempt and pity. One forever feels his twoness—an American, a Negro; two souls, two thoughts, two unreconciled strivings; two warring ideals in one dark body, whose dogged strength alone keeps it from being torn asunder. . . . The history of the American Negro is the history of strife . . . this longing to attain self-conscious manhood, to merge his double self into a better truer self. In this merging he wishes neither of the older selves to be lost. He would not Africanize America, for America has too much to teach the world and Africa. He would not bleach his Negro soul in a flood of white Americanism, for he knows that Negro blood has a message for the world. He simply wishes to make it possible to be both Negro and American, without being cursed and spit upon by his fellows, without having doors of opportunity closed roughly in his face. . . . This, then, is the end of his striving: to be a co-worker in the Kingdom of culture, to escape both death and isolation, to husband and use his best powers and his latent genius. These powers of body and mind have in the past been strangely wasted, dispersed, or forgotten.[66]

Du Bois's reference to his *dark body and Negro blood* and his self-conscious world of thought (i.e., *two souls, two thoughts; two strivings, two warring ideals*) indicates a fusion of *a biologically determined race* represented by the first reference and *sociological or anthropological theories of culture* which encompass an individual's or group's world view, thoughts, ideals, and values. His concluding desire to *cultivate his best powers and latent genius of body and mind* is clearly more a cultural reference, in our late twentieth-century interpretation of these terms. The conflation of race and culture is demonstrated even more clearly in another of his works:

> What then is race? It is a vast family of human beings, generally of common blood and language, always of common history, traditions and impulses, who are both voluntarily and involuntarily striving together for the accomplishment of certain more or less vividly conceived ideals of life.[67]

Here his references to *common history, traditions, impulses, striving together for the accomplishment of certain ideals of life* are more an aspect of what contemporary scholars recognize as characteristic of culture rather than of race.

Despite his conflation of race and culture, Du Bois describes and speaks accurately of the barriers constructed by the dominant culture because of the false notions of race prevalent during his time. The dominant culture viewed Africans and African Americans as persons devoid of culture, save that transmitted to them by their slave masters. This, however, could not have been further from the truth, as our retrieval work in the process of inculturations is revealing.

Conclusion

It is clear that in the past sacred scripture has been used erroneously by many missionaries, ministers, and Christians to justify racial injustice, segregation, and oppression in the name of a misguided notion of redemption and salvation translated into a notion of "manifest destiny." Catholic missionaries, colonial agents, slave masters, and members of other Christian churches all capitulated to the prevailing social ideological errors of their times. The separation of reality into two separate realms (the sacred and the secular), erroneous theological and moral interpretations, and a noncritical stance against the false theories of race (which were developed in the nineteenth century) delayed the U.S. Catholic church's adoption of Rome's early denunciation of the slave trade and slavery. In the U.S. context, both were originally seen as social-political issues more properly the concern of the state. However, individual voices of bishops, women and men religious, and prominent lay Catholics from diverse ethnic-racial groups condemned slavery, segregation, and racism before, during, and after the Civil War.

Despite the fact that the virus of racism still infects individuals and institutions within the Catholic church in the United States and throughout the world, men and women from oppressed ethnic and cultural backgrounds have been able to grow in wisdom, age, and grace; they have contributed to the theological, moral, and social development of our church and nation throughout the history of the Catholic church.[68]

Despite tensions that continue to exist around the issues of racism within the church and society, the church, nevertheless, has made clear her contemporary official teachings (doctrines) that any form of racism, domination, or system of oppression is contrary to the mission and message of Jesus and the will of God implicit in our human identity.

Two problems remain: first, many Catholics know little of the official social teachings of the church in general and those on racism in particular. And second, although action against racism has recently been a priority agenda for many U.S. Catholic dioceses and archdioceses, often more pressing internal issues deflect the finances and attention of church officials.

Despite these realities, Catholic Christians have nothing to prevent them from participating in the struggle for the liberation of other human beings who are dehumanized and marginalized by the oppressive dynamics of racism, sexism, homophobia, ethnocentrism, anti-Semitism, nationalism, and so forth. In fact, the church admonishes them that, by so doing, they are continuing the mission of Jesus as he confirmed his life and preaching to the will of God. Churches and groups that struggle for the liberation of the poor and the oppressed continue the mission of Jesus, whose preaching, deeds, and actions inaugurated the kingdom of God, as exemplified by the establishment of right relationships between human beings, cultures, ethnic groups, and nations. Such efforts to establish communion anticipate in small historical ways the full realization of the reign of God, which we still await.

Still there exists a contradiction between the church's contemporary teachings which affirm the essential universality and basic equality of human beings and denounce the social sin of racism, on the one hand, and the all-too-common exclusionary practices of some church members and leaders in relation to African Americans, Hispanics, Native Americans, and the poor of all cultures, on the other. This contradiction will only be overcome when the racist, white supremacist ideology, which has been legitimized by false science, is more universally condemned, and the elimination of racism is made more of an individual and institutional priority as a constitutive element of the biblical and social justice traditions of our church. The fact that many see racism as a normal and natural consequence of the history of the social construction of reality does not make it so. Fidelity to the gospel and Jesus' vision of the kingdom require the radical conversion of the heart called for in *Brothers and Sisters to Us*. Such a conversion will reveal the sinful destructiveness of racism to the whole human community and will motivate us to deconstruct racist theory and construct social and ecclesial institutions which transcend racist, white supremacist ideology.

Notes

1. This article is the initial fruit of some of the historical, theological, and philosophical research I have been doing on the themes of racism and culture in preparation for a forthcoming untitled book on ecclesiology.

2. "A Statement of the Black Catholic Clergy Caucus," in *Black Theology: A Documentary History Volume One: 1966-1979* (Maryknoll, N.Y.: Orbis Books, 1993), 230-32.

3. See James H. Cone's analysis of these two movements in *Martin and Malcolm and America* (Maryknoll, N.Y.: Orbis Books, 1991).

4. See Giuseppe Alberigo and Joseph A. Komonchak, *History of Vatican II* (New York: Orbis Books, 1995), 33.

5. Black Catholics who stayed within the church tended to follow Martin's ideals while others left Catholicism, having been inspired by the clear oratory of Malcolm X. They were also inspired by the religious discipline and focused economic and social self-determination which characterized the successful schools and small black businesses established by the Black Muslims.

6. James H. Cone, *Black Theology and Black Power,* revised edition (Maryknoll, N.Y.: Orbis Books, 1997), 31.

7. *Black Survival: Past, Present and Future: Proceedings of the Second National Black Sisters' Conference* (Pittsburgh, National Black Sisters' Conference, 1969). This conference convened at the University of Dayton, Dayton, Ohio, August 6-16, 1969.

8. *Theology, a Portrait in Black: Proceedings of the Black Catholic Theological Symposium—1978*, no. 1, ed. Thaddeus J. Posey, O.F.M. Cap. (private circulation, National Black Catholic Clergy Caucus, 1980) documents one of the first collective efforts at theologizing from the starting point of our black experience.

9. Cone, *Black Theology and Black Power*, 71.

10. Ibid., 108-9.

11. See William Julius Wilson, *When Work Disappears: The World of the New Urban Poor* (New York: Alfred A. Knopf, 1996), and Douglas S. Massey and Nancy A Denton, *American Apartheid: Segregation and the Making of the Underclass* (Cambridge: Harvard University Press, 1993).

12. See Ellis Cose, *The Rage of a Privileged Class* (New York: Harper Collins, 1993), and David K. Shipler, *A Country of Strangers: Blacks and Whites in America* (New York: Alfred A. Knopf, 1997).

13. John T. McGreevey, *Parish Boundaries: The Catholic Encounter with Race in the Twentieth-Century Urban North* (Chicago: University of Chicago Press, 1996).

14. Ibid., 89-93 provides some data on select Chicago parishes during the 1940s.

15. Ibid., 97.

16. Ibid.

17. See Marilyn Nickels, *Black Catholic Protest and the Federated Colored Catholics: 1917- 1933* (New York: Garland Publishing Co., 1988) for an analysis of black Catholic self-determination in the early part of the twentieth century. See also Martin Zielinski, *"Doing the Truth"*: *The Catholic Interracial Council of New York: 1945-1965* for a historical analysis of the extensive work for social and political racial transformation. One might expect some relief from the dynamics of racism within the church, but this is not always the case. Since the nineteenth century, black Catholics, like blacks in many predominantly white U.S. denominations within the United States, have been continuously treated as "anomalies," or second-class citizens within the church. Our presence is often circumscribed with a certain ambiguity when we encounter our nonblack sisters and brothers. In the nineteenth century, many individuals and select religious congregations of men and women initiated their ministries among African Americans. Some have abandoned this ministry and none was entirely successful in establishing a nation-wide program of evangelization specifically focused on inviting African Americans to become full and active members of the Catholic

church. During the nineteenth century, when the church commonly believed and taught that "there was no salvation outside the church," there was great ambiguity about the evangelization and baptism of blacks and their presence and contributions to the Catholic church. Despite this cloud of ambiguity and hostility toward blacks in the church, several Catholic religious congregations and Catholic apostolic associations and organizations made notable and lasting contributions to the African American ministry in the past (the Josephites, the Oblate Sisters of Providence, the Sisters of the Holy Family, the Sisters of the Blessed Sacrament and the Handmaids of Mary, the Holy Ghost Fathers [Spiritans], and the Society of the Divine Word, to name a few).

18. These pastors understand that the gospel addresses the ordinary life of its members both individually and collectively. The political, economic, educational, and medical concerns of the community are interpreted in the light of the preaching and healing actions of Jesus. The gospel is preached in a manner that has the same life-engendering hope for black people in their contemporary social context as it did for the contemporary followers of Jesus and those who joined the early Christian churches as reflected in the New Testament.

19. See Jamie T. Phelps, "The Theology and Process of Inculturation: A Theology of Hope for African American Catholics in the United States," *New Theology Review*, vol. 7, no. 1 (February 1994): 5-13; Jamie T. Phelps, "African American Culture: Source and Context of Black Catholic Theology and Church Mission," *Journal of Hispanic/Latino Theology*, vol. 3, no. 3 (1996): 43-59; and M. Shawn Copeland, "Foundations for a Catholic Theology in an African American Context" in *Black and Catholic: The Challenge and Gift of Black Folk*, ed. Jamie T. Phelps (Milwaukee: Marquette University Press, 1997), 107-47, which addresses the use of culture in theology.

20. Gerald David Jaynes and Robin M. Williams, eds., *A Common Destiny: Black and American Society* (Washington, D.C.: National Academy Press, 1989), 9.

21. Katie G. Cannon, *Black Womanist Ethics* (Atlanta: Scholars Press, 1988), 99ff.

22. National Conference of Catholic Bishops, *Brothers and Sisters to Us: U.S. Bishop's Pastoral Letter on Racism in Our Day* (Washington, D.C.: United States Catholic Conference, 1979), 11.

23. Austin Flannery, O.P., ed., *Vatican Council II: The Conciliar and Post Conciliar Documents*, vol. 1 (Northport, N.Y.: Costello Publishing Co., 1982).

24. Some other major papal social teachings of the twentieth century strongly condemned racial discrimination (e.g. John XXIII's *Pacem in Terris*, 1963:44; Paul VI's *Populorum Progressio*, 1967: 62-63; and *Octagesimo Adveniens*, 1971:16).

25. Hugh J. Nolan, ed., *Pastoral Letters of the American Hierarchy: 1792-1970* (Indiana: Our Sunday Visitor Press, 1971). See the four pastorals on racism entitled *Discrimination and Christian Conscience, Race Relations and Poverty, Racial Harmony*, and *The National Race Crises*.

26. Matthew, 25:31-40 as quoted in the U.S. Bishops Pastoral, *Brothers and Sisters to Us*.

27. National Conference of Catholic Bishops, *Brothers and Sisters to Us*, 3-10.

28. Pontifical Commission Justitia et Pax, *The Church and Racism, Toward a More Fraternal Society* (Vatican City, 1988), 9.

29. Ibid., 17.

30. Ibid., 17-18.

31. Ibid., 18-19.

32. Ibid., 19-20.

33. Ibid., 20-21.

34. Ibid., 21-22.

35. Ibid., 22.

36. Ibid., 23.

37. Besides *Brothers and Sisters to Us,* the second major Roman Catholic document written in the twentieth century was written at the request of Pope John Paul II by the Pontifical Commission on Justice and Peace and is entitled *The Church and Racism: Towards a More Fraternal Society* (Washington D.C.: United States Catholic Conference, 1988).

38. Within the two contemporary church documents condemning racism in the church and the world, biblical references are used as legitimizing "proof texts," e.g., *Brothers and Sisters to Us* refers to Mt. 7:12; Gal. 3:28; Amos 5:14, 24; Lk. 4:16-21; Mt. 25:31-40; Jas. 1:23-24; I Jn. 3:17 and Psalm 94:8. *The Church and Racism* establishes the common unity of humankind by referencing our common origin in God through Adam and Eve. While it primarily references earlier teachings of the popes and bishops, it does shore up its argument using many references to the biblical text: Ex. 19:5; Mk. 16:15; Mt. 28:19; Gen. 1:26-27, 5:1-2; 9:6; 3:20; 5:2; 9:22ff; 12:3; Thes. 8:6; Col. 1:15; 2 Cor. 4:4; Ph. 2:6-7; Rom. 1:16-17; Eph. 2:11-23, 2:14-16; Gal. 3:28; Jn. 11, 4:4-42; Lk. 10:33; Mk. 7:24; Mt. 25:38-40, 28:19; Gen. 11:1-9; and Acts 10:28, 34.

39. "*Gaudium et Spes*: Pastoral Constitution of the Church in the Modern World" in Austin Flannery, ed., *Vatican Council II.* This document's theological anthropology is rooted on the biblical teaching that human beings were made in "the image of God." This notion of human nature asserts the basic goodness and the social nature of humanity (GS, no. 12). It teaches that "the basic source of human dignity lies in humankind's call to communion with God" (GS, no. 19). Because each person is made in the image of the same God, protecting a human being's life, dignity, and ability to act as a free, responsible person is a central aspect of fulfilling God's laws of love and justice.

40. *Gaudium et Spes,* no. 29, as quoted in the Pontifical Commission on Justice and Peace, *The Church and Racism: Towards a More Fraternal Society* (Washington D.C.: United States Catholic Conference, 1988), 25. See also *Gaudium et Spes* no. 60 (for the "right to culture"), *Nostra Aetate: Declaration on the Relation of the Church to Non Christian Religions,* no. 5 (against discrimination based on race, color, condition of life or religion), and *Ad Gentes: Decree on the Church's Missionary Activity,* no. 15 (for the right to cultural self-determination) in Austin Flannery, ed., *Vatican Council II.*

41. For a basic exposition of the notion of human person as discussed in foundational moral theology, see Richard M. Gula, SS, "Part Two: The Nature of the Human Person" in *Reason Informed by Faith: Foundations of Catholic Morality* (New York: Paulist Press, 1989), 63-164.

42. See for example the ecclesiology and Christology of Edward Schillebeeckx, *The Church the Human Story of God* (New York: Crossroad, 1994). Chapter 1 particularly echoes and interprets the foundational principles found in *Gaudium et Spes,* and chapter 3 summarizes Schillebeeckx's theological interpretation of Jesus rooted in his extensive study of recent biblical scholarship.

43. Joseph A. Bracken, S.J., *What Are They Saying about the Trinity?* (New York: Paulist Press, 1979), 69. This small theological book summarizes the work of contemporary theologians who have updated the classical traditions.

44. Ibid.

45. National Conference of Catholic Bishops, *Brothers and Sisters to Us,* 10.

46. James Boggs, *Racism and the Class Struggle* (New York: Monthly Review Press, 1970), 147-148.

47. Pope Paul VI, *"Populorum Progressio,"* nos. 62-63 in *Proclaiming Justice and Peace: Papal Documents from Rerum Novarum Through Centesimus Annus,* ed. Michael Walsh and Brian Davies (Mystic, Conn.: Twenty-Third Publications, 1991), 238.

48. Francis Maxwell, *Slavery and the Catholic Church* (Westminister, Md.: Christian Classics, 1975), 10-12.

49. For a critical discussion of Kenrick's argumentation, see Jamie Theresa Phelps, *The Mission Ecclesiology of John R. Slattery: A Study of an African American Mission of the Catholic Church in the Nineteenth Century* (Ph.D. diss., The Catholic University of America, 1989), 70-75.

50. Madeline Hooke Rice, *American Catholic Church Opinion in the Slavery Controversy* (New York: Columbia University Press, 1944), 95. Phelps's *Mission Ecclesiology* discusses the view of the bishops on slavery on pages 75-81. During this period in history, Catholics were a despised minority who were under grave suspicion of having loyalties to Rome which overshadowed their loyalty to the advancement of the United States. This position within the nation, no doubt, conditioned their support of anti-abolitionist activity.

51. See Jamie T. Phelps, "Caught between Thunder and Lightning: An Historical and Theological Critique of the Episcopal Response to Slavery" (Washington D.C.: United States Catholic Conference, 1990), 21-34.
Some of Riggins R. Earl, Jr.'s research examines the Protestant participation and attitudes toward racism. He suggests that "whites' intentional misinterpretation of the anthropological nature of the slave was the core theological and ethical problem of slavery." He offers a critical analysis of the theological anthropology of Protestant slave masters and missionaries and suggests that whites seem "unequivocally certain in their beliefs that God had created them superior to those of African origins." See his *Dark Symbols, Obscure Signs: God, Self, and Community in the Slave Mind* (Maryknoll, N.Y.: Orbis Books, 1993), 5-6, 10. Read Earl's chapters 1 and 2 for his critical analysis of the various views and approaches used by Christians to defend the institution of slavery.

52. Cornel West, "The Genealogy of Modern Racism" in *Prophesy Deliverance: An Afro-American Revolutionary Christianity* (Philadelphia: Westminister Press, 1982), 47-65, provides a multidisciplinary and philosophical analysis of the rise of racism.

53. Yehudi O. Webster, *The Racialization of America* (New York: St. Martin's Press, 1992), provides a helpful historical overview of the rise of racial theory and the multicultural dimensions of racialization of experience in America. He challenges the role of social science in the construction of racial categories and the collapse of complex ethnic, cultural, and class differentiation into a flawed system of racial classifications. It is an excellent thought piece to expose the limitations and the mythical dimensions of race. John W. Cell, *The Highest Stage of White Supremacy: The Origins of Segregation in South Africa and the American South* (New York: Cambridge University Press, 1982), provides a comparative study of the historical development of the false consciousness of race ideology created by the combination of cultural-economic principles which undergirded the exploitation and power domination of blacks in South Africa and the American South.

54. West, "The Genealogy of Modern Racism," 48. Theo David Goldberg concurs with West's identification of modernity as the context of the emergence of modern race theory and its corollary dynamic of race. Accordingly, he insists that "Race is one

of the conceptual inventions of modernity." See Theo David Goldberg, *Racist Culture: Philosophy and the Politics of Meaning* (Cambridge: Blackwell Publishers, 1993), 3.

55. Goldberg, *Racist Culture*, 1.

56. Ibid., 55.

57. Cornel West, "The Genealogy of Modern Racism," 56. See also Carl von Linnaeus (referred to by Cornel West as Carl Linnaeus), "The God-Given Order of Nature" in *The Systems of Nature* (1735) as quoted in *Race and the Enlightenment: A Reader,* ed. Emmanuel Chuwudi Exe (Cambridge: Blackwell Publishers, 1997), 13. Exe argues that Linnaeus subscribed to a hierarchy of *nature* while West suggests that Winthrop Jordan argues that Linnaeus did not subscribe to a hierarchy of *races.* A review of his description of races reveals that they are not organized in any hierarchical fashion although he seems to identify "man" as "the last and best of [God's] created works." West argues, contrary to Jordan, that "the use of evaluative terms revealed at the least an implicit hierarchy by means of personal preference"(56).

58. Immanuel Kant, *"On National Characteristics"* in *Race and the Enlightenment: A Reader,* ed. Emmanuel Chukwudi Exe, 55.

59. Theo David Goldberg, *Racist Culture,* 4.

60. Ibid.

61. Ibid., 5.

62. Ibid, 6.

63. Yehudi O. Webster, *The Racialization of America*, p. 3.

64. Ibid., 33-49.

65. Edward Tylor (as quoted in Aylward Shorter, *Toward a Theology of Inculturation* [New York: Orbis Books, 1988], 4) defines culture as "that complex whole which includes knowledge of belief, art, morals, law, custom and any other capabilities and habits acquired by man as a member of society." See the first two chapters of Shorter's book for an exposition of the meaning of culture and the evolution of the Church's understanding of culture.

66. W. E. B. Du Bois, *The Souls of Black Folk*, reprint (New York: Penguin Books, 1989), 5-6.

67. W. E. B. Du Bois, *Dusk to Dawn: An Essay Toward an Autobiography of a Race Concept,* as quoted in Kwame Anthony Appiah, *In My Father's House: Africa in the Philosophy of Culture* (New York: Oxford University Press, 1992), 29.

68. See, for example, publications which reflect the contributions of African Americans to the Catholic church in the United States. The most recent publication is Jamie T. Phelps, ed., *Black and Catholic—The Challenge and Gift of Black Folk: Contributions of African American Experience and Thought to Catholic Theology* (Milwaukee: Marquette University Press, 1997). Other publications include Marilyn Nickels, *Black Catholic Protest and the Federated Colored Catholics, 1917-1933* (New York: Garland Publishing Inc., 1988); Cyprian Davis, *The History of Black Catholics in the United States* (New York: Crossroad, 1990); and Stephen J. Ochs, *Desegregating the Altar* (Baton Rouge: Louisiana State University Press, 1990). As noted in note 19, more Catholic historians, both black and white, are participating in the retrieval and publication of the history of black Catholics. Some representative samples: Jamie T. Phelps, *The Mission Ecclesiology of John R. Slattery*; Thaddeus J. Posey, O.F.M., Cap., "An Unwanted Commitment: The Spirituality of the Early Oblate Sisters of Providence" (Ph.D. diss., St. Louis University, 1993); and Cecilia Moore, "A Brilliant Possibility: The Cardinal Gibbon's Institute, 1924-1934" (Ph.D. diss., University of Virginia, 1996). These dissertations are available through University Microfilm International, Ann Arbor, Mich.

6

Black Leadership, Faith, and the Struggle for Freedom

MANNING MARABLE

What is the responsibility of people of faith to cross the boundaries of race and ethnicity, class and gender, religion and language, to help build an environment for pluralism, mutual respect, and civility? Can we think about our faith as part of a project for deconstructing racism and other forms of bigotry, while empowering the oppressed?

I would like to address three interrelated themes: First, the continuing paradox and tension between diversity and democracy. President Clinton has created a national commission to encourage a "conversation on race." What should that conversation include? It should talk about the process of "racialization," how the liabilities and barriers of race were imposed not only upon African Americans but other people of color. It should examine the processes of how African Americans and other oppressed people are marginalized at the periphery of society's resources and power.

Second, I want to highlight the contemporary social and economic consequences of racism. No one suffers more in our society than black and Latino children and youth. The statistical evidence I present will help illustrate the destructive impact of race and inequality today.

How do we understand and challenge racism as a social evil? We often think of sinful patterns of racist behavior as deliberate, conscious acts of violence or oppression. These are systemic acts of commission—the policies which segregated one racial group from another, as in the system of apartheid in South Africa, or as in the American South for many generations; the crimes of police brutality, all too frequently aimed against racial minorities, as in the infamous case of Abner Louima in New York; or the examples of vigilante violence, such as the burning of black churches. Upon reflection, we can also understand racism as a social evil which manifests itself as a series of unthinking actions, or unawareness, when white privilege is unquestioned or unchallenged; where the absence of black or brown people in our neighborhoods and schools and

77

churches is not a cause for alarm; where we are not troubled when we have few personal friendships or close relationships with individuals who have different ethnicities, cultures, or racial identities from ourselves.

For several decades, many liberals in faith communities have taken practical steps to address racism as evil. There have been attempts to bring diverse groups into dialogue, to emphasize cross-cultural knowledge, yet the greatest evil of racism is violence—the violence against both the body and the spirit. There is the violence of hunger and poverty, the violence of poor schools and substandard health care; there is the violence to the brown or black family when it has been denied a home mortgage because of a bank's redlining policies. If racism manifests itself as violence, we cannot be content simply to dialogue or just to talk over the negative consequences of prejudice. We cannot dismantle racism by fostering cross-cultural awareness. We must find the spiritual courage to speak truth to power, to take a public stand against the institutional evils of oppression. We must not just engage in conversation, we must act; we must actively, as Martin Luther King, Jr., put it, strive toward freedom. We must live our truths to transform society.

Third, given this analysis and these statistics, how do we steer society to move away from racism, intolerance, and bigotry from a liberation theology perspective? How do we make the connections for building greater democracy and social justice? What policy goals can we set which allow our belief in human justice and fairness to become real in our time?

When President Clinton announced the creation of a national commission to address the state of race relations, many African Americans were understandably skeptical. After all, Clinton had in the previous year signed a welfare bill which unfairly punished women and children of color. He had failed to offer strong support to the proponents of affirmative action. His administration had done next to nothing to rebuild and revitalize urban ghettoes. And Clinton was all but mute when confronted with widespread cases of police brutality and systematic violence against African American and Latino communities.

However, if this nation was truly committed to a real "conversation on race," we would want to put on the table many concerns which white elected officials avoid like the plague. We might begin with the observation that prejudice is never an accidental element within the makeup of a society. Hatred does not emerge in a social vacuum. Bigotry is not natural or inevitable within human beings. All white people, simply because they are born white, do not have to be racist. All males, just because they are born male, don't have to tolerate sexism or the sexual harassment of women on the job. Intolerance is a social consequence of how society is organized, and we cannot uproot bigotry unless we are also willing to examine seriously the economic and social environment which fosters and perpetuates social inequality and unfairness.

Fear is reproduced when people are taught that the other—the Latino or black or undocumented immigrant—threatens to take their jobs. Fear hardens into hatred when politicians deliberately create racial scapegoats and homophobic stereotypes to win elections. When politicians deliberately play the so-called "race card," or now the "lesbian/gay card," they create the environment for hate groups and vigilante violence.

If the presidential commission truly wants to understand the contemporary dynamics of institutional racism, it should go first to the prisons and jails across this country, conversing with black, brown, and poor inmates. The criminal justice system today has become our chief means of regulating and controlling millions of unemployed and undereducated black and Latino young men. What lynching was in the South in the 1920s, the death penalty and life sentences without parole have become in the 1990s.

In 1983, in my book *How Capitalism Undeveloped Black America* (Boston: South End Press), I exposed the brutal realities of our criminal justice system and its racist impact upon African Americans. In 1983, more than 650,000 Americans were imprisoned in federal, state, and local facilities. The U.S. incarceration rate was the world's second highest, exceeded only by that of the apartheid regime of South Africa.

By 1996, the U.S. prison population was up to 1.6 million. In the state of California alone, between 1977 and 1992 the prison population soared from less than 20,000 to more than 110,000. To appreciate this massive scale, one should consider this: the California state prison system—not including the rest of the United States—is the second largest in the world after China's. As of 1992, 344 of every 100,000 residents of the United States were in prison, another 174 were in jail. The number of incarcerated U.S. citizens doubles every seven years. We are building more than 150 new prison cells every day in the United States.

Meanwhile, the prison industry has become one of America's biggest and most profitable businesses. Between 1979 and 1990, prison construction nationwide increased by 612 percent, and annual expenditures for corrections topped $14 billion. More Americans work full-time for the prison industry than for any Fortune 500 corporation but General Motors.

What does this mean in terms of the typical daily experience of an average black male in the United States? Author Adam Walinsky cites a recent study of African American men aged eighteen to thirty-five in Washington, D.C.

> On any given day in 1991, 15 percent of the men were in prison, 21 percent were on probation or parole, and 6 percent were being sought by the police or were on bond awaiting trial. Thus, the total involved with the criminal-justice system was 42 percent. The study estimated that 70 percent of black men in the District of Columbia would be arrested before age 35, and that 85 percent would be arrested at some point in their lives.

The prisons of the United States are vast warehouses for the poor and unemployed, for low-wage workers and the poorly educated, and most especially for Latino and African-American males. White-collar criminals, those who embezzle hundreds of millions of dollars, are rarely given prison sentences. The wealthy and powerful almost never go to prison for the crimes they commit. For the most oppressed, however, prison is frequently an improvement in their life's circumstances: free health care, three meals a day, shelter, some modest training programs. Today, there are hundreds of thousands more black men in prison or stuck in the criminal justice system than are enrolled in colleges or universities.

A real conversation about race must examine critically the institutional barriers which have been erected to subordinate people of color, denying them an equal voice in society. Such a conversation would interrogate white politicians and government officials who push for so-called "race-blind" initiatives, which only buttress white racial privilege. As W. E. B. Du Bois knew, the struggle to uproot racism requires "race-conscious solutions." Only by talking honestly about the institutions and policies that perpetuate white power and privilege can we begin the long and difficult journey toward reconciliation.

What is our responsibility to create frameworks for understanding the tensions and possibilities between diversity and democracy? Perhaps the place to begin is with Langston Hughes, the poet laureate of Harlem and black America, who constantly explored the love/hate relationship our people have felt toward American democracy:

> I, too, sing America.
> I am the darker brother.
> They send me to eat in the kitchen
> When company comes.
> But I laugh, and eat well
> and grow strong.
> Tomorrow
> I'll be at the table
> When company comes.
> Nobody will dare say to me
> "Eat in the kitchen" then.
> Besides, they'll see how
> beautiful I am, and be ashamed.
> I, too, am America.

Hughes presents a powerful perspective on what the democratic project should be about. It isn't expressed in Jefferson's eloquent yet incomplete democratic arguments in the Declaration of Independence, or Lincoln's Gettysburg Address. "Difference" is coded in any number of ways: by race and ethnicity, by gender and sexual orientation, by social class and income, by physical disability. The concept of difference seems to imply that some people are defined as the norm and that others occupy a space somewhere on the periphery. From this perspective, overcoming difference means forgetting about the real variations among human beings, trying to make those who are on the outside more acceptable, more normal, more like those of us on the inside. So a generation ago, liberal educators praised their black students when they exhibited the same behaviors or spoke the same language as their white students. Dwelling upon differences between people or groups was certainly divisive. Race was something to be overcome, or at least ignored. If blacks, Latinos, and other people of color could only manage to blend themselves into the normal habits and customs of the mainstream and stop acting differently, racial distinctions could disappear. Liberal educators viewed racism as a product of ignorance, rather than a logical social consequence of patterns of inequality and institutional discrimination.

But the category of difference in itself doesn't tell us much about why American society works the way it does. All Americans are, in certain respects, different from everyone else. But not all Americans have been routinely denied bank loans, or have been refused accommodation in hotels, or have had their houses of worship burned to the ground, just because they were different. Difference has social significance only when it tells us how and why certain groups, for example, have been denied basic economic opportunities and political rights, while others have not. If we approach the study of diversity simply as an uncritical celebration of all cultures, we don't answer any of the real questions that are at the heart of the crisis in American democracy.

Growing up black in white America has always been a challenge, but never more so than today. To be young and black in the 1990s means that the basic context for human development—education, health care, personal safety, the environment, employment, and shelter—is increasingly problematic. To be young and black today means fighting for survival in harsh and frequently unforgiving urban environments.

The frightening prospects for African American children and youth have been identified by Marian Wright Edelman and the Children's Defense Fund. Today, in comparison to white children, black children are one-and-a-half times more likely to grow up in families whose household head didn't graduate from high school. They are twice as likely to be arrested for property crimes, to be unemployed as teenagers and later as adults, and to become teenage mothers. African American infants are two-and-a-half times as likely to die in the first year of life and to be born at low birth weight. They are three times more likely than white young people to live in group quarters, and/or to be suspended from school or receive corporal punishment. African American young people are four times as likely to be born of mothers dying from HIV infection. They are five times more likely to be arrested by police for violent crimes than are white youth. And they are nine times more likely to become victims of homicide.

The Institute for Research in African-American Studies at Columbia University, which I direct, is only six blocks away from the heart of Harlem, 125th Street. Every day, in our immediate neighborhood, I can see the destruction of an entire generation of our young people. In New York City, 45 percent of all African American youth dwell in poverty. In central Harlem, one out of eight households has no plumbing or toilet facilities. Every day in New York, an average of seventy thousand children, mostly Latino and black, use illegal drugs. Black and Hispanic youth unemployment exceeds 40 percent. The life expectancy of a black male in Central Harlem is forty-nine years of age.

There are many ways to measure the powerful reality of contemporary racism. For example, a 1994 study of the Office of Personnel Management found that African American Federal employees are more than twice as likely to be dismissed as their white counterparts. Blacks are especially likely to be fired at much higher rates than whites in jobs where they comprise a significant share of the labor force: for example, black clerk typists are 4.7 times more likely to be dismissed than whites, and black custodians 4.1 times more likely to be fired. Discrimination is also rampant in capital markets. Banks continue policies of redlining, denying loans in neighborhoods which are largely black and Hispanic. In New York City in 1992, for instance, blacks were turned down for mortgage applications by banks, savings and loans, and other financial institutions about twice as often as whites. And even after years of affirmative action programs, blacks and Latinos remain grossly underrepresented in a wide number of professions. For example, African Americans and Hispanics represent 12.4 percent and 9.5 percent respectively of the U.S. adult population. But of all American physicians, blacks account for barely 4.2 percent, and Latinos 5.2 percent. Among engineers, blacks represent 3.7 percent, Latinos 3.3 percent; among lawyers, blacks account for 3.3 percent, Latinos 3.1 percent; and for all university and college professors, blacks made up 5 percent, Latinos 2.9 percent. As Jesse Jackson observed in a speech before the National Press Club in 1996, while native-born white males comprise only 41 percent of the U.S. population, they are 80 percent of all tenured professors, 92 percent of the Forbes 400 chief executives officers, and 97 percent of all school superintendents.

If affirmative action should be criticized, it might be on the grounds that it didn't go far enough in transforming the actual power relations between blacks and whites in U.S. society. More evidence for this is addressed in a new book by sociologists Melvin Oliver and Thomas M. Shapiro entitled *Black Wealth/ White Wealth: A New Perspective on Racial Inequality* (New York: Routledge, 1995). They point out that "the typical black family has eleven cents of wealth for every dollar owned by the typical white family." Even middle-class African Americans, people who often benefited from affirmative action, are significantly poorer than whites who earn identical incomes. If housing and vehicles owned are included in the definition of net wealth, the median middle-class African American family has only $8,300 in total assets, to $56,000 for the comparable white family. Why are blacks at all income levels much poorer than whites in terms of wealth? African American families not only inherit much less wealth, they are impacted daily by institutional inequality and discrimination. They are still denied home mortgages at twice the rate of similarly qualified white applicants. African Americans have been less likely to receive government-backed home loans.

Given the statistical profile of racial inequality, we need to reject the economistic temptation to move away from race-conscious remedies, to race-neutral reforms defined by income or class criteria. Affirmative action has always had a distinct and separate function from antipoverty programs. Income and social class inequality affect millions of whites, Asian Americans, Latinos, and blacks alike; and programs which expand employment, educational access, and social service benefits based on narrowly defined economic criteria are absolutely essential. But the impetus for racism is not narrowly economic in origin. Racial prejudice is still a destructive force in the lives of upper-middle-class, college-educated African Americans as well as poor blacks, and programs designed to address the discrimination they feel and experience collectively every day must be grounded in the context of race. However, affirmative action is legitimately related to class questions, but in a different way. A truly integrated workplace, where people of diverse racial backgrounds, languages, and cultural identities learn to interact and respect each other, is an essential precondition for building a broadly pluralistic democracy.

Most Americans will tell you that pragmatic politics is always defined by the center. How many times have we been told that the effective battleground for determining the future of society is the great American mainstream? that to be a serious factor in politics, we need to work inside the corridors of power, not on the outside? that we need to tailor our political message to be acceptable to contented, complacent suburbanites who drive SUVs and watch cable TV? that by becoming a centrist, or even conservative, we avoid being marginalized, excluded, locked out, and isolated on the political periphery?

I respectfully disagree. Fundamental political change in a democracy almost always comes from the boundaries of society, not from the center. Conscious, dedicated minorities, not the numerical majority, become catalysts for change. And if you build a political movement to stand firmly on the middle ground, you may find that ground collapsing from under your feet.

How do we achieve democratic change within a society? We must, first, understand how that society actually works. Who gets ahead, and who doesn't? Who is rewarded, and who is punished? Usually, the people we should learn from are those not at the top of society, but at the bottom. Two centuries ago, if we had listened only to Thomas Jefferson, we would have gained some important insights in understanding the contradictory relationship between democracy and slavery. But we would have to listen to the slaves themselves, those who felt the sting of the lash, and those who were bartered and sold on the auction block, to know the reality of slavery. We would have to learn from black abolitionists such as Frederick Douglass, Sojourner Truth, and Harriet Tubman.

Less than a century ago, women were denied the right to vote in this country. Generations of white male politicians justified and rationalized the exclusion of women. We would have to listen to the early feminists and suffragists, such as Susan B. Anthony, Ida B. Wells-Barnett, and Mary Church Terrell to comprehend how sexism compromised the promise of democracy.

How do you achieve change in a democratic society? By recognizing that in a democracy, the majority can be wrong. Only a generation ago, racial segregation was legal in the United States. There were separate and unequal water fountains, public toilets, hotels, restaurants, and churches. Birmingham, Alabama's city council even passed a law making it illegal for blacks and whites to play checkers together! The overwhelming majority of good, middle-class whites in Birmingham supported their racist chief of police, Bull Connor, and their pro-segregationist governor, George C. Wallace. But they were wrong. Martin Luther King, Jr., did not say, let us wait until the majority of Southern whites change their minds about segregation. Martin did not counsel patience, or try to moderate his message of "Freedom Now" to read "Freedom Someday."

Several years ago, Proposition 187, which proposed discriminatory policies against undocumented immigrants, mostly Latino people, was being debated in California. A majority of California's registered voters supported this initiative. We must not be afraid to say that the initiative was wrong. Amendment Two was passed in Colorado several years ago, which attempted to outlaw local measures protecting the civil rights of lesbians and gays, the same rights that other Americans take for granted. We should affirm our belief in equal justice for all by saying that the homophobic politics behind that measure was mean-spirited, discriminatory, and wrong. We should never be afraid to lose an electoral campaign when we are fighting to affirm democratic rights and equal justice for all.

In a curious way, the conservatives understand this far better than most liberals. You have to be true to your values, because your principles are at the heart of what politics should be. The ideologues of the Far Right, such as Bill Bennett and William Kristol, ground their politics in a set of values. Their only problem is that they've got the wrong set of values.

How do we achieve progressive change? By celebrating our divine discontent with the way things are. Contented, satisfied people rarely want things to change too much. If you want to find out what new directions history is taking our society, don't wallow in the mainstream—stand at the edge, at the boundaries. Listen to the poets and the nonconventional music of young people. Learn from those who have little or nothing to lose. Understand the anxiety of the forty million Americans today who lack any medical insurance. Spend time working in a homeless shelter or walking a picket line with trade unionists. To be divinely discontent is to want our democratic ideals and our egalitarian hopes to be realized in the world around us. It is to challenge conformity, to push the boundaries of "the way things are" to the "way things should be."

To transform is to foster change, but it is also a healing, a reconciliation, a path from which we begin to see ourselves and others in a new way. To take a stand in the public arena and affirm our faith, the deepest beliefs we hold inside ourselves, is to link faith with positive constructive action. We strive for justice, and we begin to challenge and to transform ourselves. When we reflect that for many slaves in the South, prayer and faith were acts of resistance, we may begin to think of our faith as a site of action, a site of hope for changing our society for the better. Can we begin to think of our faith as a personal commitment to a project in liberation? Politics is, after all, a set of choices each of us makes every day.

What are we prepared to strive for in the project of social justice? The Civil Rights workers who desegregated the South in the 1960s committed themselves to "strive for freedom," in the words of Dr. King. What do we strive for today? What are the public policy challenges that truly test our understandings of faith? What is a blueprint for action for creating an antiracist theology, a gospel of racial justice?

The realization of a just society for blacks and other people of color in the United States requires radical solutions. To be "radical" means to get at the root of real problems, to seek effective solutions. What we should want is an end to economic exploitation based on racism and every other manifestation of human oppression, a truly revolutionary transformation of the state and society, and the realization of humanistic values. What should unite us in struggle is a common vision and agenda for humanity in the twenty-first century, reflecting our faith and ideals, leading to the construction of a new society and a new humankind. The best expression of our faith is found in our belief system and in our willingness to sacrifice to achieve those ideals in the real world all around us. That social justice credo starts with a commitment to freedom, self determination, and full human rights.

We must strive for the end of all forms of human oppression—racism, homophobia, sexism, discrimination against disabled people, anti-immigrant discrimination, class exploitation, and imperialism.

We must be committed to a social policy agenda which invests in human beings.

We must strive for a society in which all people have the resources to develop to their fullest potential. This can only occur when the basic needs of all people are met. At minimum, this includes free and universal health care, free child care, quality public education, lifelong access to retraining and vocational learning, and low-cost public housing.

We must strive for a comprehensive national economic policy which places the interests of people above profits. Therefore, we must support aggressive measures to restrict and regulate the power and resources of corporations. Government must halt the transfer of capital and jobs out of the country. Plant and business closing legislation should be passed which requires public hearings and direct compensation to workers who lose their jobs. We should replace the minimum wage with a mandated living wage for all Americans.

We must be committed to a society which allows for the healthy and positive development of our children. Children are society's most precious resource. But in a racist and capitalist society, poor black and brown children are frequently the first casualties. We must demand quality education, health care, housing, and safety for every child.

We must strive for justice in the legal system. One-third of all young African American men are currently in jail or prison, on probation, on parole, or awaiting trial. The U.S. prison-industrial complex has become a vast warehouse for millions of the poor and unemployed. In the past ten years, the number of black women in prison has more than doubled. Any black person is four times more likely to receive the death penalty than any white person convicted of the same crime. For these reasons, we should be in the forefront of the campaign to call for the abolition of the death penalty, the twentieth century's version of lynching. We should denounce the recent "three strikes" criminal justice provisions as inherently racist and discriminatory to black and poor people. We should call for full voting rights for people convicted of felonies, both in prison and after their release, and amnesty for all political prisoners, including those forced into political exile outside the United States.

We must strive to end police brutality and state terrorism in our communities. There are 600,000 police officers in the United States, most of whom function like an occupying army in our communities. We should call for the strict civilian control of our neighborhoods, and citizen review boards which are empowered to discipline police misconduct. We should denounce the deliberate trafficking of drugs and the proliferation of weapons in our communities by organized crime, the CIA, and other institutions of the state. We must condemn the deliberate criminalization, incarceration, and execution of black youth as a clear violation of human rights and the destruction of the human spirit.

We must strive for a clean and healthy environment for our people. We should oppose the policy of environmental racism—the fact that three out of every five African Americans live near dangerous toxic waste sites. U.S. industries today are pumping 2.4 billion pounds of toxic chemicals into our air and billions more into our drinking water. Thousands of poor brown and black people have died prematurely and needlessly because of the effects of corporate greed on the environment.

We must strive for full employment and a guaranteed income for all those unable to work. We know that twenty million U.S. residents today are either unemployed or work part-time and want full-time employment. We need a constitutional, legal right to a job, as much as a right to vote. We need government investment in community-based and cooperative institutions which generate jobs. We should demand emergency action by the government, especially in areas of concentrated high unemployment, to create real jobs at living wages. We strongly support the struggles of black working women and men inside the trade union movement, fighting for economic justice.

We must strive for civil rights, affirmative action, and compensation for centuries of institutional racism. We should defend the policies of affirmative action, race-based scholarships, and all equal opportunity legislation as absolutely essential in attacking racial inequality. We demand just compensation and reparations for the systematic brutality and exploitation our people have suffered historically and continue to experience today.

We must strive for gender equality and women's rights. We must support full pay equity and the abolition of job discrimination for women. We support strong measures to protect women's lives from harassment, sexual abuse, and domestic violence. We should defend and support women's full reproductive rights, including the right to a safe and legal abortion.

We must strive for an end to homophobia and discrimination against lesbians and gay men. We should embrace all sectors of our community, whatever their sexual choice or orientation. We oppose and reject any arguments that would exclude or marginalize the contributions of lesbians, gay men, or bisexuals to the African American community and to the goal of black freedom. Our freedom movement must struggle against every form of oppression, including the violence and discrimination of homophobia.

We must strive for quality education for all. Life-long learning should be a human right, not a privilege. We should demand greater funding for our public schools, investment in teacher salaries, classroom construction, computers, and other materials which make learning possible. We should demand an antiracist curriculum and educational programs affirming and reinforcing black history and culture. We should support academic programs for affirmative action in both public schools and universities. We should support the preservation and enrichment of historically black colleges and universities.

We must strive for liberation for all oppressed people throughout the world. The struggles of peoples of African descent are inextricably linked to the many diverse struggles of oppressed people and nations across the globe. Black liberation cannot be achieved inside the United States outside of the larger, pan-Africanist and internationalist struggle which is being waged between the haves and the have-nots. Our vision of black freedom in the twenty-first century must be internationalist.

And finally, we must commit ourselves to strive for a real democracy in the United States. Without justice there can be no peace. We are committed to the fight for the realization of a truly democratic and socially just society. We dedicate ourselves to the abolition of racism and all other forms of human oppression, and the cultural integrity and political liberation of our people.

What then should be the basis for constructing a new radical democratic politics, a politics of social transformation?

A liberation theology should ground itself in the actual conditions and perspectives of those who suffer most greatly from the disempowerment of globalized capitalism. The common points in experience and struggle, resistance and suffering, hope and human emancipation, create the context for a common social force. We may speak different languages, have different cultural and ethnic traditions, have different class backgrounds, gender and sexual orientations, but we can come together to fight the power.

To conclude: In a recent conversation with the brilliant actor and advocate of progressive causes, Ossie Davis, we talked about the challenges and problems confronting the African-American community as we enter the twenty-first century. "Every generation needs a moral assignment," Ossie told me. "We have yet to define that moral assignment for ourselves and in our time."

African American people were challenged one hundred fifty years ago by the harsh realities of slavery. The great moral and political question of that era was the abolition of human bondage. Black abolitionists, such as Frederick Douglass and Martin Delany, pursued a vision of freedom which mobilized the energies of the black community, North and South. Nearly a century later, the great moral challenge confronting black people was the oppressive reality of Jim Crow segregation. African Americans were denied access to schools, hospitals, hotels, and many other public establishments. The Fifteenth Amendment was a dead letter for several generations. Martin Luther King, Jr., and the Civil Rights movement represented the courageous struggles of a people who yearned to be free.

The struggle for freedom was like the crossing of a turbulent river. In the religious imagination of black folk, the river was frequently identified as the River Jordan. Like the ancient Hebrews who had escaped Egyptian bondage, black Americans courageously crossed their own River Jordan to seek and to claim the promised land of freedom.

Now we are in an uncertain time, filled with dangerous and destructive social forces: violence, drugs, unemployment, poverty, social alienation, and fear. Our leaders seem unsure of how to articulate a new agenda for progressive change. There are many voices within our communities which call us to turn inward, away from potential allies with whom we can work to achieve positive change. What is required is the definition of a new moral assignment, a new vision of human emancipation.

Davis says, "Now we must cross a second river, the river of equality. We must insist that the Constitution create the conditions for genuine political freedom. But *equality* is an economic function, first and foremost." It is important to distinguish between the goals of freedom and the goals of equality. Freedom is about "rights" within a democratic political process. Equality is about social justice and the material realities of human fairness—universal health care, quality education, housing, and a job or guaranteed income as a human right. Equality is about having the power to restrict the power of corporations, to stop the shutting down of factories and the economic destruction of urban communities. Equality is about having a living wage for everyone and reducing the vast disparity between the rich and working people. Equality means having a clean, healthy environment for our children. Equality means the abolition of hunger. Equality means power to the people.

Our movement must now cross the second river of equality. In doing so, we must wage the same principled struggles which were fought for political freedom during the desegregation campaigns led by Martin throughout the South. It will require the same willingness to sacrifice, the same tears, the same willingness to challenge unjust laws, and the same impatience with oppression. To end the race/class oppression within the criminal justice system, to fight for full employment and universal health care, to abolish unemployment and homelessness, to uproot discrimination based on race, gender, or sexual orientation, we must move beyond the goals of political representation and political freedom to the struggle to achieve real equality for all Americans.

7

Black Theology and the Parish Ministry

J. ALFRED SMITH, SR.

My response was one of unbelief when professor Dwight N. Hopkins asked me to give a written analysis of *Black Theology and Black Power*,[1] James H. Cone's 1969 classic text. Who am I to engage the writings of the person who gave birth to black theology as an academic discipline? After all, almost everyone knows that there is a great gulf between the academy and the parish. The gown and the town use a different vocabulary and address divergent interests. At times, these groups have been unfriendly and critical of each other. Nevertheless, the parish must be reflective, critical, and analytical, as well as honest and fair in perspective and proclamation. Moreover, Professor Cone did not write *Black Theology and Black Power* as an outsider. In fact, he wrote as an insider, as a son of the African Methodist Episcopal church, and his polemical presentations possessed the best of the black church tradition; that is, logos and pathos, reason and compassion.

Again, the question surfaces concerning my role as a minister of a black church in the inner city of Oakland, California, who has been asked to reflect on one of the seminal books challenging black theology and the black church. How can I not share my written response, unless I am willing for history to judge me as a pastoral Rip Van Winkle, whose only claim to historical remembrance is that I have slept through the most important theological revolution of the twentieth century—the rise of black theology and its impact, permanently changing the face of American theology and the vocation of the church? Unlike most respected theologians, who receive little response from the parish because most people cannot understand theological abstractions, James Cone is so lucid in *Black Theology and Black Power,* that only the ethically and morally irresponsible can remain mute upon reading his message. It is not abstract argument that turns people away from *Black Theology and Black Power*; it is pungent and powerful prophecy that pricks the consciences of those who read the first systematic presentation of black theology. Those who have had difficulty with their first reading of this work should now read the book again. Much to their surprise, they will discover truths that they had missed in their first reading. They will also observe how times have remained the same. And, in some instances, this nation and the religious establishments that profess to be moral custodians of society are in denial of cancerous manifestations of racism in private and public expressions of national life.

In this paper, I shall share the influence that *Black Theology and Black Power* has had upon my own life and thought as a parish minister. Many have said that black theology was not written for the local church. I will present the antithesis of this point of view, since I believe that too many pastors are anti-intellectuals who cease growing as students upon graduation from seminary. This is why many black pastors were not ready for the secular preachers of black power or for the theology of Professor James H. Cone. A crisis existed between so-called black church persons (on the one hand), and younger, radical, secular, black power advocates (on the other). This latter group felt that Christianity was one of the ways white power used religion to oppress black people.

The Crisis of Black Power

During the mid- to late 1960s, a crisis occurred which challenged both the faith content and existential foundation of African American people. More specifically, the question became: is it possible to be black and Christian?[2] It was this sociopolitical context which *Black Theology and Black Power* courageously addressed. Black preachers were sermonizing to compete in homiletical contests to see who was the most popular on the preaching circuit. Black denominations were using white denominations as their paradigm for imitation. Black religion had moved to the right and had avoided the issues of justice and liberation. Black college-age young people were cynical about preachers, whom they called Uncle Toms. Groups, such as the Black Panther Party and the Student Nonviolent Coordinating Committee, had written off black religion only to embrace a secular gospel of "by any means necessary" or "the end justifies the means." Liberal, white, civil rights supporters of the late Dr. Martin Luther King, Jr., were seen as enemies by so-called black power advocates. The media did not allow black power to be defined as constructive, as having dimensions of self-determination and political and economic power, or as a positive definition of blackness. Into this confused and chaotic social location, James H. Cone came with a theological definition of black power.

Cone's entrance onto the public platform was a curse to the status quo, old guard black church, but an oasis for desert survival to younger church leaders who saw God as one who works in history as the God of liberation. In the late 1960s a black power–oriented clergy group, of which I was a part, came together under the title of the Alamo Black Clergy (ABC). We met on a regular basis to study black theology and black power. We organized the Urban Black Studies Center, which became an affiliate of the Graduate Theological Union in Berkeley, California. Annually we would bring to the San Francisco-Oakland Bay area black theologians such as James H. Cone, Major J. Jones, J. Deotis Roberts, Gayraud S. Wilmore, Lucien Tobin, and Howard Thurman. The Rev.

Dr. W. Hazaiah Williams served as our founding director. The ABC charter members were the late Gene Farlough, Charles Belcher, Bishop Will Hertzfeld, James Stewart, Howard Bryan, Father Earl Neil (i.e., a Black Panther Party Episcopal priest), and J. Alfred Smith, Sr. The ABC hosted the National Committee of Black Churchmen[3] and also worked to promote constructive dialogue with Black Panther leaders Huey Newton, Elaine Brown, Bobby Seale, and David Hilliard.

As a result of my contacts with the Black Panther Party, upon becoming the pastor of Oakland's Allen Temple Baptist Church, Mr. and Mrs. Huey P. Newton became Allen Temple members. I baptized Huey Newton and I gave the eulogy at his funeral, and, in addition, I preached the eulogy for Mrs. Newton's mother. The Black Panther Party, under the leadership of JoNina Abrons, sold Allen Temple Baptist Church the headquarters property where the new Allen Temple Family Life Center now stands. Several former Black Panthers have served as Allen Temple Baptist Church pastoral staff members, as the legal counsel of the church, and as members of the Board of Deacons. All of these former Black Panthers became active agents for social change in Allen Temple Baptist Church, because they interacted in the community with pastoral leadership and lay members who seriously strove to empower persons with the social and theological ethics of black power and black theology.

Furthermore, Father James Goode (a San Francisco pastor of Ship Wreck by the Sea, and a Ph.D. student of James H. Cone's) and I (pastor of Allen Temple Baptist Church) convened a weekend of worship and study with Dr. Cone at both the San Francisco and Oakland church sites. Persons who criticize black theology as being too imprisoned within the academy are not as well informed as they could be. They lack adequate knowledge of the black church where parishes meet in ecumenical contexts to seek strategies for employing the implications of black theology and black power in a viable praxis for holistic liberation.

For instance, *Black Theology and Black Power* has motivated Mt. Zion Baptist Church of Seattle, Washington, pastored by Dr. Samuel Berry McKinney, and the Allen Temple Baptist Church of Oakland, California, to display the liberation colors of red, black, green, and gold. Both of these churches have moved past cosmetic blackness to a praxis which employs the development of a black socio-ethical power for holistic redemption. Both of these churches are engaged in linking black theology to black church history, through stained glass windows that articulate the message of women and men pioneers in the radical and revolutionary history of the African American legacy. Moreover, both churches have linked theological praxis to the global struggle of the Third World and actively support the liberating activity of the gospel in Africa.

Nevertheless, much has happened in America since 1969 when *Black Theology and Black Power* was first written. In fact, this present age is now labeled a post-modern culture, where all institutions and churches are suspect. Black churches are facing the issues of black powerlessness from the alienated grandchildren of black power. In many of his writings, Cornel West has spoken of a hip-hop culture that is dominated by the philosophy of nihilism.[4]

The Parish Church and Black Powerlessness

A cultural and class gap within black America has driven middle-class blacks and underclass blacks into two separate worlds, where each group speaks a different language and uses a different canon as a moral compass. The common ground that both groups widely embrace is historical amnesia as it relates to the Civil Rights struggle of the 1960s. Neither group has shared its story of struggle and blood sacrifice with their children and grandchildren. So what can be expected of a people who are without the historical memory of either a Martin Luther King, Jr., a James H. Cone, a Fannie Lou Hamer, or a Dorothy Heights? No longer is the issue simply one of whether black theology is imprisoned in the world of black theologians at the painful expense of the parish church's ignorance of black theology.

How did African Americans come to be in this situation and place? Should the blame be placed at the door of white racists? Is it fair to say that this natal alienation is the fruit of integration? Have both the scholars and the parish ministers failed to spread the good news of black theology and black power? Are churches simply amusement centers or places for serving people spiritual narcotics for existing in a world of the abused? Why are the new preachers and teachers of post-modern culture the purveyors of gangster rap and nihilistic rap? Why did the Million Man March,[5] led by Louis Farrakhan of the Nation of Islam, attract large numbers of black Protestant lay persons? Why were black clergy divided on the legitimacy of the march? Why has there been no significant follow-up to the march to "keep hope alive," paraphrasing the Rev. Jesse Louis Jackson? Who is at fault for the continuing damage of failed inner-city school systems? Should black theologians blame black churches or should black churches blame black theologians? Or should black theologians and church leaders, together, blame white churches for poor public policy and government inaction in eradicating institutional racism from the societal structures of American life? The growing AIDS crisis among African Americans and the very large numbers of black persons who are now filling the prisons of the nation should be enough of a wake-up call to unite the town and the gown, the pastors and the theologians into united action for survival.

For the local church, a theology of black power could educate black youth to understand that present-day gangster rap lyrics and contemporary popular music display a totally destructive conception of love. Black power and black theology, within the curriculum content of Sunday church school literature, could provide liberation and healing for the competitive, contentious, and conflicting role of gender relationships between black men and black women. Bible study groups, based on the pioneering exegetical methodology of Charles Copher, Randall Bailey, Cain Hope Felder, and Jeremiah Wright, would enable Christian black males to divest themselves of patriarchal lifestyles for free and healthy relationships with women and children as well as with each other.[6]

On the parish level, an application of black theology and black power in the area of stewardship of money would empower African American communities. For example, the Hartford Memorial Baptist Church of Detroit (pastored by Dr.

Charles Adams) owns blocks of shopping centers; the $9 million credit union of the Allen Temple Baptist Church of Oakland is, likewise, the exercise of black economic power as it opens the door for countless young families to become first-time home buyers. At the church level, the theology of black power is also seen in the far-reaching work of Pastor Ernestine Cleveland Reems of the Center of Hope in Oakland, California. With her leadership, her church provides housing, child care, and job training for unwed mothers without any funding from federal, state, county, or city governments.

In addition, black theology and black power are more than socio-economic expressions with political manifestations. Dr. Cecil Murray of the First African Methodist Episcopal Church of Los Angeles and Bishop Charles Blake of West Angeles Church of God in Christ of Los Angeles are strong pastors of strong megachurches. Why? They are leaders not simply because they excel in social justice–oriented ministries, nor because they are paragons of the incarnation of black theology and black power. They are practical visionaries in their communities and beyond because of their abilities to manifest a rich spirituality which gives clear public expression of moral and ethical power for personal and societal transformation. Other persons whose holistic ministries are well known for being nurtured in the prayer traditions of the black church are the Rev. Dr. Harold Carter[7] and the Rev. Dr. Vashti McKenzie of Baltimore. If there is one point that must clearly be expressed, it is the necessity for black theology to stress that there is no theology or power without the cultivation of centering moments of prayer and the practice of the creative encounter with the Creator, as Dr. Howard Thurman often reminded us.[8]

The history of the black church and the black community, as well as the testimony of the contemporary African American experience, underscores times in the spiritual journey of African Americans when human efforts come up short, and the activities for liberation and wholeness would have ceased had not the initiative for change moved from human hands into God's hands. Theologians and parish members must now remember that the Christian message means nothing in a post-modern culture caught up in the practice of nihilism. Therefore, the theological academy and the parish have an ontological mandate to be good news, a kerygmatic mandate to preach good news, a pedagogical mandate to teach good news, and, above all, a mandate of diaconia—to practice good news. For example, eschatological signs for the practice of black theology and black power as good news are most visible in the promising work of womanist theologians.

I am impressed with a growing number of highly educated black women theologians who are prolific in their writings. But, at the same time, they are so liberated from the "publish or perish" syndrome of scholars talking to scholars, that they will spend time producing works which will empower pastors to equip lay persons to develop strategies for personal transformation and societal change.[9] Many of the womanist scholars were either trained at Union Theological Seminary (New York) by James H. Cone or encouraged by him and Gayraud S. Wilmore. Because of the womanists' very special love for black families, and because many of them who have been hurt by patriarchal ugliness continue to give males the tough love of chiding and challenging, I am personally committed to them, their leadership, and their scholarship.

I am sure that being reared in a prayerful and peaceful home where piety was practiced by a mother, grandmother, and aunt must have opened my head and heart to womanist theology. Yet, if my social location has had nothing to do with it, I shall give God the praise for all of those influences which have helped me see the prophetic value of Dr. Cone's life of critical reflection and dialogue. I shall praise God for students of Professor Cone, like Dwight N. Hopkins who, as a former Allen Temple member, taught black theology to our congregation and ministers-in-training and, in addition, was a role model of respect for women's ministry during his tenure as a member of the faculty of Santa Clara University.

Still more work needs to be done. For example, those of us who love and embrace womanist theology must work harder for the placement of women seminary graduates, because there are not enough teaching positions for these alums. Similarly we need to recognize their pastoral leadership and appoint more black women to ministerial positions. At Allen Temple, three of the five full-time members of the pastoral staff are women.

An excellent instance of womanist theology's influence on the local black church can be found in a book by the Rev. Dr. Wallace Charles Smith. Smith, of the Shiloh Baptist Church (Washington, D.C.), has written an outstanding work called *The Church in the Life of the Black Family*.[10] In his scholarship of liberation and power, this pastor/scholar bridges any gap between the black parish and the black theologian. He knows how to communicate to a post-modern society where hip-hop culture's values of nihilism reign supreme. But, most of all, one can observe the profound influence of womanist theology upon his mind and ministry. In the D.C. area, Wallace Charles Smith has organized a ministerial association so that women ministers, who had no formal professional organization to which they could belong, could have true community and affirmation. Additionally, a woman minister, who graduated with honors from the School of Divinity of Howard University, now serves with him as a pastoral staff member. Here is one more example of a paradigm where black theology, from the tradition of Dr. James H. Cone, has drawn from the richness of the black church women's movement and is also nourished by the womanist theology writers in the context of parish ministry.

Notes

1. James H. Cone, *Black Theology and Black Power* (Maryknoll, N.Y.: Orbis Books, 1997).

2. For further analytical conversations on this question, see Forest E. Harris, Sr., *What Does It Mean to Be Black and Christian? Pulpit, Pew, and Academy in Dialogue*, vol. 1 (Nashville, Tenn.: Townsend Press, 1995), and vol. 2 (1998); James H. Cone, *For My People: Black Theology and the Black Church: Where Have We Been and Where Are We Going?* (Maryknoll, N.Y.: Orbis Books, 1984); and Dwight

N. Hopkins, *Introducing Black Theology of Liberation* (Maryknoll, N.Y.: Orbis Books, 1999). Hopkins's text is premised on answering the question: What does it mean to be black and Christian?

3. In response to the June 16, 1966, Mississippi cry of black power enunciated by Willie Ricks and Stokely Carmichael (the late Kwame Toure), a group of black preachers wrote a full page statement on black power in the July 31, 1966, edition of the *New York Times*. This theological statement inaugurated black theology as public discourse. The black preachers called themselves, initially, the ad hoc National Committee of Negro Churchmen. For more on the committee, see James H. Cone, *For My People*, chapter 1; Gayraud S. Wilmore, *Black Religion and Black Radicalism* (Maryknoll, N.Y.: Orbis Book, 1993), chapter 9; and Dwight N. Hopkins, *Black Theology U.S.A. and South Africa: Politics, Culture, and Liberation* (Maryknoll, N.Y.: Orbis Books, 1989), chapter 1.

For their July 31, 1966, statement, see "Black Power: Statement by the National Committee of Negro Churchmen," in *Black Theology: A Documentary History, Volume One: 1966-1979*, James H. Cone and Gayraud S. Wilmore, eds. (Maryknoll, N.Y.: Orbis Books, 1993).

4. See his best-selling book, *Race Matters* (Boston: Beacon Press, 1993).

5. The Million Man March took place on October 16, 1995. See Haki R. Madhubuti and Maulana Karenga, eds., *Million Man March/Day of Absence* (Chicago: Third World Press, 1996); and Garth Baker-Fletcher, ed., *Black Religion after the Million Man March* (Maryknoll, N.Y.: Orbis Books, 1998).

6. See Charles Copher, *Black Biblical Studies* (Chicago: Black Light Fellowship, 1993); Cain Hope Felder, *Troubling Biblical Waters: Race, Class, and Family* (Maryknoll, N.Y.: Orbis Books, 1989); Cain Hope Felder, ed., *Stony the Road We Trod: African American Biblical Interpretation* (Minneapolis, Minn.: Fortress Press, 1991); Randall C. Bailey and Jacquelyn Grant, eds., *The Recovery of Black Presence: An Interdisciplinary Exploration* (Nashville, Tenn.: Abingdon Press, 1995); and Jeremiah A. Wright, Jr., *Africans Who Shaped Our Faith* (Chicago: Urban Ministries Incorporated, 1995).

7. See his *The Prayer Tradition of Black People* (Valley Forge, Penn.: Judson Press, 1976).

8. See his *Jesus and the Disinherited* (Richmond, Ind.: Friends United Press, 1976).

9. In this volume, as a sampling, see the articles by Linda E. Thomas, Jacquelyn Grant, Emilie M. Townes, Jamie T. Phelps, and Renée L. Hill.

10. Valley Forge, Penn.: Judson Press, 1985.

8

An Underground Theology

JEREMIAH A. WRIGHT, JR.

During the same year that Dr. James H. Cone's *Black Theology and Black Power* was published, I was finishing up my Master's degree work in African American spirituals under Dr. John Lovell at Howard University. Under John Lovell's tutelage, my research caused me to end up in a very different place from the position articulated by Dr. Cone in chapter 4 of his monumental work.

Dr. Cone states that the existence of the black church "symbolizes a people who were completely stripped of their African heritage as they were enslaved by the 'Christian' white man" (Cone: 91). My research at Howard University and my research across the past three decades makes this premise highly suspect. The problem this has created in the field of black theology is more than a problem of semantics and more than a problem of the century-old debate about "Africanisms."

From my perspective as a pastor-scholar, the problem this false premise has created is this: When you *start* from the wrong place, you are going to *end up* in the wrong place. Or put another way, faulty assumptions lead to faulty analyses; and faulty analyses inevitably produce faulty conclusions. The assumption that African people were completely stripped of their African heritage during the period of enslavement is a faulty assumption.

One can start with the work of Lorenzo Dow Turner (*Africanisms in the Gullah Dialect*), Melville Herskovits (*The Myth of the Negro Past*), or Margaret Creel (*"A Peculiar People": Slave Religion and Community-Culture among the Gullahs*). One can use an interdisciplinary approach (as linguists did forty years ago) and add to the foundations of Turner, Herskovits, and Creel the findings of Janice Hale in early childhood education (*Black Children: Their Roots, Culture and Learning Styles*), Elkin Sithole in ethnomusicology (*"Black Folk Music": Rappin' and Stylin' Out: Communication in Urban Black America*), and Geneva Smitherman in linguistics (*Talkin' and Testifyin': The Language of Black America*). Or one can go to the slave narratives and let the enslaved Africans speak for themselves. The results will be the same, and that is that Africans were *not* stripped of their African heritage during the period of enslavement.

The age-old argument between "Merchant of Venice" historians like E. Franklin Frazier and cultural anthropologists like Lorenzo Dow Turner (a linguist) and Melville Herskovits does not add to our discussion here. It will, therefore, not be included as a part of this essay. Suffice it to say that there was a major assault on the African heritage launched by the slave traders, the colonizers, and the slave holders to "season" the Africans in the Caribbean and "break them in," so they would be more suitable as slaves. That is true, and that is undeniable. However, the assault, though devastating, could not destroy those aspects of culture which my advisor in the History of Religions, Dr. Charles Long, used to say were stamped in the Africans' DNA! That is what my research at Howard University back in 1967-69 had shown me, and that is also what the research of several scholars (and many different disciplines) has proven across the past thirty years. Let me start with my research.

My exhaustive study of the spirituals among the holdings of the Mooreland-Spingarn collection at Howard University and in the Rare Book Room of the Library of Congress contradicts what Dr. Cone says about "most of the spirituals [being] otherworldly and compensatory in character." What I discovered among the slave narratives was just the opposite! I discovered that just as there was an "underground railroad" or an "invisible institution" (Cone: 100) in the history of the black church in North America, there was also an "underground theology" which was part and parcel of that black church, a theology that was not visible to the eye of the uninitiated observer.

Perhaps my being at Howard and taking courses under Sterling Brown and Arthur Davis (editors of *The Negro Caravan*), taking courses under Leo Hansberry and Chancellor Williams, and being exposed to an African-centered methodology by these scholars and others like Stanley Alsop and Olive Taylor informed my perspective profoundly and caused me to see things so differently from Dr. Cone. For whatever the reason, however, this perspective has shaped both my ministry and my research for more than thirty years.

While reading slave narratives that talked about freedom in the here and now and the coded messages of the Spirituals in which "heaven" was often equated with "goin' up" North or going back to Africa, I was also studying the texts themselves. "Didn't my Lord *deliver* Daniel? Then why not every man?" (italics added) is neither otherworldly nor compensatory. "Go Down Moses," "Joshua Fit de' Battle of Jericho," "Oh Mary, don't you weep, Oh Martha, don't you moan. Pharaoh's army got drowned!" and "If I had my way, I'd tear this building down" are neither other-worldly nor compensatory. They speak of changing the system of slavery in the here and now. They speak of destroying slavery and slaveholders if necessary. In addition, songs like "I Got Shoes!" are saying that slaveholders and racists, overseers and "Christian" hate-mongers are missing the message of Jesus Christ entirely. *"Everybody talking 'bout Heaven ain't goin' there!"*

In looking at the spiritual "Oh Freedom," for instance, as Dr. Cone does on page 94 of his work, what is missed by most students of the spirituals is the word "*before.*" This song is not a song which simply says that death is preferable to life if life "must be in slavery" (Cone: 94). Much more profoundly, I submit to you, is that when the African poet said "an' *be-fo' I'd be a slave, I'd be buried in my grave*," (emphasis added) what he or she was saying was that their bodies might have been in chains, but their minds were free.

Dr. Na'im Akbar points out that in order to be a slave, you must give psychological assent to the person(s) or the systems that are trying to enslave you. In the 1700s and 1800s the vast majority of Africans never gave that psychological assent! They were saying that they were *not* slaves and that they would never be slaves! They refused to bow down psychologically. They refused to give psychological assent to their enslavement!

Dr. John Kinney, dean of the School of Theology at Virginia University, says, however, that the real tragedy is that in the 1990s most African Americans have now given psychological assent to their oppressors and to their enslavement. We have gotten the chains off our bodies and put them on our minds!

That was one level of research which let me know that the enslaved Africans had a theology which was diametrically opposed to the "Slaves-be-obedient-unto-your-masters!" theology of the dominant culture. Another level of my research opened up areas of possibility which Eurocentric education had never allowed me to entertain. I discovered at Howard that there were spirituals on the *African* side of the Atlantic Ocean.

Some Africans were Christians in Africa before coming to these shores. Those Africans created spirituals on the continent that I had never heard about in American schools. I also discovered how tremendous the influence of the "Triangular Trade" was upon the African Christian community in North America. Remember! Most of the Africans who were enslaved in North America did not come straight from Africa to North America. They were carried first into the Caribbean. Depending on who the trading company was, to whom the slave ships belonged, where the trading was taking place, and/or where the demand was, the enslaved Africans were sold to a slave owner either in Puerto Rico, Cuba, Hispanola, Haiti, St. Croix, San Maarten, Jamaica, Trinidad and Tobago, and so on. Their subsequent location "colored" their situation—both linguistically and religiously (and, by the same token, theologically!).

The cross-fertilization (to use Cornel West's terminology) that then took place as they were traded from one island to another, as they learned one new language after another, and as they were exposed to one religious tradition after another had a tremendous effect on the Africans in North America as they were then shipped from the Caribbean into the North American enslaved community. The linguistic, the musical, and the theological implications of this reality are awesome—especially given the fact that Africans were not persons with *tabula rasa* for brains!

What they got in the New World (first in the Caribbean and then in North America) was added to an African storehouse of knowledge, wisdom, folklore, belief, and practice. That is the basis of black religion and black theology—not just what the white "Christian" slaveholders brought to the table.

While uncovering these findings in the slave narratives and the texts of the spirituals (plus the research of Dr. Lovell), my methodology was altered tremendously by the brilliant mind of Dr. Stanley Alsop. Dr. Alsop was the dean of the Jamaican Campus of the University of the West Indies and he was "on loan" to the English Department at Howard University. Dr. Alsop was a linguist with a Ph.D. from Oxford. He taught me two invaluable lessons that have changed my methodological approach to the study of African people forever. First, he taught me the importance of the interdisciplinary method, where findings from several different disciplines are considered, e.g., linguistics, ethnomusicology, the spirituals, sociology, cultural anthropology, sociolinguistics, literature, psychology, and early childhood education. It is this methodology that made the scholarship of Dr. Cheikh Anta Diop so profound. The years have taught me, incidentally, that theology needs to be added to and/or informed by this interdisciplinary method—especially when studying Africans in the Diaspora.

Dr. Alsop's second lesson, however, is the one that has literally changed my life and my ministry. He taught me that starting in Africa for an understanding of African Americans yields a much more wholesome picture than starting in 1619 (or 1919 for that matter)! The tragedy of such misguided scholarship as the pitiful work of Joseph Washington (Cone: 113) is caused by the failure to start in Africa when undertaking an analysis of the African religious tradition(s). Donald H. Matthews puts it this way, "Black Theologians have seriously neglected the African roots of African American religion" (Matthews: 38).

Dr. Alsop, as a linguist, started in Africa. He looked at the African roots of the speech of African Americans and Africans in all three Americas to demonstrate that without an understanding of the *roots*, there will never be any understanding of the *fruits*! His methodology caused me to examine the spirituals and the religion of enslaved Africans by starting in a very different place from where Dr. Cone started. As a result, our findings (at times) are at opposite ends of the (East-West) spectrum.

Janice Hale does the same thing in her study of early childhood education. She found out that for years and years we had been mislabeling African children because we had been trying to understand them by comparing them to European children. In her landmark study, Dr. Hale compared European children with European American children and African children with African American children, and her findings are still earth shattering! Dr. Hale discovered while doing her Ph.D. at Brigham Young University that European children are left-brain oriented and are object oriented. The entire educational system in the Western hemisphere is set up on the European educational model. A child is left with objects from the time he or she is in the crib up through their Ph.D. level, where they can study in a carrel in silence with an object (a book).

African children, however, are not left-brain oriented. They are right-brain oriented. African children are also subject oriented as opposed to being object oriented. They are more interested in the teacher, a person, and a subject than they are in a book (an object). They come from an oral-aural culture where learning takes place by paying attention to a subject!

In the 1950s during the early days of school desegregation, white teachers found out just how different these African American children were when they had them in their classrooms for the very first time. The black children kept getting in the white teachers' "space," because they wanted to come up close to the teacher and touch the teacher while learning. That is simply a part of African tradition.

Perhaps Janice Hale's primary premise is one that needs to be utilized in the study of theology, cultural anthropology, speech, and music if we are to ever break the cycle of Eurocentric, hierarchical thinking. Hale profoundly proves that difference does not mean deficiency. Difference simply means different. African children have a different way of learning. African children have a different way of singing. African children have a different way of dancing. African children and African adults have a different way of thinking theologically!

What Dr. Hale did in the field of early childhood education, Dr. Elkin Sithole replicated in the field of ethnomusicology. Dr. Sithole points out that one can never understand African American music (all of the *genres* of African American music) without understanding African music. Unfortunately, however, most African Americans are not taught any African music. We are taught European music and the European classics. Almost no one reading this chapter can name four African composers! Sithole maintains, however, that one can never fully understand jazz, the African style of common meter singing, the field shouts, the hollers, the camp meeting songs, the spirituals, blues, or gospel music without a full appreciation of the African roots of that music and those genres.

What Dr. Hale did in the field of early childhood education and Dr. Sithole did in the field of ethnomusicology, Dr. Geneva Smitherman has done in the field of linguistics. Smitherman has demonstrated that unless one starts in Africa, there can never be any understanding of African speech in the Diaspora. The American Society of Linguists, incidentally, calls African American speech a language in and of itself. It does not classify it technically as a dialect. The African language in the Americas contains all five subsets of what every language contains: grammar, syntax, semantics, phonics, and pragmatics!

Smitherman's methodology is consistent with the methodology of Janice Hale and Elkin Sithole. It is also consistent with the methodology of Stanley Alsop. Stanley Alsop hammered his methodology into my head while at Howard and challenged me to approach the religious tradition and the music of our people using his methodology. This was twenty years before Molefi Asante coined the word "Afrocentric."

Using Dr. Alsop's approach, I discovered in the spirituals and in the religious traditions of black people a motif of resistance and refusal. There was a resistance to oppression and a refusal to bow down to the oppressor that runs from Queen Nzinga's resistance in Angola through Harriet Tubman's insistence on carrying a pistol! Harriet Tubman, please remember, was an African Episcopal Zion minister.

That resistance and refusal motif runs through the Maroon communities in North America and South America. The Maroons were Africans who refused to be slaves! They ran away into the hills and into the woods and swamps, determined to be free! Those communities stretch from the bayous of Louisiana and Florida all the way down through Surinam to Guyana in South America.

That same resistance and refusal motif runs from the African who wrote, "be-fo I'd be a slave," all the way through the nineteenth-century "Black Apostles" who confronted racism and oppression (See *Black Apostles: Afro-American Clergy Confront The Twentieth Century* by Burkett and Newman).

In disagreement with Dr. Cone, who thirty years ago thought that the "creativity of the Black Church which characterized the pre-Civil War [was] missing after the war," I see this same strand of creative resistance and refusal running from Charles Tindley through Thomas Dorsey and the creation of what I call "the sacred blues"—or gospel music—all the way up through the creation of the Spiritual church in North America (See Hans Baer's *Black Spiritual Movement*).

What I have tried to implement (or "embody") in my ministry is the truth that I have discovered in my research. At Trinity United Church of Christ in Chicago, we have a worship service each week which affirms our African-ness (our Africanity) and our having roots on the African continent and in the African experience. Our Bible classes are taught from an African-centered perspective, starting from the premise that Christianity did not start in Europe. It started in Africa. Our Bible Study Department is called "The Center For African Biblical Studies"!

Our seventy different ministries proceed from an African-centered world view (our mission statement is at the end of this chapter) and several of those ministries use Swahili names such as *Imani Ya Watume* (Messengers of Faith), *Siveni* (Hear Us), *Kujichagulia* (Self-Determination), *Isuthu* (Coming into Manhood), *Intonjane* (Coming into Womanhood), *Wailika* (Little Angels), *Kemba Efuru* (Faithful Daughters of Heaven), and *Alama Ya Sali* (Signs of Worship).

We affirm our African roots and use Africa as the starting point for understanding ourselves, understanding God, and understanding the world. We use Africa as the starting point for our music, our worship style, and our pedagogy. We understand Africa as the place where civilization began and the place where our story begins. We affirm that story, we embrace that story, and we tell that story. Our story is God's story. It is a story which contains a theology of resistance and refusal. It is the underground theology that has been a part of our story since the first European set foot on the Motherland; and it is the story that must be told.

The theology of resistance and refusal is just part of the underground theology, however. The *style* of the music found in the black church is also a carrier of meaning and a part of the counterpoint theology produced by blacks who have "been through the fire." All of the ramifications of this underground theology and all of the various levels that have fed it (Malcolm X, Marcus Garvey, Martin Luther King, Jr., Ida B. Wells-Barnett, the Underground Railroad, jazz and Rock 'n' Roll) are areas of study which scholars of this rich religious tradition will be investigating in years to come. I anxiously await their findings, and I anxiously await the dialogue that will take place as a result of their studies!

Bibliography

Baer, Hans A. *The Black Spiritual Movement: A Religious Response to Racism.* Knoxville, Tenn.: University of Tennessee Press, 1984.

Brown, Sterling, Arthur P. Davis, and Ulysses Lee. *The Negro Caravan.* New York: Arno Press, 1970.

Creel, Margaret Washington. *A Peculiar People: Slave, Religion and Community-Culture among the Gullahs.* New York: New York University Press, 1988.

Hale, Janice E. *Black Children: Their Roots, Culture and Learning Styles.* Baltimore: Johns Hopkins University Press, 1982.

Herskovits, Melville. *The Myth of the Negro Past.* Boston: Beacon, 1958.

Lovell, John. *Black Song: The Forge and the Flame.* New York: Macmillan, 1972.

Matthews, Donald H. *Honoring the Ancestors: An African Cultural Interpretation of Black Religion and Literature.* New York: Oxford University Press, 1998.

Sithole, Elkin T. "Black Folk Music," in *Rappin' and Stylin' Out: Communication in Urban Black America.* Thomas, Kochaman, ed. Chicago, Illinois: University of Chicago Press, 1977.

Smitherman, Geneva. *Talkin' and Testifyin': The Language of Black America.* Detroit: Wayne State University Press, 1987.

Turner, Lorenzo Dow. *Africanisms in the Gullah Dialect.* Ann Arbor: University of Michigan Press, 1974.

Mission Statement of Trinity United Church of Christ

Trinity United Church of Christ has been called by God to be a congregation that is not ashamed of the gospel of Jesus Christ and that does not apologize for its African roots! As a congregation of baptized believers, we are called to be agents of liberation not only for the oppressed, but for all of God's family. We, as a church family, acknowledge that we will, building on this affirmation of "who we are" and "whose we are," call men, women, boys and girls to the liberating love of Jesus Christ, inviting them to become a part of the church universal, responding to Jesus' command that we go into all the world and make disciples!

We are called out to be "a chosen people" that pays no attention to socio-economic or educational backgrounds. We are made up of the highly educated and the uneducated. Our congregation is a combination of the haves and the have-nots; the economically disadvantaged, the under-class, the unemployed and the employable.

The fortunate who are among us combine forces with the less fortunate to become agents of change for God who is not pleased with America's economic maldistribution!

W. E. B. Du Bois indicated that the problem in the 20th century was going to be the problem of the color line. He was absolutely correct. Our job as servants of God is to address that problem and eradicate it in the name of Him who came for the whole world by calling all men, women, boys and girls to Christ.

Part III

Black Faith and Women

9

Searching for Paradise
in a World of Theme Parks

EMILIE M. TOWNES

This presentation is, in itself, an exercise in the different styles of public discourse that are part of the very fabric of and the modes of analysis and critique employed by black theology and womanist theo-ethical reflection in doing the work our souls must do. I mix prose and poetry, exhortation and critique, as literary and analytical tools. I employ this overarching methodology to address the layered realities of African American life and the religious experience. In part, the joint task of black theology and womanist theo-ethical reflection is to open public space for the African American church and larger community to, as Katie Geneva Cannon states, "remember what we never knew." In part, it is to explore the tremendous complexities and multiplicities of the nature of realities, truths, lies, and damned lies in which African American critical religion finds its home, offers strategies of resistance, and seeks to embody a liberating transformatory praxis.

This presentation contains two levels of conversation. One is a very public one with black theology and other modes of theological discourse from my own methodological framework as a womanist Christian social ethicist. The other is intracommunal. On this level, I want to suggest a prior set of questions and observations about the nature of the public and the private in African American life and theological reflection that I believe are significant, if not crucial, to the trajectories and content of black theology as it moves into the next century.

I. The Beginning

when i was a little girl

      i spent a good deal of time trying to conjure up heaven

i thought that if i could just imagine those angels, those harps, those clouds

          then i wouldn't be so scared of this big angry white-haired, white-
          bearded, white furrow-browed God the minister preachified about on

105

those Sunday mornings in Southern Pines, North Carolina
i thought if i could see those fluffy clouds

    sit on those soft-with-goose-down couches

    move around with grace and style as my walk was a *glide* all over
heaven

    always being good, never having to worry about being bad

    smell the tasty (cause i just knew anything that had to do with heaven
had to be tasty) food

        the fried chicken

        the hot-with-butter rolls

        the spoon bread

        the gravy made from chicken grease

        the fresh greens

        the fresh string beans

        the big-grained rice

        the macaroni and cheese

        the mashed potatoes

        the candied yams, coming right from the ground

        the rib roast

        the salmon croquettes

        the salads—lettuce and tomato

        the cakes—pound, coconut, chocolate

        the pies—apple, sweet potato, chess, pecan

        the kool-aid

        the lemonade

        the sweetened tea ('cause there was no such thing as *un*sweet-
            ened tea when i was growing up)

        and butter, butter, butter, butter

            i realize now that i was associating heaven with the
            way my grandmama's house smelled on Saturday
            night and Sunday

i thought if i could hear the good music—'cause even my playmates and i knew
that all angels knew the beat, could carry a tune, and played a mean harp

    then i wouldn't worry so much

        when the men in white sheets marched through the black sec-
        tion of town where my grandmother and all the other loving
        people i knew lived

i thought if i could just conjure up heaven in my mind

and in my heart

and in my prayers

then maybe

    just maybe . . .

it seems interesting to me now, years later, that i never once consciously associated paradise with what i saw and felt on earth when i was a little girl

and now in our worlds of knowledge and our ability to create and shape our environment to fit our own levels of comfort

    it is hard to imagine paradise

        sometimes

    that isn't beyond our technical expertise

we seem to be mired in a world of facts

           statistics

           data

           numbers

           flow charts

           pie charts

           forecasts and projections

we seem to delight in our abilities to prove or disprove

    anything

    everything

    and the reality of nothing

we use our technical brilliance to explain

           codify

           compartmentalize

           delineate

           elaborate

we have created our own worlds and oceans of fun

      flags over Texas

          Georgia

          St. Louis

    river boats of delight

    funhouses of sex

    peep shows on paper and video and flesh

    shooting galleries of death

    citadels of holiness

    and

enclaves of scholarship

we seem to have so much knowledge

     so much ability to theorize and cogitate and construct

     that it often feels like womanist reflection and work

     is like searching for paradise in a world of theme parks

far too many of us have become beggars at the table of religions that sanction our own destruction

     and we find ourselves content to live out the weary drama of an outdated carousel of momentary ecstasies

     and some of us think that this is holy

II.

i, quite frankly, have renewed my search for paradise

This paradise is not collapsed solely into a terrifying apocalypse howling in the end of human history. It is connected to an understanding of humanity and our value systems and our world. As an echo of James Cone's work in *Black Theology and Black Power*,[1] this paradise I seek is largely focused on this life, for it is intimately linked to a Hebraic focus on a good and long life as the goal of each person. This paradise causes us to hope to live on into the next generation, and it expects God's judgment and salvation in this world. This prophetic eschatology envisions God accomplishing divine plans within our context through human agents. And like the prophets, it calls to the pyramidal towers of evil to beware. Yet it yokes with an apocalyptic eschatology that finds hope and judgment in the future.

Therefore, this paradise is eschatological and salvific. Eschatologically, the tension is between our present social order and the coming Day. It is historical and temporal in this regard and provides a theo-ethical foundation for the transformation of society. This search for paradise is not a desperate search for just any kind of revelation. It is a soul-deep and wish-filled conviction that our current circumstances are not ultimately definitive or inevitable. This eschatological hope seeks consolation and fortitude in the difficult reality that far too many of us live in whirlpools of catastrophe.

The search for (and the living) of a grounded paradise that is not confined solely to human history is tied with tensile thread to our time—one of crisis and one of hope. The very nature of this apocalyptic and prophetic eschatological vision is that it refuses to accept or tolerate injustice and faithlessness masquerading as piety. It shudders at the fact that we no longer know how to value life in its fullest. We rarely cry tears of genuine joy or absolute sorrow. We find few occasions in which we laugh from the wells of our souls, because we have lost the depth of our compassion; we can no longer dance for joy, because we no longer do justice. This vision does not delight or support the status quo—for this often does not reflect the will of God—but is the architecture built from our own stiff necks.

This paradise is rooted in our biblical faith, in our lives, and in our future as we work with God for a world of peace and wholeness, as we model and live so that we can be radical advocates for a justice of substance and concreteness. Yes, this is a search for a paradise that stares down evil. But it is not an apocalypse exhorting a fascination with utter destruction—that simply begets a passivity of inaction and, worse, one of indifference. This search for paradise demands a cold, hard, faith-filled stare at evil, rejects its inevitability, and chooses life over extinction.

This, then, is a passionate paradise that bends toward justice as it poses the question much as Micah did and still does for us: Is it not for us to know justice? Consequently, this paradise is not found beyond nuclear annihilation or ecological suicide. It is, as the tradition from Isaiah to 2 Peter to Revelation suggests, a new heaven and a new earth: one in which the very is-ness of life is challenged and debunked; one in which a new reality and hope for full humanness emerges; one that envisions God accomplishing divine plans within the very fabric of our lives, one in which we are to stand with God and lend our hearts, minds, souls, and energies to the task—relentlessly.

Theological Roots

Along with feminist theology, black theology is one of the more contemporary foundations for womanist theological reflection on the nature of this search for paradise. Womanist thought can and does also stand in the theological streams of evangelicalism, liberalism, neo-orthodoxy, and liberation theologies. Certainly, as foundational texts, James Cone's *Black Theology and Black Power* (along with *God of the Oppressed* and *A Black Theology of Liberation*) have had and continue to have a profound effect on all of the liberationist social postmodern theologies, of which womanist thought is only one. Cone's recognition, reformulation, and restatement of W. E. B. Du Bois's most prophetic words, "The problem of the twentieth century is the problem of the color line," combined with both an appreciation for and critique of black nationalism and also the ways in which African Americans experience the religious, have pushed womanist theological reflection to consider and reconsider the ways in which building an interstructured theo-ethic requires patience, hard work, perseverance, and a relentless commitment to rigorous critical and analytical scholarship that addresses the general public, the religious communities, and the academy.

As black theology has matured from the firm foundation laid by Cone, it has taken, in these latter days of the twentieth century, a measured look at the quest for human freedom and justice. One of the major methodological linchpins of black theology has been this quest for the equality of all persons under God. Indeed, ethicist Peter Paris calls this *the* fundamental principle of the black Christian tradition in which human equality under God is understood as categorical, absolute, unconditional, and universally applicable.

Black theology has articulated a strong doctrine of sin in relation to racism and an equally strong doctrine of virtue on the part of those who oppose racism. Black theology is forged from the moral conviction that God cares about the poor and the oppressed. Cone and other black theologians in the liberationist tradition understand that God is deeply involved in the human condition, God understands and knows human suffering and will deliver us from suffering. However, there is not an other-worldly impulse in this. This is, again, the yoking of prophetic and apocalyptic eschatology to deal with the concrete and tangible situatedness of human suffering in our world. Because God is the highest source of moral good, God in Jesus Christ identifies with the poor and outcast as liberator *and* redeemer.

Black theology also has biblical roots. There is, as is the case for many other theologies, the search for moral laws, wrestling with the Ten Commandments, and seeking to understand the ethical mandates in scripture from deontological and teleological frameworks. For many black theologians, loyalty to God means discerning the meaning of existence and the moral truths of the universe primarily in light of scripture. However, there is a profound search for recovering the African presence in the Bible. This is not, to my mind, a revisionist search, for the revisionism began when Eurocentric thought misapprehended the biblical world and refused to see it and its peoples in their richness. As scholarship emerged out of this misapprehension, so did the loss of the African presence in the biblical world. Somehow Egypt was taken out of Africa as European biblical scholarship, from the fourth century to the eighteenth century, recast the Bible into what Cain Hope Felder calls the "saga of European people."[2]

There is a strong emphasis on community. Community is more than a place or a common territory where people meet. It is more than a social organization or a collection of individuals living in close quarters to each other. In black theology, community is the exploration of a "we" relationship through seeking to understand the dynamics of belonging, group identification, and social solidarity. There is a consideration of the black family as the center of values-shaping that can be both orthodox and heterodox in its understanding of the composition of the family. There is a concern for moral achievement in the collective life of the black community and the social advancement, growth, and improvement of the condition of African Americans in the United States.

Within black theology today, various motifs have appeared with some regularity, although not with the same emphasis. There has been a concern for inclusive community. This community is both intra- and intercommunal in nature. As such, it is more precise to name this "communities" with an emphasis on the plural. There has been the ever-present interest in the worth and dignity of all persons. The imago dei, the creation, the Fall, the cross, and the resurrection all have varying sites of prominence. There has been the concern for just political, economic, and social systems. As such, black theology is rarely "just theology." It has within it a strong impulse toward ethics—philosophical, theological, and social. More recent motifs include the equality of women, intersections with the Third World, globalism, the environment, war and peace, and class.

Womanist Self-Critique

However, it is in the last chapter of *Black Theology and Black Power*, "Revolution, Violence, and Reconciliation," where Cone issues a critical reminder to womanist thought: the problem of racism will not be solved through talk but through action.[3] As womanist theo-ethical reflection features an inter-structured look at class, gender, and race, Cone's message contains a striking methodological warning about the challenge of holding fast to a praxis-based analysis in ethical and theological discourses that often feature abstraction and nuance.

Yet as much as womanist theology and ethics have gained from black theology and other liberation theologies, the very rise of womanist thought signals major methodological omissions in its precursors. Cone himself notes these omissions in the introduction to the twentieth anniversary edition of *Black Theology and Black Power*.[4]

Therefore, taking its cues from black theology and feminist theology, womanist theology cannot and must not merely accept methodologies or constructs of theological reflection that do not consider with ongoing rigor the experience of African American women and the diversities found within black womanhood and the larger African American community. In both an intercommunal dialogue with other racial and ethnic groups and an intracommunal conversation among black folk, womanist thought seeks to explore the nature of oppression as it has a peculiar impact on the lives of black women. This is done with an eye toward the nature of how this may or may not manifest itself in the lives of men, children, the aged, differing sexualities, persons of various class locations, and so forth. What this means is that race is only one consideration for womanist theo-ethical thought. Race is joined with a host of other materialities of black life in a hermeneutic of liberation and transformation.

This requires that womanist theo-ethics accept the challenge to be as self-critical as it is rigorous and analytical in its methodology. One entry point for this challenge can be found in the work of Toni Morrison.

> There is a certain kind of peace that is not merely the absence of war. It is larger than that. The peace I am thinking of is not at the mercy of history's rule, nor is it a passive surrender to the status quo. The peace I am thinking of is the dance of an open mind when it engages another equally open one—an activity that occurs most naturally, most often in the reading/writing world we live in. Accessible as it is, this particular kind of peace warrants vigilance. The peril it faces comes not from the computers and information highways that raise alarm among book readers, but from unrecognized, more sinister quarters.[5]

Morrison's essay is based on her acceptance speech for the National Book Foundation's Medal for Distinguished Contribution to American Letters in 1996. As such, Morrison focuses on the dangers, the necessities, and the pleasures of the reading/writing life in the late twentieth century. For her, the dangers are captured in two anecdotes she tells. In one, it is the danger that, in her words, "our busied-up, education-as-horse-race, trophy-driven culture poses even to the entitled." In the second, she teases out, again in her words, "the physical danger to writing suffered by persons with enviable educations who live in countries where the practice of modern art is illegal and subject to official vigilantism and murder."

Morrison's essay is instructive to womanist thought as it intersects with black theology and other theological reflection. It is in the dancing mind that we all meet each other more often than not. It is in our books and essays and lectures and papers that those who are not womanists most often meet us for the first, if not the only, time and way. It is in this dancing mind—where we tease through the possibilities and the realities, the hopes, the dreams, the nightmares, the terrors, the critique, the analysis, the plea, the witness—that womanist work is done in the academy, in the classroom, in the religious gatherings of our various communities, in those quiet and not-so-quiet times in which we try to reflect on the ways in which we know and see and feel and do. This is the world of public discourse and methodological paradigms and challenges.

This womanist dancing mind that is in search of paradise is more than our attempt to make sense of the worlds surrounding us, sometimes enveloping us, sometimes smothering us, sometimes holding us, sometimes birthing us. It is more than our desire to reconfigure the world and then invite others to come and inspect the textures, the colors, the patterns, the shapes, the sizes of this new order, this new set of promises.

No, the womanist dancing mind is one that comes from a particular community of communities yearning for a common fire banked by justice and hope. As such, our particularity marks us with indelible ink. Our task is to explore the twists and turns of the communities from which we spring and from which we take our very life and breath. It is to be very particular about the particular— and explore the vastness of it.

The womanist dancing mind—the one that weaves in and out of Africa, the Caribbean, the U.S. South, North, East, and West; the Christian, the Jewish, the Muslim, the Santeria, the Vodun, the Native American; the caste of color, the sexuality, the sexual orientation, the socio-economic class, the age, the body image; the environment, the pedagogies, the academy— has before it an enormous intracommunal task that is both gendered and racial, one in which we are trying to understand the assortments of African American life. If we do this task well, we will realize the ways in which black life is not our life alone, but a compendium of conscious and unconscious coalitions with others whose lives are not lived solely in the black face of United States life.

In this womanist dancing mind, I believe that the search for paradise is not one concerned with the universality (or not) of the womanist field of vision. What womanist thought is interested in is exploring the depths of African American life—female and male. For it is in exploring these depths, in taking seriously this particularity—not as a form of essentialism, but as epistemology—where womanists can meet and greet others. For we are intricately and intimately interwoven in our postmodern culture.

In this particularity, womanist thought must stand toe-to-toe with the damaging and destroying effects of the African American color caste hierarchy—even for those, who like myself, are relatively light-skinned black women, we who are the natural inheritors of its toxic benefits. Womanist thought must explore gender—sexuality, sexual orientation, sexism—(and continue to challenge Black Theology to do so) to get at not only a hope for wholeness, but also to understand the ways in which age and body image, and a history that contains the castrating matriarch, the ultimate mammy, and the lascivious whore, the black buck, the rapist, and the black male stud, continue to ooze from the pores of videos and magazines and television and radio and music and the pulpit.

Because womanist thought sits in the academy, the church, the classroom, and the community, it must explore socio-economic class as it moves in and out of black life with blazing speed—taking the poor *and* the wealthy out of sight. Because we all have to live somewhere, the environment is something I cannot forget to call continually back into my consciousness and work. Black womanist thought must work to broaden the black community's understanding of what is at stake in the atmosphere we breathe, beyond the pristine and irrelevant images of Sierra Club calendars that rarely, if ever, put people in nature. This helps us understand that postmodern culture and the air it spawns will kill us if we do not start paying attention to and then strategizing for a more healthy environment for all of us to live in.

This said, let me deal more directly with the topic of the universality of womanist discourse through the lens of particularity. For it is in this particularity that I am challenged to deromanticize the African continent by coming to know its peoples on their terms, not mine. I am compelled to search out and recover my Caribbean streams of consciousness and memory to understand the different ways in which black folk have survived and not survived our own Diaspora and the different manifestations of the latent Middle Passage in our historic and contemporary lives. I must listen to the different rhythms of blackness that come from the different geographies that shape peoples bodies and health. I am drawn, sometimes with enormous reservation and circumspection, to understand the different ways in which other religions, beyond my own Christian identity, have shaped me and my communities and to understand what is at stake when we have lost, forgotten, or been stolen away from the rich medleys of the religious in black life. As I reach further into my particularity, I am brought face-to-face with the tremendous loss of touch with Native American peoples.

It is through the particularity of the womanist dancing mind that I can meet and greet those parts of myself that have been lost through neglect, ignorance, well-practiced amnesia, or malicious separation. I am challenged to look at those places that the "isms" that I impose on others are turned back at me, and I am asked to see myself through the eyes of those whom I would and do reject. It does not matter that this rejection is not intentional or malevolent. What does matter is that if I say, as a womanist, that I am engaged in race, gender, class, and environmental interstructured analysis, then I must face those places within myself and within my work that ignore the ways in which that interstructuring takes place.

This womanist dancing mind that is in search of paradise, says Morrison, requires "an intimate, sustained surrender to the company of my own mind as it touches another." For Morrison, this is done in reading. For me it is in reading and listening. It is my own need, which Morrison names so well, "to offer the fruits of my own imaginative intelligence to another without fear of anything more deadly than disdain." For Morrison, this is writing. For me this is writing and speaking and working to bring in justice. As I engage my work within communities of communities, I find both celebration and anguish.

But mostly what I hope to find is that peace of which Morrison speaks, the peace of my mind as it dances, and dances, and dances into a new future that I have had some small part in helping craft with other people and other communities of resistance and hope. This is a future (and a mitigating hope-filled present) that is more vibrant, more life bringing and giving, more welcoming, more humane. What is at stake in womanist discourses is deadly serious: it is challenging the ways we know (epistemology) and the ways we think (orthodoxy) and the ways we act (orthopraxy). And we make judgments on these.

It is with a kind of self-critique—one that considers the role of particularity and universality—that I approach the topic of black theology as public discourse. I want to look at one prospect, and a vexing one for black theology as public discourse, that arises for me out of the interplay between particularity and universality: the nature of the public and the private in black life and scholarship. I do so from a womanist rubric that, in the final analysis, believes that the search for paradise, rooted in concrete material life with an eye to the future as well, is absolutely necessary in these modern-postmodern times.

The Split between the Public and Private Realms

The very nature and scope of black theology means that it must maintain its public voice. This public voice has and, judging from the more recent writings in black theology, will continue to make the connection to the changing dynamics of the church, society, and the academy. I make this claim even while hearing the echoes of manifold discussions of a specious dichotomy between the public and the private realms. Formulations of such a split manifest a position of privilege that can and does define separate worlds of existence in humanity and in nature. Further, it suggests the power to construct and maintain these worlds often at the expense of everyone: those who hold the power, those who suffer the powerful.

In our academic lives, one manifestation of this dichotomization is in conversations about the nature of objectivity. Objectivity is, in many ways, a beguiling methodological construct. The rise of reason within modernism, for all its positive rewards, has lulled far too many of us within the academy into the erroneous belief that there is in fact an Archimedean point from which we can do our work within the humanities. The reality is that we stand, even on our best theoretical, methodological, critical, and analytical days, on an Archimedean verandah. We survey the territory of postmodern culture by moving our bodies and our perspectives in an attempt to respond to questions of ethics and politics as well as aesthetics and epistemology. But we are, ultimately, immured by the subjectivities, the particularities that make us both distinctive and finite.

Black theology and other liberation theologies constructed out of the concerns of social postmodernism are often easily dismissed. Perhaps much of this stems from the very way in which black theology questions and challenges liberal, neo-orthodox, and evangelical discourses that are, historically speaking, still quite young. Ironically, these forms of theological reflection often look at black theology as the interloper and the heretic they were once charged with being as they emerged on the theological scene in the United States in earlier eras.

With the Christian church, one manifestation of the false public-private split is in a negative dualism that separates the body and the spirit. This Cartesian separation does more than split us apart, it fractures us in such a way that we often believe and live as if our bodies and spirits have no influence on each other. We live together in a somewhat uneasy coexistence within the splinters of this fracturing.

The theological root of the body-spirit fracture is the traditional Christian theological formulation of the meaning of incarnation in which being is that which is in the body yet not of it. This Cartesian formulation belies the ways in which the body is basic to much of the imagery we have concerning Jesus from nativity to crucifixion as well as our own embodiedness. The nativity is a very embodied experience. The smells, sounds, and sights of a stable are tangible and *very* concrete. Yet our representations of the nativity, our conscious and unconscious imaginings of the scene, often take all the is-ness of the birth of Jesus away from us. We imagine and often worship an antiseptic scene that is pleasing to a deodorized faith.

The gospels are full of stories of Jesus sharing meals with others. We tend to spiritualize these stories and name them miracles—which they were, but we do so before we recognize the ways in which they provided concrete bodily sustenance to people. These narratives spark the mystery of miracles for us, yet they are also stories that point to the physical needs we have for food and drink. When we separate the mystery from the way in which it touches our humanity to offer a window *into* the mystery, we invite a fracturing of body and soul.

There is a very concrete and physical aspect to Christian faith that we often ignore because of the body-spirit fracture we have in our faith and in our understanding of faithfulness. When we live out of an incarnational understanding that takes us out of the *dynamic* dualism we have of body *and* spirit, then we lapse into the *deadly* dualism that tells us that the body is inferior, if not evil, and must be transcended by the spirit of Jesus.

This devaluing of the body takes many forms in our society. In some cases it manifests itself as ageism, in others it is racism, sexism, heterosexism, classism, nationalism. All of these fracturings of the body and the spirit slaughter genuine public discourse. The private discourses that serve as undercurrent and foundation for the public are also shattered, through reactionary violence to the challenges of genuine diversity and the search for universals from which we can craft common strategies and visions.

In terms of one social manifestation of this public-private dichotomization, the rise of a rhetoric of victimization within African American life and within the larger cultures of the United States is dangerous. This rhetoric of victimization is, of course, distinct from political and social forces conspiring to create victims by constructing an architecture of annihilation. What troubles me about the rhetoric of victimization is that it fails to acknowledge the individual and collective choices we make in how we live our lives—even in the midst of death-dealing socio-economic and cultural realities. If black folk refuse even a limited agency then we abdicate our agency and place our fate in the hands of a powerful and absolute dominating other that is not divine but all too human, if not inhumane. To assent to victimization—be that assent conscious or unconscious—is to live lives of hopelessness and despair. It is to believe the inaccurate but very effective media portrayals, that African Americans are hopelessly trapped in pathologies of our own making, without any recognition or analysis of larger social structures that defeat caring, compassion, and respect for all humanity and the earth itself.

The sometimes mindless, other times calculated, assertions and declarations of victimization are sinful. They do not place any of us on a higher moral ground but allow us to make claims that are often unjust and allow us to abdicate from our responsibility to work in partnership with God. To give victimization such a large hand in black lives means that we are no longer seeking mutual or harmonious relationships. Rampant individualism, which often fuels this rhetoric of victimization, has turned back on African American life in such a way that the moral arc of the universe bends toward the self (and its gain) rather than the community (and what it means to work and live in mutuality). Rather, we are falling into a weird solipsism in which we are bound within the walls of our ideologies rather than expanding our vision into a radical future based on justice.

Despair and the rhetoric of victimization are the natural enemies of hope. However, if black and womanist theologies cannot provide a hefty hope, one that moves in transformatory ways that are concrete and specific as they also call for vision and trust, then we cannot expect the theo-ethical musings that are needed to address the very real inequities of life to have meaning for those who have either fallen into despair or been placed there by hegemonic forces.

Maintaining a Public Voice

Hence, as I consider the prospect of black theology as public discourse, I find that it must begin to address with much more rigor and precision the ways in which this false split between the public and the private has functioned and will continue to function as a form of intracommunal genocide for African Americans. This genocide will extend from the community to the church and into the academy for African American scholars of religion who find their theoretical and methodological home in black theology.

with a history that includes such vulgar spectacles as auction blocks and lynchings

      it is ludicrous, in womanist thought

          to believe for one second

that there is any such thing as a public and private split in the
worlds of the communities from which i come and now live

for as when i was growing up

it was clear that black folks did not have a private life that was not at
the beck and call of hegemony

even my search for paradise was tinged with the blinding
white hot evils of white and male and economic supremacies

we did have citadels of hope

and outposts of resistance

we did have separate but equal

and Jim Crow

but what we really had to struggle *for* was a private world that was genuinely
our own

one that wasn't shaped and formed by dominating others

but one that we could actually call and know to be home

given that this is the place from which i move and try to understand the stump
from which i speak, it is clear to me that

a dominant gaze makes that which is named private invisible in the
public realms of the dominating others

this mournful gaze does not recognize the richness of african american
culture

it resorts to collapsing black realities into postmodern min-
strel shows

it seeks to freeze frame black life

without recognizing that even when we all share a common
language

the rhythms and cadences of living are different and rich
within themselves

and within the communities of african american life
as well

the private has never *been* private in the hegemonic rhetoric of public/private
splits for communities of the dispossessed

it has been controlled and manipulated to fit the news at 5, 6, and 10
(central time)

it has been a place where various forms of the police state could, did,
and do enter at will

it has produced casualties in see-through body bags

so that even our pain and our sorrow become the stuff of
romanticization and novels

it has vented an endless stream of stereotypes and prototypes of black wickedness and sexualized body parts

and sadly, oh so sadly

many of these brutalized and brutalizing images have been internalized in african american communities

and in the individual lives of black women and children and men

for far too many of us

this not so private sphere is a place of paralyzing demons

some, in my community, have slipped into an endless spiral of horizontal violence

some have neither martin's dream

malcolm's nightmare

walker's color purple

or mama day's lightening powder

there is no split between public and private realms in womanist thought

for oppression is not seen as a static process

it is dynamic and it is relentless

so, quite frankly, womanist thought engages in a renewed search for paradise

one in which the public and private are not antagonistic dualisms

but very natural dance partners

the private: that place of home

is a place for health, healing, identity formation, resistance, celebration, transformation

it is the place where the "real lives" the "real worlds" of african american peoples take place

not the media-driven images of african american living that trick all of us into believing in and/or living grotesque stereotypes of african american life

it is the place where the realities of colorism, intracommunal gender oppressions, class and caste, racism, ethnic tensions, geographical differences/commonalities all exist

it is the place that shapes the radical differences within african american life, such that we are not a monolithic community, but an eclectic and diverse compendium of communit*ies*

it is the place of core resistance to devaluing oppressions

the private is the place of rest

that we are still learning to create in a social order that features a suffocating regime of interstructured inequality

it is the place of morrison's dancing mind

walker's world in our eye

sanchez's house of lions

it is a place, that we are building, life by life

in which we yoke our individual lives with communal
accountability

and learn a communal hope that teaches us as we
learn

to love our eyes
backs
hands
mouths
feet
shoulders
arms
necks
inside parts
lungs
life-holding wombs
life-giving private parts
hearts
spirits
souls

womanist thought and the worlds out of which it comes

has the historic reminder that we must lift as we climb

and so the private is not to be a place of withdrawal with no return

but a place to gain strength for the journey

so that we learn to live creatively in the tight circle of choices that are
given to us by this social order we all live in

but also plot, scheme, and realize ways to craft that tight circle into a
spiral of possibilities for this generation

and serve as the standing ground for the next generation and
the next generation and beyond

yes, it is true that the public *and* the private are realms in which the choices we
have are within a cultural and socio-economic reality

that is geared for warring

violence

destruction

and the annihilation of the enemy, the other

this is a sad and weary refrain

but it is still the truth

and this makes the idea of autonomous public and private realms
     at times
         an obscene phone call
         a dirty joke
     one, which at times chokes
     because anger and rage come so quickly
         and completely
         that we cannot draw our collective or individual breaths
     because it implies a choice or a set of choices that have not been part
     of the historic reality of the lives of most, if not all, african american
     women
for you see,
     choice, like poetry, is not a luxury
         it is a right
one that is denied
     subverted
     violated
     pillaged
so womanist wit and wisdom holds fast to dreaming a world
     public *and* private
     this is a more powerful
     more real
     more concrete world
     in its now intentional and strategic yoking of the private, the personal
         with the public, the communal
a world that shakes with liberating fury and passion
     as it designs and sets in motion the plot lines of justice and freedom
     because we know that liberating hope is the only defense against
     despair and ruin
this transformatory nature of womanist recognition that the private, the personal
     and the public, the communal
     must form a near-seamless thread
helps our communities to realize that
we live in structures of evil
     not just *a* structure
the isms of all of our lives come in dolby sound
     they are layered upon layered

woven with a thin thread

with tensile strength

and a tight pattern

we can't get at one without dealing with the other

if we are careful *not* to use the masters' tools

the yearning and struggle for freedom is the kind of thing

that brings out the biggest, best, and most seductive of the masters' tools

because freedom means those tools will be banished

forbidden

made obsolete—and even *tools* want to survive

transformatory womanist reflection, thought, and life recognizes that

freedom is fleeting

elusive

and frustrating

we can lose it as soon as we gain it

we can never attain it without understanding the political and economic systems of the world

and not just the contemporary stuff and how it functions

but the details of its evolution

we have to organize ourselves *for* freedom

which means strategies—that will be put into action

talking loud

shouting down opposition

silencing dissent or conflict

are, at best,

short term solutions

freedom means pitching in

listening for the voices

accepting the variety

allowing the voices within our community

the young and the old

the lesbian and the gay

the propertied and the propertyless

the heterosexual and the celibate

the dark and the light

the bisexual and the transgendered,

the female and the male

the conservative and the radical

the thoughtful and the clueless

all these and more

to have a full and authentic and *valued* place within our public/private discourse

realizing that there are many paths to freedom—and slavery—and death

debunking the notion of a public/private split means that black folk learn to love our eyes

backs
hands
mouths
hearts
spirits
souls

for this is to love our bodies

which means tackling the gross iconization of our lives

that comes from the false dichotomy of public and private in white western self-absorbed penile thought

for when womanists talk about the body

it is both the personal, the private, the individual body

and the public, the group, the communal body

i first learned about this body from the older black women in my life

and it was years before i realized that they were not just talking about *my* body

they included miss hemphill down the road
miss rosie across the street
miss montez around the corner
and cousin willie mae down by the juke house

my body was placed in a witness of women

who knew violation

enjoyed sex

moved with dignity

and shook from religious ecstasy

i learned that there was always the possibility that some injustice might be done to my body

and bodies of other black folk

but also knew i had a home to come to and they would stand by me there would be times when it seemed my options were few

>but i had a right to scream

>>to say no

>>to fight back

>>to do what i thought best to protect any violation against the dignity of my body

>*and i had an obligation to teach this right to other black boys and girls as well*

they crafted a community of healing that was a refuge of loving women and sometimes men

>>to heal a scarred throat

>>or bruised knuckles

>>or brutalized body

they taught me that i was a child of God

>>and in some strange, if not halting way

>>that meant i was free

>>>but i'd have to fight for it

almost all those women are gone now

>>but what they left me with is the deep knowledge that the community they created and gifted me with

>*must* be re-created

as public discourses, black theology and womanist theo-ethical reflection should be the praxeological base points for this work

as public discourses, we must be clear to the public what is at stake and what are the ingredients in crafting an embodied healthy community of renewal, resistance, hope, and transformation

it begins with the strong and the weak *together*

>>who will refuse to accept inept silence or self-abnegating sacrifice as the only options for life and scholarship

>>who will hold themselves accountable to the spirit

>>who *will* choose to live rather than die

>>>because silence suffocates when it is prompted from violence and fear

>>>and this is a truly slow and obscene death

it also means that we've got to understand the system

>>in order to maneuver it into places which celebrate our bodies

and learn how to turn racism and sexism and classism and ageism

>>and even homophobia and heterosexism

into occasions to not only speak, but also do justice
and when women (and men) gather
in our pain and in our joy
holding
loving
and wrapping life with glory
we can name the violation and abuse
and then act to eradicate it
we will understand that we live in a world
in which i'm not sure even the elite have control anymore
because so much of the world has gone mad on violence
we understand that choices are often tight
but that some of us come from the tradition of the trickster
and there *are* ways to create new options
but it will take courage and cunning and faith
to get there
those women did not tell me how you do all this
but they did teach me how to use an oyster knife
womanist oyster knives
are made with craftiness
calculation
joy
care
and faith
and we are sharpening them
polishing them
yes, i *am* looking for paradise in this world
but it is not a paradise of theme parks with jury-rigged thrills and
fears
but a paradise of hope, love, justice, joy, and resistance
it is a paradise built on an enduring faith
for ultimately, it's not so much about *who* possesses this enduring faith
but our will and willingness to go to God in search of such a faith
recognizing our humanness
recognizing the promises found in each of us
and holding our selves together

It is to this task of holding our selves together that I want to see black theology join womanist theology as public theologies committed to move beyond analysis, methodology, and theory to strategies and actions rooted in justice. We must do so as public theologies dedicated to exacting scholarship and confessional (but also analytical and critical) alliances to the black church. These are not antithetical impulses. Rather, it is to turn again to a paradise that is both prophetic and apocalyptic in its eschatology. Yoking scholarship with apologetics is not a panacea nor is it arcane intellectual camouflage. It is hard work, close and respectful listening, an openness to learn and grow, a willingness to admit—if not confess—one's limitations and awfulnesses, to grow our lives, our scholarship, our preaching, our mission, our teaching large.

For as we turn into the twenty-first century, there isn't anybody else who will do this for us.

Notes

1. James H. Cone, *Black Theology and Black Power* (New York: Seabury Press, 1969), 121-27. Current edition published by Orbis Books, Maryknoll, N.Y.: 1997.

2. Cain Hope Felder, "Introduction," *The Original African Heritage Study Bible*, King James Version (Nashville: The James C. Winston Publishing Company, 1993), viii.

3. James H. Cone, *Black Theology and Black Power*, 135.

4. James H. Cone, *Black Theology and Black Power* (New York: Harper & Row, Publishers, San Francisco, 1989), vii-xiv. Current edition published by Orbis Books, Maryknoll, N.Y.: 1997.

5. Toni Morrison, *The Dancing Mind* (New York: Alfred A. Knopf, 1996), 7-8.

10

Servanthood Revisited

Womanist Explorations of Servanthood Theology

JACQUELYN GRANT

Introduction

When Jesus declared that he "came not to be served, but to serve" (Mk. 10:45), one could say that he was presenting a new understanding of leadership. Some have attempted to capture this different understanding through the concept of "servant-leader." Whereas this presentation may be helpful in beginning the process of rethinking the leadership question, the problem of leadership is but a small reflection of the real structural or systematic problems which continue to violate humanity.

Service, servant, and servanthood are concepts of the Christian faith that are thoroughly integral to the practice of faith. Yet, these concepts have been thoroughly corrupted by many presuming leadership historically, as well as by the general dominant/white Christian community. In effect, the Christian notion of servanthood has been fused and confused with the oppressive, unjust, social, and political designation of servanthood—which in fact has meant servitude. Historical evidence of this fusion is clearly traceable to the institution of slavery, when the brainwashing of the slaves masqueraded as religious indoctrination. The masters intended that the slave would understand his/her servanthood status not only to be ordained by God, but to be of God.

What followed slavery and replaced it was the institution of domestic service wherein blacks were still perceived to be the servants of white masters. Though slavery was no longer legal, many of its practices were carried out as if it still existed. By and large, relations between the races had not changed significantly. The superior/inferior, master/servant, dominant/subordinate models were still in effect.

In effect, the institution of domestic service replaced the institution of slavery as the place where the reality of servanthood continued and yet continues to be corrupted. The notion of servanthood, as we have come to use it, has in fact become a mechanism for perpetuating evil and suffering among people because of race, gender, class, or other humanly applied categories.

It is no accident that our images of Jesus and God are quite unlike those of the servants of the world. God is not black; God is not female; and God, who is rich in houses and land, is certainly not poor. Our images of God are totally unlike those whom we have historically relegated to the servant arenas of life. Whatever else Jesus and God may be, servants (as we understand it) they are not.

Explorations into the theme of servanthood and its impact on the daily sociopolitical positioning of persons in the church and society, historically and even today, demonstrate not only how distasteful the position of servant is, but how oppressive and in fact sinful it is. An examination of the conditions under which black women have been forced to live throughout their existence in most societies provides a prime example of this oppressive system of servanthood. From slave girl, house girl, pickaninny, mammy, cook, to cleaning woman, or whatever the form of domestic servant or service, black women have essentially been defined by others as objects. The institution of domestic service, even as we know it today, facilitates the continuation of this attitude, which extends from antebellum times. Studies continue to demonstrate that black women are disproportionately represented in the domestic service industry, and that conditions there still significantly impact and reflect the attitude that whites harbor of blacks in general, and black women in particular.

In this study, I explore three themes: (1) The institution of domestic service as a place to analyze human relationships as we know them in and under structures of oppression. The conditions and practices which exist under this system are not accidental to the theologies which undergird dominant culture reality; to the contrary, they are integral to them. (2) The doctrine of humanity as a central problem in our understanding of servanthood. What makes for the exploitation of servants is perhaps the inability to see the servant as human. The historic practice of relegating some to the servant class while others are exempt from this category begs the question, "Why are some people always more servant than others?" (3) The use of (servanthood) language as a tool of oppression or liberation in Christian community. Using servanthood language as a point of departure, the argument in actuality is far reaching. What is the function of language in creating reality? How have racist language and sexist language been tools for insuring institutionalized oppressions both inside the church and in the larger society?

By focusing on the experiences of African American women, this study challenges us to move toward developing theologies which can empower us to free our language and our social political structures, theory, and praxis from assumptions and practices which prevent us from creating the reigndom of God.[1]

Domestic Servanthood and the "Servanthood" Problem

An exploration into the area of black women's work reveals that black women have always made up a significant portion of domestic servants in the United States. The problematic being addressed is the historic relationship between the people of the servant class and the victimization of servants both in the secular (social/political/economic) world and the Christian/church world.

A study in the area of domestic service enables us to see how, historically, life in these two arenas (the secular world and the church world) has been distorted and defined to serve the social and political interests of the dominant oppressors. Some of the ways in which black women function vis-à-vis domestic service illustrate how this happens. This analysis enables us further to see not only that some people are more servant than others, but more specifically, that relationships among women of the dominant culture and minority women merely mirror the dominant/subordinate model of the larger society. Within the institution of domestic service, this model prevails.

Emancipation did not change the basic relationship between black women and white women in particular and black people and white people in general. For some, emancipation meant slavery without chains; for others it meant mere servanthood, and in fact, often servitude. After slavery there was neither change in the image nor significant change in the condition of black people in the United States. The image was still that blacks were inferior and that they were intended to service white America. Consequently, when blacks, now free, sought work, they were relegated to the service jobs and menial work of slavery days, which they did forcibly during slavery. Both black men and black women were limited in vocational options. Studies of domestic servants show that black women are more often in this category than any other group of people.[2] Between 1890 and 1920, while white female servants decreased, black female servants increased, such that by 1920, 40 percent of all domestic servants were black women. Black women's representation was disproportionately high, resulting in significant numbers of them being permanently relegated to that work.[3] This was and is because blacks and servants (especially in the South) were considered synonymous. Katzman described domestic service in the South as a caste system. In contrast to the South, in the North and West, he notes that servants were rarely found in lower-middle-class or working-class families. However, in the former slave states, black servants were as common in these households as in households headed by white-collar workers.[4] He further notes that the South has been called a "housewife's utopia."[5] This system in the South was a part of a larger racial caste structure in which, reminiscent of slavery, blacks were servants and whites were masters and never the two should be changed. The dominant/subordinate relationship within the household mirrored the white/black relationship in general, especially in the South.

Even in the North, however, the social-political gap between black women and white women differed so radically that even the changed attitude on the part of black women maids, after migrating from the South to the North, did not significantly change their status. White women were still dominant and black women were still subordinate.[6]

Though legal slavery was abolished, much of the character of slavery remained for decades thereafter. This meant that basic relationships had not changed significantly, as we can see in two areas of the country, for black domestics.[7]

A Modicum of "Humanity" in the Midst of "Inhumanity"

One of the reasons that domestic service has taken the form that it has is that the humanity of the servant has been denied. This is clearly seen as we look below the surface of the industry itself. Two areas of domestic service provide an opportunity for a deeper look, enabling us to examine the "servanthood problem." The black mammy tradition and the "live-in" tradition are quite similar. In these traditions, we see the consistent and persistent violation of the humanity of black women.

Jessie Parkhurst[8] provides a snapshot view of the life of the black mammy tradition in North America. It can be used to demonstrate that the black woman was seen as useful only to the extent that she was a servant. For all intents and purposes, she was at best an object to be used by her master and mistress, before and after emancipation. In describing the role of the black mammy, we can see how the humanity of the black woman is negated. Several points are to be made about the black mammy tradition.

The black mammy represented not only a status symbol, but it insured a way of life for white people. Having a black mammy became another notch in the belts of white men and women who were of (or who wanted) stature. Providing comprehensive services, from child care to field work in some situations, the black mammy became a central part of the white household. Not only was the black mammy tradition commonplace among the aristocracy, but also among the middle class and poorer farmers. The black mammy is objectified and loses her identity. Yet, she cannot act as though she is white—for to do so would certainly be stepping out of her place. She was like another manufactured order betwixt and between white humanity and black reality. She shared the ideals of the white family and in the public's eye was associated more with the white family than with her black family. In other words, in the public realm she existed only for the whites.

The story of the black mammy is in fact the story of the white owner/employer storytellers. It is through the eyes of the owners/employers and their children that we are introduced to the black mammy figure. Images presented of her were, more often than not, those characteristics important not to her, but to them. Among the characteristics given her were loyalty, affection, strength, piety, trustworthiness, faith, patience, discretion, devotion, and truthfulness. In her relationship with her white owners, certainly these characteristics would be of great significance, since these qualities were directed toward them and aided in keeping the system intact.

In accenting these qualities, the black mammy is placed into a category unto herself. The qualities listed above, in addition to others such as good, popular, regal, courageous, neat, tender, and warm-hearted are denied other black women. Other black women are dirty, undesirable, promiscuous, and the like. They are kept at a distance. It is in this sense that perhaps we could argue that there is a modicum of humanity allowed, in that she suffered fewer indignities than other black women.

The black mammy had to minimize her family interests for the sake of those of the master/mistress. Her primary function was the care of the family of the master/mistress. She was to facilitate the whims, will, and the needs of the entire white family. This meant that she had to be conveniently located to do so. If she was not sleeping in the children's room, she was sleeping in a cabin, closer in proximity and distinguished in either size or structure from the quarters of other servants.[9] Only in old age was she able to experience any real sense of home life, for she was of no longer of significant use to the master/mistress/employer.

The quasi-different treatment of the black mammy and other black women was evident. Generally, black mammies were not sold, rather, they were passed from generation to generation. In addition, they were generally not physically punished, and were given more latitude with regard to their behavior. Still, the black mammy was a nameless object, a traveling servant, a convenience, whose personhood and name were of no importance. She, therefore, was known always as "Mammy," and not by her given name.

The relationship of the black mammy to the children of the master was a peculiar one. She cared for their every need, at home as well as while traveling. She was nurse-maid as well as playmate.[10] Perhaps among the most cynical aspects of the relationship was the expectation that the black mammy was responsible for orienting white children into the oppressive culture designed to keep the black mammy system in place. Teaching the children about proper "places" in society, Parkhurst said:

> As for example, the question of the child who asked, "Mammy, who made you black?" And the answer, "Child, who been puttin' notions in your curly haid? Gawd made mammy black and He made you and your ma white, for the reason that when Noah came out'n de Ark, Ham was disrespectful to his pa and laughed at him, and Gawd told Ham he and his children should be always servants; so He made him black, and dat's where we all black people come from."[11]

The relationship between the black mammy and the mistress was one of inequality and contradictions. It is said that often the best friend of the mistress was the black mammy. They shared the same space, though with a qualitative difference—the mammy's space was always a controlled space. That relationship was also characterized by self-destroying behavior designed to keep the oppressive system intact. During the war, the black mammy was saddled with the responsibility of "keeping up the spirit of the mistress," and feeding and nursing Confederate soldiers back to health.

It is interesting that Parkhurst seems to present this picture of the black mammy as though it is a complimentary one. The sources, those who spoke about their memories of their black mammies, represented their impressions as quite positive and acceptable. It is interesting to note that when in 1923 the Daughters of the Confederacy attempted to have a monument in memory of this group of women erected in the nation's capital, the black community rejected it and proposed instead that a better memorial would be to extend the full rights of American citizenship to the descendants of these Mammies: The blacks included in their counterproposal a plan which advocated the discontinuation of the following: lynching; inequality in education and educational facilities; all practices of discrimination; the humiliation of blacks in public conveyances; and the denial of voting rights of blacks.[12]

The mammy tradition had its origin in slavery, though it survived and continued, with many of the same characteristics, as a common phenomenon well into the twentieth century. Servants were almost as controlled as they had been during slavery. Domestic service is personal service, related so much to the personal property of slavery times, that it was unregulated by law. Under the conditions of servitude, black women, as black people, were considered subordinate property and unequal in pursuit of life, liberty, and happiness. Katzman credits racial stereotypes as the justification for the subordination of black women in the South. According to popular views, blacks "were childlike, lazy, irresponsible, and larcenous." They were worthless, dirty, dishonest, unreliable, and incompetent.[13] In ruling over them, white women were only acting in the best "interest of all concerned."

As in slavery, the humanity of black women was violated and often denied in other expressions of domestic service. This denial of the humanity of black women meant that they could still be the subjects of continued violations. Since black women were considered property rather than humans, they could be used to do the drudgery work of white women; as Zora Neale Hurston later stated, they have been treated as the "mules of the world."[14] Essentially, they were indispensable to the ongoing work of many white households. The stereotype that blacks are more suited for service work reflects the fact that even after slavery, and to some extent today, the term "chattels personal" can still be used to describe the way blacks are treated, especially in the area of domestic service.

In her book *Living In, Living Out*,[15] Elizabeth Clark-Lewis analyzes the life world of "live-in" domestics during the early part of this century. What she demonstrated was a continuation of the distressing situation of black women servants and the oppressive attitudes and expectations of white women. Black women spoke of the problems ranging from indecent accommodations to unreasonable time requirements. Esther Lawson talked about her inadequate living conditions: "This woman had me a room fixed up in the basement. Well, it was more like a garage. No door on it, or nothing. They pulled the car right in. . . . When I'd go down at night from the kitchen I'd go right in this little room. Car sitting up there. That's where I slept."[16] Clark-Lewis reported that the women in her study all talked about the proverbial "good servant" lecture given by the employer. "Good servants were to be efficient and meet all of the rigid standards of the household. The introduction unfailingly emphasized the employer's lofty status, unparalleled standards, grand moral obligations, and unbounded benevolence. The main message, of course, was that a good servant must assume the role of humble subordinate at all times."[17]

The role of black women was to be the primary worker in the household. Work which was considered heavy and dirty was reserved for them. Even when white women were employed, it was to do lighter, more respectable work. Essie Octavia Crockett described the work and the workers in the household in which she was employed. Clearly, the distinction between black women's and white women's work was important to be made.

> In that house only colored people worked; did everything. Now she some-times has a white lady to make up her menu for her fancy parties . . . or to do her . . . invitations . . . [and] to do fancy writing for Christmas cards. . . . These is things they'd never want us to do because we might have to sit down or get talked to like a human person.
>
> But they didn't work. No serving, running for this or that, in uni-form. . . But I started work in 1918, and I never . . . saw any [white women] serving for a family. No, they don't do no work.[18]

Not only is hard work the normal expectation, but "around-the-clock" work is also. Bernice Reeder said: "When you live-in, you must do everything but chew they food. Do this, do that, run here, run there, and when you get through—do this!" In support of this, Weida Edwards confirmed:

> You had to do everything, twenty-four hours to the day. You were up with the mister. . . . Then the children had to be cared for and . . . she'd finally start calling for this and that. . . . The whole place is cleaned daily and all meals are from scratch. . . . Now [after 10 P.M.] she'd be up to all hours worrying everybody to do this or that. Why not? She'd sleep 'til noon if she wanted to—it was you that had to be up, dressed in your gray by six-thirty.[19]

The life of the domestic was not her own. It seems that the primary agenda of the white mistress was that of total control of the black domestic. This control was best exercised by filling every minute in the servant's day. It was further insured by the institution of low wages. Even in those instances when the work was similar or the same, black women were paid at a much lower rate than white women.

I have considered some of the social and economic contradictions which black women experienced in the institution of domestic service. I have left unad-dressed the matters of sexual exploitation, political exploitation, and major eco-nomic exploitation. Certainly, there were many such exploitations in and beyond the institution of domestic service. But two things stand out in relation to the issues identified in the black mammy and live-in traditions: (1) the lives of black women were controlled and therefore, the domination/subordination model necessary in master/servant relationships was always present; and (2) the wholesale violation of the black women's humanity. In effect, domestic service was but a microcosm of the larger society.

Servanthood and the Question of Being Human

There are several questions that emerge as we consider the institution of domestic service as a context wherein we see some of the contradictions and violations against black humanity in general and black women's humanity in particular. As Dorothy Sayers asked a few decades ago about white women, the question that we are forced to ask is, Are black women human? Are servants human? Even though all black women are not domestic servants, black women are often treated as servants by the larger community. How has the institution of servanthood negatively impacted the perceived humanity of black women?

Further, one could explore the question, how do these different experiences of women impact the direction and contents of theology? Upon whose experience(s) are our theological conceptualizations based—the daughters of slaveholders/masters or the daughters of slaves/servants? The data presented above clearly reflect the fact that black women were not considered human. What, then, does it mean to be human?

What we've learned recently from various expressions in liberation theology is that the recognition of the humanity of people must be a basic part of our search for the reigndom of God. Components of this sense of humanity are: (1) an affirmation of human dignity; (2) the practice of justice in human relationships; (3) the establishment of equality among human beings—men and women, differing racial and ethnic groups, etc.; (4) self-affirmation as a necessary category of human reality; (5) self-reliance, self definition, and self-control as components of humanity; and (6) economic empowerment for historically oppressed peoples. Individual, social, economic, and political relationships are the focal points in determining the perceived humanity of individual persons and groups of people.

Perhaps the most often cited articulation of this quest for full humanity has come in the form of equality language. In addressing its usage in the black church tradition, ethicist Peter Paris recalled:

> The doctrine of human equality under God is, for [black churches], the final authority for all matters pertaining to faith, thought, and practice. In short, its function in the black experience is categorical, that is, it is unconditional, absolute, and universally applicable. Consequently, all action (religious or political) that is aimed at correcting the social injustice of racism is viewed as moral action.[20]

Paris summarizes two of the most important theological implications of this aspect of the doctrine of humanity. "First, the black churches, under the norm of the black Christian tradition, are characterized by their common quest for human freedom and justice, that is the equality of all persons under God. Second, that aim implies a strong doctrine of sin in relation to the problem of racism."[21]

Womanist analysis draws our attention to the fact that the various expressions of violations of humanity are in fact acts of sin. Specifically, womanists argue that personal and institutional expressions of oppression are in fact sin actualized. After reviewing notions of sin in slave songs, slave narratives (autobiographies), and black theology, Delores Williams proposes an understanding of sin as devaluation and defilement of black women's bodies. Certainly, the institution of domestic servanthood represents a devaluation and defilement.[22]

In general, womanist principles accent the move toward full humanity for all. To this end, the eradication of all forms of oppression is primary. Womanist theology argues for a multidimensional analysis which fosters a liberative and holistic model for understanding humanity. That is to say, violations against/of humanity can be reversed by consistently challenging those structures which mitigate against human dignity.

What we saw in the data on the black mammy tradition and the stories of live-in domestics is the presence of racism, sexism, and classism. The primary reason for the discrimination is the belief that "to be black is to be servant and to be servant is to be black," a feeling which is particularly present in the South.[23] As the (black) South migrated north, the attitudes greeted them there as well. Blacks were associated with servanthood in a way that whites were not. Even when whites were employed in this capacity, it was always at a much higher rate.[24] This intertwining of race, gender, and economic contradictions kept black women disproportionately among the servant class. So much so that servanthood became, not a state of employment, but a station of life which was not deserving of the privilege of basic human rights and dignity. We see this in both traditions discussed: South and North, the black women were little more than objects; they were expected to be oblivious to political issues, particularly those in their own interests. This is not Christian altruism, but it is forced service.

Servanthood Language Revisited

There is nothing more basic to our understanding of Christian living than the notion that we are all called to be "servants." The concept of servanthood had both a positive and negative connotation in biblical times. The negative notions of servanthood are represented in the fact that there were clearly class divisions in the Bible that were unfavorable or undesirable.

The positive dimension of servanthood is seen in the fact that Jesus declared that he came to serve. The notion of servanthood in recent times has been used primarily as a mechanism of control. In order to ensure that the slaves were properly accepting of their station in life, they were often taught a catechism which declared that they were created to be the servants of whites. Some were more to the point than others. Whereas one answered that slaves were created "to serve our earthly master," the Jones catechism taught slaves that they were to look upon the master "'with all fear,' they are to be 'subject to them' and obey them in all things, possible and lawful, with good will and endeavor to please them well. . . . God is present to see, if their masters are not."[25]

Even after slavery, it appears that the attitude survived, for black people in general and black women in particular have always been disproportionately relegated to being servants of white people. Still, they were given to believe that it was not only their worldly duty, but their Christian or heavenly duty to obey. In other words, Christian servanthood and sociopolitical servanthood were taught to be the same. In serving white people, blacks were being obedient to God. The critical factor is one of control. Servanthood language is designed to get and maintain that control.

Theological language is symbolic language. But in reality how has it functioned? Anthropologist Clifford Geertz said, "Religion is a system of symbols which acts to establish powerful, pervasive, and long-lasting moods in [people] by formulating conceptions of a general order of existence and clothing these conceptions with such an aura of factuality that the moods and motivations seem uniquely realistic."[26] Geertz goes further to argue that symbols actually have the power to transform our world views. If this be so, those who control our symbol systems, control reality. Those who control the language, meaning, and applicability, control reality.

The Theological Challenge

In my article "The Sin of Servanthood . . ." an answer to the Christian theological problem is proposed. It is suggested that we move from the language of servanthood to a language of discipleship. However, a rushed answer to this question would be premature. Further theological wrestling is warranted.

In her description of the relation between the black mammy and the white mistress, Parkhurst said: "Frequently the best friend the mistress on the plantation had was the 'black mammy.'"[27] It is important to realize that friendship requires some sense of integrity in the relationship. Can friendship be based upon such inequality as that which existed between these two groups of women?

The entire system of religious/theological language needs to be transformed. One piercing question to be asked is: what happens when political and social language and interests are used to give content to theological language? Certainly, during most of America's history, there has been an infusion of theological teachings with the unjust political and social agendas of the oppressors.

Perhaps we could say that the central question being raised here is how shall we image ourselves as human beings? How shall we structure ourselves in light of this collective image—personally and institutionally? Further, how shall we image God? In the human/God relationship, is the master/servant model helpful or harmful?

It is clear from this discussion that my answers to these questions are not obvious, given the oppressive nature of most of Christian history. Christianity in all of its majesty, has not enabled us to solve basic relational problems. I contend that this is related to the distortions of doctrinal issues such as the doctrine of humanity. As long as some people are always more servant than others, the destructive relationships will continue. As long as both divinity and humanity are held captive to the limitations of human sinful need for control and domination, we will never liberate humanity, Jesus Christ, and God.

Notes

1. In an article entitled "The Sin of Servanthood and the Deliverance of Disciple-ship," in *A Troubling in My Soul: Womanist Perspectives on Evil and Suffering*, ed. Emilie M. Townes (Maryknoll, N.Y.: Orbis Books, 1993), 199-218, I began explo-rations into the theme of servanthood theology. This study further explores this sub-ject. I discussed some modest attempts on the part of feminist theologians to redeem the concept of servanthood, but suggest that their resolutions are inadequate. In the section "But some people are more servant than others," I attempted to use relation-ships between black women and white women as an occasion to demonstrate the problem in continuing to employ such relationships and language in the context of Christian practice.

2. This is true, perhaps, with the exception of some Third World peoples today, and particularly in certain areas of the country. See notes 3, 4, and 5 below.

3. Whereas for white women, domestic service was merely a stepping stone for more respectable work—office clerks, stenographers, typists, bookkeepers, cashiers, accountants, store clerks, saleswomen, and telephone operators—for black women it defined their being in the eyes of white America. As the number of white women decreased in that area, the number of black women increased (David M. Katzman, *Seven Days a Week: Women and Domestic Service in Industrializing America* [New York: Oxford University Press, 1978], 72-73).

4. Ibid., 185.

5. Ibid.

6. Trudier Harris, *From Mammy to Militant: Domestics in American Literature* (Philadelphia: Temple University Press, 1982). Harris cites some literary sources to argue that the mammy from the South turned militant in the North. There is evidence to suggest, however, that black women did not exercise any more significant power in the North than they did in the South. See, for example, Ella Baker and Marvel Cooke, "The Bronx Slave Market," in *The Crisis* 42 (November, 1935): 330.

7. Statistically, black women remain highly represented in the category of domestic service. See David H. Swinton, "The Economic Status of Black Americans during the 1980s: A Decade of Limited Progress" in *The State of Black America—1995* (New York: National Urban League, Inc., 1995), 153-79. However, the primary focus of this study is not necessarily statistics. It is the character and the content of the rela-tionships between the parties involved in the system of domestic service and the larger ramifications for life, particularly as attitudes about each group are shaped.

8. Jessie W. Parkhurst, "The Role of the Black Mammy in the Plantation Household," *Journal of Negro History* 23 (July 1938).

9. Ibid., 354.

10. Ibid., 356.

11. Ibid., 361.

12. Ibid., 349; originally from *Washington Tribune* (2-3-23); *National Baptist Union Review* (Nashville, Tenn., 5-4-23).

13. Katzman, 186, 188.

14. See Zora Neale Hurston, *Their Eyes Were Watching God* (New York: J. B. Lippincott Company, 1978).

15. Elizabeth Clark-Lewis, *Living In, Living Out: African American Domestics in Washington, D.C., 1910-1940* (Washington: Smithsonian Institution Press, 1994).

16. Ibid., 99.

17. Ibid., 101.

18. Ibid., 105.

19. Ibid., 106.

20. Peter J. Paris, *Social Teaching of the Black Churches* (Philadelphia: Fortress Press, 1985), 14.

21. Ibid., 15.

22. Explorations into the physical and sexual violence, which are not part of this study, are reflections of the defilement of black women's bodies.

23. Katzman, passim.

24. Clark-Lewis, 105.

25. Albert Raboteau, *Slave Religion: The "Invisible Institution" in the Antebellum South* (New York: Oxford University Press, 1980), 163.

26. In *Created in Her Image: Models of the Feminist Divine*, ed. Eleanor Rae and Bernice Marie-Daly (New York: Crossroad, 1990), 6.

27. Parkhurst, 365.

11

Disrupted/Disruptive Movements

Black Theology and Black Power 1969/1999

RENÉE LESLIE HILL

I live at the intersection of many rebellions, resistances, and struggles for liberation. Black power, women's liberation, gay/lesbian rights: all three movements crisscross, intersect, move through my life, and I in them. I could not have known as a child thirty years ago the impact that these movements would have on my life now. Coming out as a black lesbian has reconnected me with these struggles for liberation, both as a part of my history and as critical components of an ongoing life of struggle and celebration. I have long since stopped trying to acquiesce to the demands that I choose between my race, my gender, and my sexual orientation as a starting or ending point for protest against personal or communal oppression. My life is lived fully only in the intersections, in-between places, and borderlands of identities. My survival, growth, and power are based on the flexibility and consciousness that are essential to negotiate the shifting terrains of the social, political, and spiritual contexts of my life.

It has become more and more clear to me that all of us who do not fit into the concept of the white heterosexual male "norm" live most honestly in these intersections. Most of us do not fit into the neat categories that are required by a society that uses rigid definitions to control, to construct, and to maintain oppressive hierarchies. Coming into consciousness about the social and political power embedded in multiple social locations is essential to any seriously comprehensive liberation movement or ideology, including movements for and theologies of black liberation.

This consciousness is not necessarily new. The struggles and movements for liberation that were happening when *Black Theology and Black Power* was first published were not all uniformly rigid, nor were they based solely on finite, limited notions of identity, as many popular representations of them might have us believe. There certainly were struggles and silences around gender and sexuality within and among black activist communities. However, male-centered black nationalism and the essentializing of black identity were not always conflated. At times solidarity and cooperation resulted in powerful and creative alliances. As Angela Davis writes, "Contemporary representations of nationalism in African-American and diasporic popular culture are far too frequently reifications of a very complex and contradictory project that had emancipatory moments leading beyond itself."[1] She goes on to describe an instance of political alliance between black, Chicano, and progressive white students to demand the creation of an alternative college that would serve their interests. She also describes an article written by Huey Newton in 1970 in the Black Panther Party newspaper in which Newton was "urging an end to verbal gay bashing, urging an examination of Black male sexuality, and calling for an alliance with the developing gay liberation movement."[2] Acts of political solidarity such as these signified an understanding of both the diversity within marginalized communities and insight into the types of alliances that are necessary to successfully challenge oppressive power. It is critical today to develop and maintain these types of alliances. It is equally critical to look to the diversity within black communities, to name current challenges, and to identify new solutions. This is the necessary task of black power and black theology today.

Theologies of liberation must be examined, constructed, modified, or rejected in relation to social, political, and historical contexts. Theology is a dynamic and living process. Any theology that claims to be in the service of freedom from oppression for all marginalized people must have at its heart the contemporary political, cultural, social, and economic conditions from which they arise and which have an impact on them. Many of the conditions that people of African descent faced in this country thirty years ago have changed and not necessarily for the better. The violence of legal race and class oppression has fallen away in some of its forms. It has resurged in other forms, such as the dismantling of affirmative action programs, repressive immigration policies, and criminal sentencing policies that disproportionately target the poor and people of color.

Theological method is faced with new challenges, such as growing gun violence and crime committed on the part of younger and younger people. The devastation of AIDS and drug abuse and the implication of law enforcement for drug supply to certain areas in black communities are also parts of the new and changing landscape from which theologies of liberation arise and to which they need to respond. The impact of the power of multinational corporations, "natural" disaster, genocide, and war are all a part of the current context of black theologies. When all of this is added to the multiple social locations and complex identities that comprise black life and being, we must be willing to take a new look at the categories that define black power and black theology. What does it mean today to be "black?" How is "power" to be understood in the face of global, community, and personal complexity? What does this understanding of blackness and power have to do with "theology" and theological methodology committed to the radical reordering of social, political, and economic relationships in a world that continues to be devastated by white supremacy, Northern and Western political dominance, and unregulated global economic greed?

James Cone wrote out of his own context, limited by his own experience, and yet his work allows for greater complexity than he could imagine in 1969.

Blackness: "Black is ... Black ain't" [3]

Recent discourse about race, along with gender and other aspects of identity, has come to the conclusion that race is not to be understood as a matter of essence or biology. Race is socially constructed. Being black or any other race is defined and understood within a broad context of history and culture. Race is given meaning within and by society for any number of socio-economic and political reasons. Within the social group that is defined as black there is a variety of cultural and ethnic expressions. There is not one way to be black, no single image to hold up as the norm for what it means to be black. Blackness can have different and changing meanings, depending on other aspects of social location. "Blackness" as described in *Black Theology and Black Power* is not an essentialized identity. In spite of a lack of attention to gender, sexuality, and Third World issues in this early work, there are distinctions that are made between blacks to whom black power is dedicated, and liberal whites and "middle-class Negroes" who help to perpetuate the marginalization of too many blacks. What is described is not ontological blackness, but ideological blackness in relation to needed social change. Blackness in this instance is not simply a description of a victim status, it is an ideological statement along with a type of consciousness that is infused with the desire and the power to challenge a white supremacist society. "Black Power is an affirmation of the humanity of blacks in spite of white racism."[4] Recognizing the power of the ideology described above does not excuse the ways in which the understanding of black identity has been limited and limiting. The norm for black communities was and still is for too many a male heterosexual image. An amplification and clarification of ideological blackness is critical to a re-examination of the meaning and relevance of black power and black theologies today. The affirmation of the humanity of blacks needs to be understood not only in the face of white racism, but also in the face of sexism and heterosexism both within and outside of black communities, in the face of the abuses of global capitalism, and in the face of disease and violence not known in past generations. Indeed, an amplified and expanding sense of the meaning of affirming black humanity would be refreshing and challenging in the face of the consumer and media derived apathy and disempowerment that plague too many black communities. We need to know who we are beyond the images and roles that have been constructed for us by the dominant culture for the purpose of control. We need to excavate our own sense of blackness in order to resist the categories and false unity that we retreat into when we feel threatened.

Shaping a New Black Consciousness

What is needed, then, is not "integration" but a sense of worth in being black, and only black people can teach that. Black consciousness is the key to the black man's [sic] emancipation from his distorted self-image.[5]

Affirming black humanity means shaping a new black consciousness that will serve as a catalyst for developing new ways of building communities, doing politics, and constructing theologies. Black consciousness today includes a sense of intragroup/intraracial diversity. This black consciousness emancipates black humanity from a distorted self-image of heteropatriarchal primacy. Black identity is not simply limited to black heterosexual male identity. A truly emancipatory black consciousness embraces all of black humanity. Therefore, a black "sense of worth" *is* in fact a sense of worth in being gay/lesbian/transgendered/bisexual or heterosexual; in being immigrant, non-Christian, working-class, middle-class, Spanish-speaking, French-speaking, female, or male (I could go on), because this (and much more) is what it means to be black. What I am describing is not an "ontological" blackness but the reality of diversity within black communities. The sense of worth that is at the core of black power is one that values the rich complexity and diversity of black being.

The challenge of ideological blackness moving as a force into the twenty-first century is the task of recognizing and challenging multidimensional oppression. Part of that challenge is the paradoxical necessity to recognize the interconnectedness of black humanity and, at the same time, to not universalize blackness or take away the power of self-determination for those who would use another name.[6] Ideological black consciousness provides an opportunity to draw on the power, knowledge, and experience of survival that comes from complex and diverse identities within the world of blackness. We have skills that we have learned to draw on in experiences of survival under historical manifestations of white supremacy. Ingrained in our communities are many other "habits of surviving"[7] that can be drawn on to confront oppression both internal and external to black communities. The skills, setbacks, wisdom, and opportunities for growth that come from the lives of black gay men, single black mothers, biracial teenagers, African child soldiers, black lesbians with AIDS, and transgendered black activists are all examples of the depth of power and knowledge for change and survival that are available to all black people and, in turn, to our theological methodologies and reflections. U.S. Third World feminist theorist Chela Sandoval points to these possibilities in her description of how, in working with a diverse group of women of color, new resources for challenging oppression emerged:

Through compassionate inclusion of our differences and the self-conscious understanding that each difference is valid in its context we are awakened to a new realm of methodological, theoretical, political, and feminist activity—with a pool of differences, born of survival and resistance, at our disposal. These differences give us access to ever new and dynamic tactics for intervening in the systems which oppress us—tactics which are capable of changing to confront the ever-changing movements of power. And if we are courageous enough to legitimate this multiplicity of tactical approaches as valid, our movement will be less likely to oppress its own people through the forcing of certain "correct" political lines.[8]

Instead of reacting against difference, trying to silence it, or make it invisible or separate, we need to learn to embrace the differences within and among communities of African descent in order to move with comprehensive and flexible power for social and political change for all members of black communities and ultimately for all marginalized people.

This dynamic and complex understanding of blackness reaches far beyond an individual sense of identity or interpersonal politics. The compassionate embrace of difference within black communities moves political and theological perspectives from limited black nationalist perspectives to expansive internationalist perspectives. The black consciousness that is needed to undergird our political activity and our theologies of liberation is one that takes into account the politics, life, and cultures of people of Africa and the Diaspora. It must also take into account the need for solidarity with other marginalized and oppressed peoples around the world. Blackness is global citizenship. Black power and black theologies must be able to respond to a sense of "African-ness" that is impacted by multinational economic, political, and social forces as well as by racism and neocolonialism.

Power

Power is the ability to make things happen, to make changes for better or for worse. Power is neutral until political choices are made about how to use it. Power is agency and the ability to be self-determining.

I am one who wrestles with the efficacy and limitations of identity politics. Because of my hybrid identity/multiple social location I have always resisted the ranking of oppressions. I still believe that this resistance to ranking is a commitment to freedom, especially in light of the diverse and varied ways that oppressive power is made manifest in the world. The struggle for freedom and full humanity must be complex and comprehensive, flexible and innovative.

Race, gender, class, sexual orientation, and other markers of identity are important in our culture. They are important focal points for celebration and pride. They are important for remembering and learning from our histories of both oppression and resistance. However, markers of identity are also used for control and repression. Race is the marker that became the basis for the enslavement of Africans in this country. Women have been excluded from positions of power and leadership based on oppressive notions about gender. Class, the unacknowledged identity marker, restricts access to power from those who are not already in the ruling class through unspoken and unacknowledged rules and practices. Sexual orientation has been used to define everything from pathology to sinfulness.

What threads all of these markers together are the ways in which exploitative power is used first to oppress and marginalize based on identity, and second to encourage a rigidity in identity politics that inhibits practices of solidarity and justice for all people. We are told that we are either one thing or another, never both/and. Life is defined as either black or white; there is no complexity, no shades of gray. There certainly are no vibrant colors, textures, or spontaneous movements. I know this only too well in my own life when I have been asked to choose individual aspects of complex identity against the prevailing norm, which continues to be white, male, and heterosexual.

The time is well past for us to talk about and act out of narrowly defined and compartmentalized identities. The principalities and powers have never focused only on one group or on one aspect of identity. How often have we seen racism combined with classism, misogyny intertwined with heterosexism? The decision to exclude, more often than not, is inclusive.

What is needed is the development of strategies for challenging the complex, intertwined, and ever-changing nature of oppressive power. In order to do this, as stated above, we need to mine the rich resources of our complex identities and differences as individuals and as communities. The use of the unitary voice is at times an important tactic in the struggle for full humanity for marginalized people. However, when we always speak and act only or simply from a unitary identity, "we blacks," "we women," "we lesbians," we risk at best ignoring and at worst repressing our complexities and therefore the constructive power that is hidden within that "we." We also risk losing important connections and opportunities for developing networks of solidarity. Oppressive power is complex and multifaceted. The struggle for justice needs to be equally complex and multifaceted.

I continue to be struck by the ways in which we limit our political and spiritual power by limiting our knowledge of who we are. For example, in the dominant discourse and imagination, not only does "black" still signify male and heterosexual, "women" still means white women, and "gay" means white and male. The political and spiritual alliances that have the potential to be built within the complexities of these markers of identity are tremendous. In our political action as well as in our theological methodologies we need to embrace the truth that gender, race, class, sexuality, and age are not inherently oppositional.

The urgency for developing networks of solidarity and resistance is illustrated by the way in which destructive power is made manifest in the ongoing violence against those who are marked as other and therefore out of bounds of what is deemed acceptable and normal in our society. Hate crimes perpetuated against people of color, gay men, and all women, as well as children are not uncommon; they are not isolated. The graphic violence of the contemporary lynching of African Americans; the bashing and murder of gay men, lesbians, and transgendered people; child murder; and the ongoing violence against women illustrate the painful reality of the ways in which oppressive power works in the consciousness and murderous actions of human beings.

Contrary to most popular assumptions, white supremacy, misogyny, and the hatred of lesbians, gay men, bisexuals, and transgendered people are not simply the product of extremist people, groups, or institutions. The vast majority of the population does not identify with the Ku Klux Klan or with the Nazi party. Most would not even readily identify as or with gay bashers. The roots of oppression are much more insidious and pervasive in their ordinariness. It is the gross violence that gets our attention; it is the subtle persistent messages that create the climate for that violence to happen. The power that infuses the black theological work as we move into the next millennium, the power that affirms black humanity in all of its complexity, has the ability to identify and resist the subtleties and multiple manifestations of oppressive power. It is this ability that will ultimately be able to address the multidimensional oppression that we face as whole, complex communities.

What is enraging is that white communities seem not to have changed much over the past thirty years. White racism and white supremacy are deep and virulent. Much of it today is disguised with new masks. Some of it is just the same hatred that was out front in the hate-filled faces of white parents and children who opposed busing, the white cops wielding billy clubs, and the white preachers who preached segregation. Some say that we as a nation are making tremendous progress in terms of gender equality (even with the defeat of the Equal Rights Amendment) and race relations. And we should acknowledge that for some there has been some progress. Perhaps this progress is why the backlash against people of color, immigrants, and the poor has become so powerful. The appearance of progress is acceptable in the post–Civil Rights era, whereas real change, real transformation of a racist, sexist, classist, heterosexist culture does not go unchallenged. The dismantling of affirmative action programs, the demise of welfare programs, the attack on immigrant rights, and the rapid growth of the "prison industrial complex" are all concrete instances of backlash that signal the viability of those systems and structures of oppression that are at the foundation of this country. This foundation, built on slavery and genocide, is even today demonstrating an unbroken commitment to the use of oppressive power that has yet to be completely dismantled or transformed.

The truth is that power, including oppressive power, has the ability to shift and change. It cannot be addressed outside of the complexity and flexibility that it thrives in. Resistance and liberation movements must be equally complex and flexible. Sandoval writes that "power centers can perhaps be best visualized as clusters of choices on an electromagnetic field—that is capable of movement and change into ever new and different designs."[9] We need to be prepared for the fact that what might not seem lethal to us in our particularity might become lethal if we remain ignorant of our own complexities, or if we lose track of our need to form networks of solidarity with other marginalized people. The homophobia that we ignore because it is "not our issue" might well turn out to affect a dearly loved family member. The sexism that is "not at the top of our agenda" might be followed up by racism that is used to deny us our livelihoods or even our lives.

Black Power as Liberating and Healing Power

One aspect of human identity that holds potential resources for new forms of black power, black affirmation, and healing is sexuality.

A black theology that claims to represent, challenge, empower, and embrace the diversity of black peoples must be a theology that is deeply concerned with supporting healthy sexuality within black communities. This attention to sexuality includes encouraging and nurturing healthy heterosexual, lesbian, gay, bisexual, and transgendered selves and relationships. The powerful black theologies that will lead us into the twenty-first century are theologies that understand and address sexuality in its totality, as spiritual and physical intimacy, as well as private, public, and political expression. Black theology must engage sexuality as a personal, public, and political force that helps to shape and define, build up and tear down black communities. Even in the face of hostile voyeurism on the part of American white supremacy and sexual obsession within and outside of theology, black theology must expose violent and antisexual forces and claim creative sexual power. Black theologies of liberation must insist upon the examination and re-examination of what constitutes Christian sexual ethics and models for relationships both personal and communal.

This examination must be done in light of the realities of domestic and sexual violence, child abuse, teen pregnancy, AIDS, STDs, and other stress factors that impact domestic life and personal relationships. Black theology must move questions of sexuality out of the realm of the private and into a conversation about what it means to be human, what it means to be created by God, for God's freedom and love. These questions about sexuality that need to be raised in and by black theologies must challenge black peoples and black communities to develop and maintain a deep and abiding love for all black bodies in all shapes, sizes, and expressions of who we are.[10]

Theology

Christianity has been on many occasions if not simply inadequate, downright destructive. As a black lesbian I wrestle mightily with a Christian religious heritage that has had its share of supporting and promoting misogyny, white supremacy, and the hatred of homosexuals. For too many people, the Christian message has not been a message of liberation. The Bible has been used as a weapon to enslave Africans, silence women, and abuse lesbians and gay men. Racists and misogynists have hidden behind church tradition to justify their destructive policies and actions. The black theology that was taking shape thirty years ago certainly recognized this fact in its recasting of Christianity as black power itself:

> If the gospel of Christ, as Moltmann suggests, frees a man [sic] to be for those who labor and are heavily laden, the humiliated and abused, then it

would seem that for twentieth-century America the message of Black Power is the message of Christ himself.[11]

This is a radical renaming that is necessary to rescue Christianity from the oppressive forces that wished to coopt it. This recasting is still essential if Christianity is to be a relevant, positive force for contemporary social change and liberation struggles today. This recasting of the gospel and the liberationist claim to the Christian message must be done in light of the more complex understanding of blackness and of power as described above. Christianity *as* black power cannot be limited to a racial definition. Therefore, it is necessary to extend Cone's original statement about white perceptions of Christianity that "what they [white people?] fail to realize is that in America, God's revelation on earth has always been black, red, or some other shocking shade, but never white."[12] The "shocking shade" that is at the heart of liberating Christianity is now joined by shocking textures and shapes, shocking expressions of gender and sexuality, and even shocking images of God that symbolize the diversity within black communities.

For example, womanist theology has challenged black male theologians to examine gender justice in the work of theological construction and in black communal life. This critical and constructive work by black women theologians was a response to the limited and limiting male-centered understanding of black identity. In constructing theologies from womanist perspectives, black women further participate in recasting Christianity as a force for justice in contemporary society. However, the limitations of the strict application of identity politics are quickly revealed even in this move from black to womanist theology. In the earliest expressions of womanist theology the images of black women were depicted fairly narrowly. For example, the voices and lives of self-identified black lesbians were silent and invisible. To be black and female apparently meant being heterosexual. Because heterosexuality was assumed, discussion on sexuality, including heterosexual privilege, was not included in the discourse. As with the absence of reflection on dominance and privilege within black communities around sexism and male privilege, there was no discussion about or challenge to black heterosexism and homophobia. All theologies constructed on limited notions of identity fail to address the political and social complexities of power, oppression, and liberation that we are faced with globally. Opportunities to learn from intragroup diversity and various experiences of struggle and survival are lost.

In learning from the histories of theological construction, theologies of liberation must include in their methodology an internal mechanism that encourages and even insists upon flexibility, internal critique, self-reflection, the ability to revise, expand, and even draw in when necessary to challenge oppressive power inside black communities, in broader communities of color, and when engaging the oppressive power of dominant white communities.

A good example of this flexibility can be found in Cone's preface to the 1989 edition of *Black Theology and Black Power*. Here he reflects on the critiques that were made about the European sources that he used in writing his theology, as well as his own self-critique around his failure to link the struggles of African Americans with the struggles in the Two-Thirds world, his lack of attention to classism, and his lack of challenge to sexism. In reflecting on these shortcomings Cone identifies a crucial tool in the construction of theologies of liberation, that is, the tool of memory, which leads to transformation. He states, "Amnesia is an enemy of justice."[13] We need not get stuck in our omissions or shortcomings. If we have the ability to be self-reflective, open to the diversity and complexity of our lives and communities, we retain the possibility of entering into a dynamic and powerful theological discourse and practice of justice making. There is no theology that will make sense for all people and for all time. There is, however, a commitment to God's freedom and human dignity for all which requires a radical openness to transformation both internal and external. Flexibility and self-examination are essential to building the future of theologies of liberation.

Multireligious, Multidialogical Process for Doing Theologies

My multiply intersected life has necessarily had a deep influence on my theological reflection and religious practice. With an understanding that boundaries are both permeable and are to be respected, I have come to view and experience theology and religious practice from the multilayered and diverse world of religions in the African Diaspora. Black Christian theologies cannot afford *not* to be in dialogue with other religious traditions. As expressions of transformative power and resistance, black theologies cannot function in isolation. The Christian hegemony that has controlled and defined African American religious discourse is being challenged by African Americans who practice Islam, African-derived traditional religions (including Santeria, Akan, Yoruba, and Vodun), Buddhism, Judaism, and Humanism among other traditions. As part of their internal mechanism for critique, black Christian theologies of liberation first must be aware of themselves within the history of Christian dominance in relation to other religious expressions in the United States. Second, as a result of this awareness, black theologies must be willing to be open to learning from other traditions on a variety of different matters, including the meaning of freedom, oppression, and full humanity. This openness will necessitate wrestling with the ambiguity and anxiety that arise when the absoluteness of Christ as the one and only way to God and to salvation is called into question. If the person of Jesus Christ is not at the absolute center of all black theological reflection, what or who is? Perhaps there is no center at all. Being knocked off-center requires black Christian theologies to enter into a multidialogical process, in which the definition of ultimate truth is called into question. Being knocked off-center provides opportunities to explore core beliefs in order to renew or reject them. It invites the kind of creativity and openness that black theologies of liberation will need to navigate the questions and unknowns of the future. Again, the challenge is to engage the diversity of our communities even when that engagement calls our theological foundations into question.

Disruption and Change—New Movements: Black Theologies and Black Power

One image that I have for black power and black theologies is that of a river and its many moods, the different terrains that it runs through, and its changing currents. As the river water encounters different conditions, it is able to adapt, to encompass obstacles, to go over or around them, to move things when necessary. It changes and is changed in the process of moving and being. Theologies of liberation, including theologies that arise from African American experiences, must have a similar character. The ability to move with and through difference, the ability to use power to shift, change, and adapt are all characteristics that are well suited to the tasks that black theologies and black power are facing. This image of theology is one that will certainly be disconcerting to some. It appears that there is no center, no framework to work in. The reality is that justice is the guideline. Faithfulness to God's instruction to "do justice, and to love kindness and to walk humbly with God"[14] is the center of the black power and the black theologies that seek to affirm black humanity and all marginalized humanity today. This center is able to shift and change according to the needs of individuals and communities and in response to the tactics of oppressive power.

Theological methods that can be most effective in the contemporary contexts of the complexity of black life are methods that might be comprised of more questions than answers. What is the meaning of Jesus Christ in relation to other faiths? Where is God in the suffering of black communities faced with AIDS and addiction? What does it mean to "love kindness" in the face of continued white racism? What does it mean to walk humbly with God in class-stratified black communities? The questions point to the contradictions that give rise to new theologies and new forms of power.

In this vision for black theological methodologies, a traditional hermeneutical circle characterized by movements of action, reflection, celebration, and more action might be revised to look more like an open circle, perhaps with broken lines, punctuated by layers of questions, disruptions, and moments of ambiguity and uncertainty that are in fact necessary for creative, relevant theological construction.

As an African American lesbian, Christian, theologian, and worker for justice, I have learned the importance of not relying on maps that other people have designed. I know the importance of the ability to improvise, to change direction, and when necessary to invent new pathways. This is how I live, grow, and struggle within Christian community and in the world at large. I recognize that the reality of the boundlessness of God's love and justice is testified to in the existence and survival of all who are considered to be outside of the norm, out of bounds. It is this love and justice that ultimately disrupts all that we take for granted, whether theological reflection or our understanding of who and what we are. It is this love and justice that disrupts cycles of oppression and calls us to new and powerful ways to live in all of the intersections of our lives.

Notes

1. Angela Davis, "Black Nationalism: The Sixties and the Nineties," in *Popular Culture: A Project by Michele Wallace,* ed. Gina Dent (Seattle: Bay Press, 1992), 322-23.

2. Ibid., 323.

3. Ralph Ellison, *Invisible Man* (New York: Vintage, 1947; 1972), 10.

4. James H. Cone, *Black Theology and Black Power* (Maryknoll, N.Y.: Orbis Books, 1997), 16.

5. Ibid., 19.

6. I am thinking here especially about the history and naming of womanist theologies out of black women's experience.

7. Kesho Y. Scott, *The Habit of Surviving* (New York: Ballantine Book, 1991), 10. Scott describes the "habit of surviving" as "the external adjustments and internal adaptations that people make to economic exploitation and to racial and gender-related oppression. Such habits, first and foremost, are responses to pain and suffering that help to lessen anger, give a sense of self-control, and offer hope" (10).

8. Chela Sandoval, "Feminism and Racism: A Report on the 1981 National Women's Studies Association Conference," in *Making Face/Making Soul,* ed. Gloria Anzaldua (San Francisco: Aunt Lute Books, 1990), 67.

9. Ibid., 65.

10. I thank my colleague Lisa Anderson, a doctoral candidate at Union Theological Seminary in New York, for her work and reflections on black love and black bodies.

11. James Cone, *Black Theology and Black Power,* 37.

12. Ibid., 50.

13. Ibid., xi.

14. Micah 6:8.

12

Reimagining Public Discourse

REBECCA S. CHOPP

This essay focuses on the basic theme of black theology as public discourse, by placing black theology and feminist theology side-by-side to consider, retrospectively, how they function as public discourse and how they have shaped public discourse, and, prospectively, how they might function in one possible vision of the future. I assume that, as David Tracy has argued, all theology is in some sense public. I want to examine how these two theologies, taken together, are to be interpreted as public discourses and how, in turn, they redefine or add to our notion of public discourse.

I will bring together black and feminist theologies for both personal and cultural reasons. As a theologian whose whole career has been spent participating in liberation theology—indeed, as someone who is part of the first generation to grow up with these movements and whose career has been deeply formed through the emergence of feminist theology—I find myself wondering about the past and future of my theological home and inescapably drawing comparisons between it and the retrospect and prospect of black theology. These two theologies share a common cultural context, some common theoretical resources in ideology critique, hermeneutics, and the retrieval of the prophetic or mystical/prophetic strand in Christianity. By bringing these together we may be able to understand that something quite distinct has been happening in theology and public discourse during the last thirty years.

To bring these two movements together and ask, "What do they tell us about public discourse?" is a problematic task! Indeed, such theological movements have said so resoundingly that there is no abstract public, no unmarked voice in the center, and that one can only speak from one's own place, that I falter a bit before I begin. How can I, a white feminist Christian, say anything about black theology? But, of course, the whole point of discourse and public discourse is to communicate, to be heard, to engage in what Hannah Arendt would call simply "debate." So in bringing together these two discourses—feminist theology and black theology—to inquire into public discourse, I do so recognizing that my own location may well prejudge how and what I hear. While I do not intend to read black theology through feminist theology, I am openly bringing along my place as a feminist theologian, rather than abstracting from it, in order to be honest about the perspective I bring—and my own retrospective.

I also fear that by bringing these two discourses together I might be heard as not dealing significantly enough with the differences between these two and mitigating or belittling the problems of sexism in black theology or the problems of racism in feminist theology. The differences are very important. Womanist theology has had the double burden of pointing this out in both theologies: Thinkers such as Jacquelyn Grant and Delores Williams have had to analyze the structuring of oppression in each discourse.

It is, therefore, important to keep these multiple and complex problems in the foreground as we examine the ways in which black theology and feminist theology function as public discourse and how they have helped transform the nature and status of public discourse. I will organize my argument under three rubrics: (1) Narrative Identity and Public Discourse (how these theologies function), (2) Public Discourse and Testimony (how they have shaped discourse), and (3) Imagining the Public as a Space for Cultivating Compassion (a prospective proposal).

Narrative Identity and Public Discourse

Let me begin by locating "public discourse." Let us assume that public discourse can mean, from the work of thinkers such as Jürgen Habermas and Nancy Fraser, the sphere of rational discourse in which citizens are free to debate matters of interest in the social order. Habermas and historians of the "public sphere" argue that the public arose with liberal democracy and depended upon a number of historical factors, including the emerging urban geography of pubs, libraries, civic associations, and other arenas of and for discourse.[1] Habermas recognized that this public failed to ever be completely realized, perhaps rightfully so, since, as alternative public sphere historians have shown, it depended upon exclusions of gender, race, and class. As Fraser points out, there is a certain irony: the public sphere is developed as a place of free speech, but it, in turn, creates and secures distinctions and calls into question the "public" nature of it all.[2]

This broad sense of the social public must be supplemented, in the case of theology, by the publics of church and the academy. Especially in late industrial capitalism, the church and the academy are also publics—spaces to which persons belong and, in some sense, determine interests in common. These are not three separate publics, but overlapping and reinforcing ones. The autonomous rational citizen of the social public was trained in the academy and received legitimation and comfort in the church. The academy and church shared common assumptions with the social public about rationality, anthropology, freedom, discourse, and identity. And, as Fraser notes, there are also sub-publics and counter-publics—such as the black church within the ecclesial public—though, I would suggest, these counter-publics are such by virtue of what we perceive as public and, thus, are a constitutive part of the larger, over-lapping publics.

It is, of course, calling into question this irony of publicness that is the aim and work of so many black and feminist theologies. One way to understand the retrospective aspect of black theology and feminist theology is to sketch out in broad strokes how they have called into question the narrative identity of the social and ecclesial publics. (I will leave the public of the academy for another day.)

To analyze how black and feminist theologies called into question the narra-tive identity of the public, I need to define, briefly, what I mean by "narrative identity." A public depends on what Raymond Williams would call a "selective tradition," i.e., a narrative of rationality, of rational human beings, of human rights, of revolution in politics, economics, law, and, yes, even religion.[3] I like to adapt the phrase of Benedict Anderson, and say that a public is an "imagined community" based on the narration of memory, inclusivity, shared common-ness.[4] By "narrative identity," I mean the "we," the story we tell ourselves that defines our "we." This is not the only feature of the public, but it is, from a the-ological viewpoint, a very important characterization, because it provides our fundamental assumptions, our images upon which we build our norms, our val-ues such as courage, respect, dignity, and compassion. As Paul Ricoeur would suggest, the "we" is an ideological construct, a means of social and public cohe-sion, though the "we" fails to fully represent the real.

Black theology and feminist theology used what Gadamer and Ricoeur might call an "applied hermeneutics" to remember and retell the history of the American and Christian publics. The social public and the ecclesial public formed their identities through their narratives, and these narratives were shaped through the prejudices of those who—in the best Gadamerian sense—told the story. Black and feminist theologians criticized the assumed narrative identity of America and American Christianity by remembering and retelling how things really happened and constructing new narrative identities for these publics. So black and feminist theologians had to engage in ideology critique, an ethical responsibility to retell the story that had been told from the viewpoint of hegemonic discourse. But along with such critique, to engage in what Ricoeur and Kearney might call "poetic license"—as well as historiography—these the-ologians created new narrative identities based on alternative memories and experiences not yet represented as real in the public. Narrative helps us repre-sent the past as it really was and reinvent it as it might have been.

Central to both the ideological critique and the new sources for narrative identity—in both black and feminist theology—is the memory of suffering. It is suffering and oppression in multiple forms that provide the impetus both for ide-ology critique and for the speaking and hearing of voices forgotten or silenced. As Richard Kearney has observed, our identity—be it national or communal—is inextricably linked to our memory.[5] Questioning which memories we recall and which ones we repress is how both black and feminist theologies have func-tioned in the public domain, enlarging and expanding our narrative identity.

Cone's *Black Theology and Black Power,* to take the "classic" example, is about questioning the narrative identity of the public; it is about the memory and expression of suffering and oppression. His insistence on remembering and telling the story of suffering was striking and upsetting to the "real" of the narrative identity of white, male, American public discourse. It sounded angry; it was.

In reading back over *Black Theology and Black Power* I am struck by how Cone used the basic tools of American narrative—such as freedom, hope, and existentialism—and the voices of its public intellectuals—Tillich, Camus, Barth, and others—to remember. Narrative identity can remember new things, but it does so through present signifiers. To make an analogy, therapy can allow you to remember what you have forgotten, but it does it through what is very present to you: your own values, beliefs, perspectives. Remembering what really happened occurs, not so much by telling the rest of the story, but first by using the assumed values and sacred doctrines of the present against themselves or by using them to question back history.

I am also struck by the clarity with which Cone understands the irony of exclusion in both publics, church and society, and the irony of the complicitous relations. He understood quite well that only by remembering could the irony of the social public and the ecclesial public be exposed. But beyond this, remembering brings out the irony of how America and the church were complicitous in forgetting what really happened. Cone says it this way:

> It is ironical that America with its history of injustice to the poor (especially the black man and the Indian) prides itself as being a Christian nation. (Is there really such an animal?) It is even more ironic that officials within the body of the Church have passively and actively participated in these injustices.[6]

Providing what Ricoeur would call "eyes to see and weep," Cone, and other theologians with him, remembered a history of suffering and told new stories—sometimes through songs and sermons as well as narratives—to shape the American and the American Christian narrative identity. It was not only remembering and telling within the social public, but it was also remembering in the ecclesial public. Theological constructs are, in relation to narrative identity, always poetical: telling the truth but telling it in performative ways in which, perhaps, we can see the real differently. Cone remembers and retells, in *A Black Theology of Liberation* and *God of the Oppressed,* the story of God on the side of the oppressed, of Black Christ, of historical transformation rather than other-worldly liberation.

The narrative identity of society and of Christianity takes on a new shape, one gained through remembering what others have forgotten, denied, ignored. This reshaping of narrative identity can also be seen as the function of feminist theology, whose quest for narrative identity focused not only on remembering and telling of the suffering of women, but also on figuring new voices and new stories in the publics of society and church. From Mary Daly's *Beyond God the Father* to Ruether's *Sexism and God-Talk,* the real of the social and ecclesial publics were written in new ways.[7] Women rushed to talk of women's experience—accepting, at first, an oppositional definition. We also ignored and forgot particularities of race and class for the sake of universal, and thus hegemonic, experience. But the point is that feminist theologies—like black theologies—functioned as markers for fields of experience, opening up multiple voices, contestation, difference. In these texts and many others, narrative identity is shaped and reshaped through interlacing rhythms of remembering, of telling of suffering, of ideology critique, of new voices, experiences, expressions.

It is important to note that from the beginning these stories themselves were contested, they were fought over and retold in many different ways. Very soon African American women and lesbian women added their memories and stories to the narrative identity of feminist theology. The critique of "essentialism" led to the exploration and inclusion of diverse voices in the works of theologians like Mary McClintock Fulkerson and Paula Cooey. Similarly, black theology underwent criticism within its own ranks for borrowing white academic discourse and criticism from other liberation theologians for ignoring structures of oppression in class and gender. A further development came with the second generation of black theologians who, as Shawn Copeland has observed, shifted "their attention to both their enslaved ancestors and to their children," finding new theological memories and sources for narrative identity in slave narratives, music and rap, literature and poetry.[8]

My first point, then, is that as public discourse, black theology—as well as feminist theology—functions as public discourse in terms of narrative identity: identifying the real through the memories of suffering and inclusion of new voices. As public discourse these two theologies have criticized and reshaped who "we" are, as a social public and as Christianity, by making public the memories of suffering and giving public hearing to new voices, experiences, and expressions of life, while calling into question essentialist and hegemonic definitions of these publics.

Public Discourse and Testimony

If black theology and feminist theology have criticized and reshaped the narrative identity of the publics of American society and American Christianity, they have also modeled new forms of public discourse. It is not only what they have said and why, but how they have said it that has shaped public discourse. In what I will call the "poetics of testimony," black and feminist theologies not only added new voices, but contributed a genre to public discourse, one that invites these diverse voices to speak and be heard, questions the politics of the public/private separation, and requires the ethos of the public to be guided through an ethical responsiveness to the other or an ethos of cultivating compassion (see p. 161 below).

Black and feminist theologies have been identified with the theological movement known as liberation theology and, indeed, have self-consciously accepted or debated this term. Liberation theology refers to theological discourses from oppressed and marginalized groups that speak in their own voices and criticize the oppressive practices, values, and structures of the hegemonic center of church and society. It exposes the suffering and oppression caused by the center and guides the praxis of oppressed groups to interrupt, critique, and transform the center.

Well into the fourth decade of liberation theology, we can identify various generations or stages of how it has functioned. Liberation theology has pursued its work through radical movements of empowerment, through cultural separatism by finding one's voice, through appropriating cultural stereotypes in what Henry "Skip" Gates calls "profound acts of artistic exorcism," and through theoretical critiques utilizing Marxism, poststructuralism, and liberal theory (in thinkers such as Cornel West and Mary McClintock Fulkerson). In feminist theology one can talk about stages of asserting equality, romantically embracing difference, transforming cultural rules through gender analysis. Similarly, a number of scholars of black theology such as James Cone, Dwight Hopkins, and Shawn Copeland have identified various movements or generations of thought operating in these last forty years.

As someone who writes both in and on liberation theology, I accept these dimensions as strategic practices that, depending upon the cultural situation at a given point in time, give voice to the particularity of one group's experience, as well as criticize and transform the dominant social order. In my judgment, liberation theologies were and are directed to the movements from which they arise and to which they are accountable. Cone has been justified in insisting that black theology is, first and foremost, for black people and the black church.

My claim is not to replace the term "liberation theology," but to argue that, as public discourse, liberation theology is best understood as a poetics of testimony. Through this phrase, "poetics of testimony," I want to suggest that black and feminist theologies have sought to shape public discourse by combining diverse genres with an ethical summons to be responsive to those who suffer. If liberation theology aptly names how these discourses function as interruptions of the center, the poetics of testimony helps us understand how these discourses transform the shape of the public at the center—where the price of access is the acceptance of the dominant code—to a reimagined and embodied public, a public where what I will call "an ethos of cultivating compassion" is foregrounded, a public where the texture of narrative identity is woven through particularity and difference. In this section, I will attend to the questions of poetic narrative, and in my concluding section I will attend to the ethical demand of imagining the public as a space for cultivating compassion.

The genre of the "poetics of testimony" gathers together poetry, theology, novels, and other forms of literature that express how oppressed groups have existed outside modern rational discourse. You may recall Elie Wiesel's observation, "If the Greeks invented tragedy, the Romans the epistle, and the Renaissance the sonnet, our generation invented a new literature, that of testimony."[9] Wiesel's invention names the work of black and feminist theologians, writers, and artists. The poetics of testimony as a genre provides a strong critique of dominant cultural practices and provokes refiguration of the social imaginary, i.e., the basic presuppositions, metaphors, and rules that frame cultural operations. The poetics of testimony challenges how the real is both represented and created through public discourse. In other words, through the poetics of testimony, both our narrative identity and our understanding of discourse are constituted and shaped by multiple rather than univocal representations.

Though I use this trope of the *poetics* of testimony, I do not want to limit it to poetry proper. I use poetics to draw our attention to the fact that public discourse, at least in some forms of black and feminist writings, asks us to reimagine the real both in terms of the narrative memory of the public—who we have been and are—and in terms of the very nature of public discourse. Such discourse is an invention, in and of itself, for it must create language, forms, images to speak of what, in some way, was ruled unspeakable or not worthy of speech in the public. Indeed, here we could even point to the transcendent, which modernity relegated to the private sphere or ruled out of court as unspeakable, and to the contemporary need to rethink and recreate our notions of transcendence in relation to narrative and public discourse.

Poetics is discourse that calls into question, reshapes, fashions in new ways, and enlarges the ordering of discourse within what Julia Kristeva and Homi Bhabha have called "the social imaginary." While our efforts here are directed at theology, my argument suggests that theology, poetry, fiction, music, films, all participate in this genre of public discourse. Understood in this way, one realizes why so many theologians such as James Cone and Will Coleman, Elisabeth Schüssler Fiorenza and Katie Cannon use not only traditional doctrine, but the ecclesial practices, music, and literature of their movements to create theological discourse.

As a type of public discourse, the poetics of testimony has three fundamental characteristics. First, the poetics of testimony seeks to tell the truth or the real represented in and through narrative identity, by combining a legal sense of giving a true account with a religious sense of pointing to the absolute through the conditions of the particular. Second, the poetics of testimony functions as an ethical summons to attend to the other in a responsive fashion. Third, the poetics of testimony requires that forms of public discourse become more tensive, more poetic, open to more diversity or what I will call multilinguistic or polyglot public discourse.

The first characteristic of the poetics of testimony as public discourse, in both church and society, is truth-telling or reconstructing that which constitutes or forms the real of the narrative identity. Truth-telling combines a legal or juridical sense of providing a true account, as in a trial, with a religious sense of pointing to the real of the absolute, in and through the conditions of a particular experience; here, the experience of a cultural movement. Ricoeur has pointed out how testimony blends this juridical notion of being on trial with a religious or prophetic claim to the irruption of the absolute, all within the narration of the "facts," or what I have suggested is the narrative identity of the public.[10] There is both a historical-cultural dimension and a recognition of transcendence, of the power and spirit of transfiguration, evoked by testimony.

As the narration of facts that seeks to remember accurately, to correct the existing narrative, and to describe the real, testimony is neither a symbol of a depth dimension or whole nor an analytic example of the structure of consciousness. Rather, testimony in public discourse narrates a story, a story that allows the transcendent, the possibility of the new, to break in and open us to change and transformation. Such testimonies are not just expressions of a prelinguistic experience or even of a religious code; they are neither subjective nor objective; they are, instead, collective and social. In addition, testimony is both private and public. One testifies, after all, in and to the public space about what one has seen, what one has experienced, what one knows to have happened.

Testimony, in its religious sense points to the absolute through the relative and particular, not as a claim about cognitive limits nor as a foundational grounding, but as a narration of suffering and hope that is witnessed to within the particular but in terms of the absolute. Because the witness tells the story out of a determination to live, to survive, the juridical sense of testimony points to the conflict of life and death that is at stake, but more importantly, it also points toward the prophetic sense, or how we salvage, transform, ensure life and survival in the face of oppression, suffering, and death. This movement of testimony from the historical to the transcendent and back again allows us to rewrite the narrative, to retell the truth, to enlarge the narrative identity.

For Cone this is represented, for example, by the slave songs which moved from the particular experience of suffering to the hope placed in the transcendent God and back to living in the present context with a different story to tell. It is represented by the black and Third World theologians and peoples who utilize the resources within their own cultural contexts to point beyond oppressive regimes and who draw upon the spirit and power of the transcendent God to rewrite and relive the story toward economic and political liberation. As Cone argues in *My Soul Looks Back,* the slaveowners and missionaries weren't going to provide liberating resources or facts; rather, these facts have to be found within the particular historical realities and the transcendent possibilities embodied within and recognized by a cultural movement.[11]

The second characteristic of the poetics of testimony has to do with its ethical summons to attend to the "other." Testimonies enact a moral consciousness and a social, even at times, global responsibility. They invoke an ethical claim— they are from someone to someone about something. And in testifying, one summons the hearer to respond. A decision is called for, a change in reality is required. Within testimony lies something like Levinas's claim that we are constituted through responsibility to and for the other, a responsibility that is not reciprocal, a responsibility that exists within historical and cultural realities. Testimony summons the public space to serve those who suffer and hope, those whose voices testify to survival, those who dare to imagine and enact transformation. It summons the public space to serve them in their particularity, rather than drawing them into the image of an existing and partial "we."

The poetics of testimony functions as a moral discourse, as a summons to otherness, and this discourse works by requiring that the public be ethically constituted through hearing those who suffer, who have been forced to be the others of history. But testimony is not simply in terms of the social reality, it is also in reference to the absolute. In the ecclesial public, the church is the space of God and the people of God working on behalf of the oppressed. As Cone insists, God is on the side of the oppressed. But God is never confined to or equated with the ecclesial public. The church, as a public, is defined in and through its ethical responsiveness to the other of history, which is impacted by and through God's liberating work. Recall Cone's section on the prospects for the future in his book *For My People* where he summons church and community to be responsive to the others of history:

> As black churches and black theology prepare for the future, it would be wise for them to move beyond their mutual ignorance and antagonism and begin to recognize their need of each other. We must ask not what is best for the survival of black churches or black theology, but rather what is best for the liberation of the black poor in particular and the poor of the whole world in general. Unless we black preachers, theologians, and lay persons are prepared to measure our commitment to the gospel in terms of our participation in the liberation of the poor, then our gospel is not good news to the poor but instead an instrument of their oppression. We must be willing to submerge our personal ambitions, transcend denominational differences, and overcome personality conflicts in order to bear witness together that God's liberation of the oppressed is at hand in the words and actions of black Christians.[12]

Here, too, we see that for Cone, testimony and the summons to responsibility is always in relation to the otherness of both the historical realities of culture and the transcendent possibilities of God's liberating action which must be enacted.

The third characteristic of the poetics of testimony is its sensitivity to diverse voices, broken language, and multiple discourses. In relation to this characteristic the debates in black theology and feminist theology over the use of "white European, patriarchal discourse" have been very important. This is not to say, however, that using the "master's tools," to employ the phrase of Audre Lorde, is wrong or unhelpful. Indeed, Cone and other black and feminist theologians use these discourses to further their own claims. But if black and feminist theologians used only the categories, resources, and argument structures of the dominant discourse, then public discourse would have been confined to functioning as integrationist or substitutional discourse. The debates over the utilization of African sources, of slave narratives, of music and literature in black theology and the use of women's stories and women's art in feminist theology expressed the demand to add new sources, voices, and types of argument as public discourse in both society and the church. Public discourse, in all its voices and shapes, can no longer be monological (monotonal) or translated through one type of argument, style, or voice. Public discourse must now be polyglot, not a tower of Babel hoping to be translated into one primal voice, but a fluid, empowered, and spirited gathering space, understood in its differences, its connections, in ever changing re-creation of common places or tropes.

This characteristic of public discourse as heterogeneous or polyglot functions in two ways. First, the diversity of genres in public discourses means that the public itself is implicitly shaped as a kind of multilinguistic space. The norm of a general "we" who hear in one voice or way is put aside, as are translation models of the diversity of discourse. The public is reimagined as spaces where voices are spoken and heard. The second aspect of polyglot discourse refers back to the ethical imperative of black and feminist theologies. This aspect has to do with the genre of discourse that summons the public to hear the other and to respond through the cultivation of compassion as integral to the public space that is shaped by the ongoing movement of the historical and transcendent realities.

In summarizing this section, it is important to observe why the "poetics of testimony" is the term best used to describe these theologies as *public* discourse. There are other ways to describe black theology and feminist theology as public discourse, including interpreting them through current cultural theory and/or through a kind of practical systematic theology (the former working best in the social public, the latter preferable in the church). But such interpretations fail to give full weight to the substance of the claims of black and feminist theologies and the new shape they give to public discourse. Black and feminist theologies are not merely examples of cultural theory nor are they variations of some structure called systematic theology (though they are both exemplar and variation). More properly understood in their own measure, black and feminist theologies call the publics of society and church into a conflict over truth and freedom, both in their representation (the narration of the real, the reference to the absolute) and in terms of the ethical imperative (the summons of responsiveness to the other, the pluralism of voices and shapes of discourse). Black and feminist theologies insist that our narrative identity and our public discourse be expressed in diversity and in historical-cultural particularity.

But transformation or liberation is never abstracted or isolated from the transcendent dimension, the new possibilities, the hope of liberation that breaks into the historical-cultural realities and is enacted in and through these particular cultural movements. This work of "naming God" or tracking the spirit and power of transfiguration in the midst of social and ecclesial publics—which is so central to Cone's theology—means theology, itself, is summoned to respect, to hear, to respond to the otherness in and through reflection and praxis.[13] The purpose of these discourses is to testify to what really happened, to shape the narrative identity with true words and forms and, in so doing, to change the direction and outcome of the story. Through the phrase, the "poetics of testimony," we can best give these theologies, as public discourse, their full ethical and poetical force.

Imagining the Public as a Space for Cultivating Compassion

If testimony tells us who we are and shapes us in the present through remembering those forgotten in the past, we must also ask how it helps us to imagine ourselves and others living differently in the future. As Ricoeur has suggested, testimony has a utopian, prospective sense, as well as a historical, retrospective sense. One testifies not only so the truth will be told but, according to both the juridical and religious senses of testimony, so that the future might be lived differently in light of the history of suffering. Testimony requires truth about the past and insists on justice as the goal for the future. When we understand black theology and feminist theology as poetics of testimony, we are challenged to imagine the public as a space for cultivating compassion.

By the term the "poetics of testimony," I have been trying to uncover both the substance of the discourse—the narrative identity—and the form of the discourse—the poetic resources of stories, songs, fictions, theologies. I have been trying to show that liberation theologies as poetics of testimony insist that our narrative identity and public discourse be constituted in diverse and multiple ways. When we ask about the future, we can see how the convergence of form and substance, how the poetics of testimony enables us to trace and to imagine the future of the public in new ways. This convergence of form and substance, of ideology critique and poetic possibility, creates what I will call the "ethical imaginary," for it has to do with how the poetics of testimony requires us to understand and shape the future as a space for cultivating compassion—the basic other-regarding attitude that resists hegemonic integration, that struggles against denying the other or making the other into the dominant, hegemonic image. This futuring work of testimony develops the ethical imaginary and cultivates compassion through three characteristics which function to keep the public space from moving toward closure or univocity: (1) the phronesis of empathy, (2) solidarity in difference, and (3) transcendence as possibility and praxis. I will figure these three characteristics of the ethical imaginary as concentric circles.

The first circle of the ethical imaginary is the space of what Aristotle would call *phronesis,* or practical wisdom, of empathy. As a public space, it is an imagined community where the texture of our interactions shapes and forms who we are and how we live together. Here the poetics of testimony is at work shaping the ethical imaginary through the voices of those who question back history and draw upon poetic resources. Challenging and retelling the story in songs, fictions, and theologies stirs up emotions and creates a plot in which we can imagine ourselves, others, our world in different ways.

To imagine ourselves living in difference and living differently, requires the phronesis of empathy. As Kearney, Martha Nussbaum, and others point out, narrative identity functions within an ethical context that cultivates character, virtues, an ethos, or practical wisdom. A primary value guiding the ethos of cultivating compassion within the public space is the phronesis of empathy, or the ability to identify with and understand someone different from one's self. As Diana Tietjens Meyers has suggested, empathy requires the ability to imaginatively conceive of what life is like for the other person. One's own experiences can contribute to the phronesis of empathy, but cannot be the sole basis for understanding the other. Empathy, according to Meyers, requires us to mobilize our "powers of attentive receptivity and analytic discernment." She continues, "Particularly when the other's background or circumstances are very different from one's own, empathy may require protracted observation and painstaking imaginative reconstruction of . . . the other's viewpoint."[14] The phronesis of empathy requires complex intellectual and emotional capacities. It reconceives the public space in terms of what Iris Marion Young has called "asymmetrical reciprocity," and forms social relations and individual character consistent with this empathic quality.[15]

If we are the stories we tell ourselves, then the stories of black and feminist theologians call and invite the public space to cultivate compassion through empathy for the other as other. Without the ability to hear the otherness, to promote understanding, and to live with difference on a most basic and fundamental human level, the publics of church and society cannot and will not be communities where diversity is recognized and encouraged.

Sisters in the Wilderness, by Delores Williams, is a collection of narratives that urge us to hear and understand our narrative identity as Christians and Americans in new ways, by remembering women who have served and suffered.[16] Through the story of the slave woman Hagar, we hear the stories of African American women cast out, of struggles, and of suffering. Building her own theological discourse on the Hagar story and placing it into dialogue with other womanist and feminist theologians such as Renita Weems and Elsa Tamez, Williams forces the reader to imagine all of the narratives at once, to imagine a world where there is no *one* public discourse, a world where all engage in asymmetrical reciprocity.

The first circle, then, suggests that cultivating compassion requires the phronesis of empathy. Indeed, this collection of essays may represent the phronesis of empathy at work—perhaps we are learning to hear James Cone, Delores Williams, and other diverse voices; perhaps we are beginning to understand. Our narrative identity is being re-formed as testimony allows us to imaginatively understand difference and differently.

The second circle of the ethical imaginary—which draws in closer to the ethos of cultivating compassion—is the space of solidarity in difference. Cultivating compassion requires not only that we hear and understand difference, but—as Delores Williams's multiple narratives demonstrate—that we learn to live together in our differences, to enact transformation, to redeem suffering. Here again, the poetics of testimony of black and feminist theologies is essential to shaping the ethical imaginary toward cultivating compassion. Ideology critique serves as an ethical responsibility to bring to light and remember the stories of those who suffer and to resist being drawn into the image of a partial and hegemonic "we." And poetics offers new ways for different voices to speak and to keep public discourse open and fluid. But the poetics of testimony suggests that recognizing and encouraging such diversity through the phronesis of empathy is not enough; rather, it requires us to fashion the public space as a space of solidarity. Solidarity in difference, or the flourishing of polyglot discourse and the furthering of survival, is the frame within which compassion is cultivated.

The public space as a place of solidarity is a polyglot texture of different bodies, different voices, different people. It means that the "we" of the public is not and cannot be one singular voice, cannot be reduced to a least common denominator, cannot promote sameness as the basis for our interactions. As Janet Jakobsen has suggested, the public must not be shaped in terms of an overarching body, but must be imagined instead as a network of interrelations among multiple and overlapping or contending public spheres.[17] The ethical imaginary cultivates compassion when we create networks of diverse and complex voices, bodies, and publics. In forming such networks, our ethical imaginary—in the largest and most utopian sense—fosters solidarity in difference so that no one suffers as a result of oppressive hegemonic public spaces.

Elisabeth Schüssler Fiorenza and other feminists show us a vision of the ecclesial public as a place of solidarity in which ecclesial citizens participate fully no matter what their sex, race, class, or sexual orientation. The images feminists use, such as the *ekklesia,* the community of friends, and the round-table, all suggest that the public is a place where differences are embodied and embraced and no body suffers or is rendered invisible because of its difference. This second circle of the ethical imaginary is thus figured as a public space where, in and through our solidarity, we understand difference, understand differently, and seek to redeem suffering, to struggle against hegemonic integration, to enact change.

The third and most tightly drawn circle through which testimony forms the ethical imaginary is the space of transcendence as possibility and praxis. Transcendence is not about other-worldly hope, the neo-orthodox hope of God interrupting history in one brief point. Rather, transcendence requires us to continually think of the public in new ways in and through the embodied memory of particular stories, to continually enlarge our imaginary. The poetics of testimony as transcendence empowers us to imagine the public space differently, to think the "we" in new ways, to sing new songs, to live in ways that enact and embody transformation. The otherness of transcendence breaks into the public sphere in and through these testimonies; it empowers and requires us to imagine and enact a public space in which compassion, regard for the other, is primary.

Testimony is not finally about redemptive suffering; it is, first and foremost, about hope figured as the future of justice. The testimonies of black and feminist theologians speak of transcendence as the spirit and power of the transfiguration that vetoes the law of slavery, breaks the chains of classism, and rewrites the social customs that erase and deny women's dignity through various practices of abuse and so-called protection. Calvin Schrag has suggested that this is a transcendence coupled with alterity, with otherness, that exceeds the bounds of what we might call ordinary transcending. In Levinas's notion of radical alterity or Tillich's claim of God beyond God, one finds this strong sense of transcendence as both the source and dynamic of transfiguration. Schrag observes,

> Neither a metaphysical designator of a being in some supernatural realm
> nor an epistemological protocol positing conditions for knowledge . . .

transcendence is more like an existential-pragmatic alterity—an alterity that registers its efficacy by making a difference in the experience of ourselves and the world.[18]

Precisely in this "other" space of transcendence, we receive the ability to glimpse other spaces, to change the "we" of the imagined public, to enlarge our ethical imaginary in ways that perceive new possibilities and enact transformation. In this space of transcendence as possibility and praxis, the public space for cultivating compassion can be figured as hope.

From his earliest writings, James Cone has asserted the importance of hope in black and liberation theologies. But Cone's hope, and the hope of testimony, is not only about the neo-orthodox hope of God interrupting history in one brief point—though in the early writings of Cone, the Wholly Other God is quite present in order to interrupt racism. God's transcendence, witnessed to, in, and through these testimonies, is also the power and dynamism of historical transfiguration, the enactment of justice in and through the public space. As Cone states in *God of the Oppressed*, "While the meaning of liberation includes the historical determination of freedom in this world, it is not limited to what is possible in history."[19] In resisting the movement toward closure of the public space, compassion requires the transcendent possibilities and praxis that open and enlarge our imaginary and empower our enactment.

The ethical imaginary that cultivates compassion is thus constituted through these three concentric circles representing the basic characteristics of the future public space: the phronesis of empathy, solidarity in difference, and transcendence as possibility and praxis, or hope. But, perhaps, drawn in an even tighter circle, forming the heart or the reshaped center of the ethical imaginary, is the ethical responsibility of testimony to the memory and the presence of the dead and those who suffer. The circle of the suffering, the oppressed, the dead—figured as the center of the ethical imaginary—summons us to see them, to hear them, to remember them, and in compassion, to rewrite and relive the narrative toward a future and a present of justice.[20]

Notes

1. Jürgen Habermas, *The Structural Transformation of the Public Sphere: An Inquiry into a Category of Bourgeois Society*, trans. Thomas Burger with Frederick Lawrence (Cambridge: MIT Press, 1989).

2. Nancy Fraser, "Rethinking the Public Sphere: A Contribution to the Critique of Actually Existing Democracy," *Social Text* 25/26 (1990): 56-80.

3. Raymond Williams, *Marxism and Literature* (Oxford and New York: Oxford University Press, 1977), 115.

4. Benedict Anderson, *Imagined Communities* (London: Verso, 1991).

5. Richard Kearney, *The Poetics of Modernity* (New Jersey: Humanities Press, 1995), 98-101.

6. James H. Cone, *Black Theology and Black Power* (New York: Seabury Press, 1969), 36.

7. Mary Daly, *Beyond God the Father: Toward a Philosophy of Women's Liberation* (Boston: Beacon Press, 1973); and Rosemary Radford Ruether, *Sexism and God-Talk: Toward a Feminist Theology* (Boston: Beacon Press, 1983).

8. M. Shawn Copeland, "Black, Hispanic/Latino, and Native American Theologies," in *The Modern Theologians*, ed. David F. Ford (Cambridge, Mass. and Oxford: Blackwell, 1997), 362.

9. Elie Wiesel, "The Holocaust as a Literary Inspiration," *Dimensions of the Holocaust* (Evanston: Northwestern University Press, 1977), 9.

10. Paul Ricoeur, "The Hermeneutics of Testimony," in *Essays on Biblical Interpretation*, edited with an introduction by Lewis S. Mudge (Philadelphia: Fortress, 1980). Reprinted by permission from *Anglican Theological Review* LXI:4 (1979).

11. James H. Cone, *My Soul Looks Back* (Maryknoll, N.Y.: Orbis Books, 1995), 106.

12. James H. Cone, *For My People: Black Theology and the Black Church* (Maryknoll, N.Y.: Orbis Books, 1984), 116-17.

13. I am indebted to Mark McClain Taylor for the notion of "tracking spirit." See "Tracking Spirit: Theology as Cultural Critique in America," in *Changing Conversations: Religious Reflection and Cultural Analysis*, ed. Dwight N. Hopkins and Sheila Greeve Davaney (New York and London: Routledge, 1996), 123-44.

14. Diana Tietjens Meyers, *Subjection and Subjectivity* (New York: Routledge, 1994), 33.

15. Iris Marion Young, *Intersecting Voices: Dilemmas of Gender, Political Philosophy, and Policy* (Princeton, N.J.: Princeton University Press, 1997), 39.

16. Delores Williams, *Sisters in the Wilderness: The Challenge of Womanist God-Talk* (Maryknoll, N.Y.: Orbis Books, 1993).

17. Janet R. Jakobsen, "The Body Politic vs. Lesbian Bodies: Publics, Counterpublics, and the Uses of Norms," in *Horizons in Feminist Theology*, ed. Rebecca S. Chopp and Sheila Greeve Davaney (Minneapolis: Fortress Press, 1997), 136.

18. Calvin O. Schrag, *The Self After Modernity* (New Haven: Yale University Press, 1997), 138.

19. James H. Cone, *God of the Oppressed*, new revised edition (Maryknoll, N.Y.: Orbis Books, 1997), 145.

20. I want to express my deep gratitude to Elaine Robinson, my research associate, who researched and edited this essay, shaped the narrative of the third section, and contributed useful insights into the role of transcendence in the poetics of testimony.

Part IV

Black Faith
and
the Third World

Liberation Theology
and African Women's Theologies

ROSEMARY RADFORD RUETHER

This essay will focus on the emergence of African women's theologies in the context of the development of black and African theologies. I wish to give a special tribute to James Cone as one who has played a unique role in the inspiration of black theology in South Africa and also within the assemblies of the Ecumenical Association of Third World Theologians (EATWOT), the main forum for the theologies of Africa, Asia, and Latin America. For more than twenty years James Cone has been a supporter of this organization and has persuaded EATWOT to accept American black theology as a Third World theology. He has been in attendance at all international meetings of EATWOT.

When the Women's Commission of EATWOT was formed in the 1980s James Cone also promoted the presence of womanist theologians as members of this commission. Today the North American delegation includes womanist, mujerista, and Asian American women theologians who form a member group of the commission. This unique role played by American black theology and now by womanist, mujerista, and Asian American women theologians in EATWOT owes a special debt to James Cone for their presence and influence in this body.

Feminist theologies arising from the so-called Third World (Latin America, Africa, and Asia) have generally developed in relation to the liberation theologies of their regions. Latin American liberation theology was pioneered by priest-theologians, such as Peruvian theologian Gustavo Gutiérrez,[1] in the mid-1960s in response to the growing crisis of poverty and revolutionary violence in their regions, and the failure of the capitalist developmental model promulgated by North American and Western European corporations and governments to promote social justice.

In 1976, in the wake of the rise and destruction of the socialist reform government of Salvador Allende in Chile, Latin Americans, such as Sergio Torres, reached out to Asian and African theologians to form the Ecumenical Association of Third World Theologians. Latin American liberation theology has focused on the questions of poverty and economic oppression both within their countries and particularly between Latin America and the First World. These Latin American theologians were challenged by Asian and African theologians to be more sensitive to the questions of race and culture as well.

However, questions of sexism and gender were virtually ignored by these male theologians from all three regions. By the late 1970s a growing cadre of women theologians were attending the international meetings of EATWOT: Mercy Amba Oduyoye from Ghana, Virginia Fabella and Mary John Mananzan from the Philippines, Marianne Katoppo from Indonesia, Sun Ai Park from Korea, Ivone Gebara and Elsa Tamez from Latin America. These women began to challenge the lack of attention to gender in Third World liberation theologies. The issues surfaced in the 1981 EATWOT Assembly in New Delhi when the plea of Marianne Katoppo for inclusive language brought jokes and trivializing comments from the men.[2]

In 1983 an international dialogue between Third World and First World theologians was convened in Geneva with a mandate to make the five delegations from Asia, Africa, Latin America, Western Europe, and North America gender inclusive. The result brought together a considerable number of women theologians from across the globe to discuss feminist issues in theology and social analysis. This brought further resistance from some of the male Third World theologians who wanted "their women" to stay in "their place"; i.e., behind the agenda of the men of their region. These men argued that feminism was a First World, middle-class women's issue.[3]

At the end of the conference the women theologians from Africa, Asia, and Latin America rose together and demanded a Women's Commission within EATWOT that would meet separately in order to allow Third World women to dialogue and to develop their own feminist theologies in their own contexts. "We have to decide for ourselves what feminist theology means for us," they said. "It is not for First World women to tell us how to do it, nor is it for Third World men to tell us it is not our issue."[4]

This proposal was accepted by the EATWOT organizers and a four-stage process was planned: national meetings, continental meetings, then a Third World intercontinental meeting. These took place in 1985 and 1986. The papers for these conferences made their way into major publications.[5] The fourth step in this process was a planned world consultation that would bring Third World women theologians into a new stage of dialogue with First World feminist theologians. This finally took place in December 1994 in Costa Rica, bringing together forty-five women theologians from fourteen countries.[6]

By 1994 the definitions of First and Third World were themselves in question.[7] The paradigm of dialogue expanded to include an Eastern European woman, an Arab Christian woman, and a delegation of women theologians of both European and Indigenous ancestry from the Pacific. The boundaries of the two "worlds" were further complicated by the presence of a white South African and a Japanese feminist theologian, both seen as First World within the Third World.

This process of developing Third World feminist theology led by the Women's Commission of EATWOT is of great importance. Without it it would have been much more difficult for women theologians of these regions to develop and publish their thought. Thanks to funding from the World Council of Churches, women theologians who could not have afforded such consultations themselves were able to gather regionally and internationally. They were able to organize networks of communication, develop a sense of their own identities as women theologians from Africa, Asia, and Latin America, receive the stimulation of South-South dialogue, and found journals and publications.

I now turn to a focus on African women's theologians as these are developing in the context of black and African theologies. The Circle of Concerned African Women Theologians, which emerged in the late 1980s, has become the major vehicle for the exchange and development of African Christian women's theological work.[8] The context in which these African women do their work is that of postcolonial (now postapartheid) Africa, yet an Africa still very much shaped by the colonial experience and ongoing neocolonial relations with the Western world.

Like Latin America, sub-Saharan Africa was Christianized as an integral part of European colonialism, but this took place in the mid to late nineteenth century, rather than five hundred years ago. The African peoples still retain their historical indigenous languages and cultures, even if their relation to these cultures is somewhat altered through Western Christianizing and cultural imperialism. Thus the question of the relation between Christianity and indigenous culture is a central one for African Christian theology, while this issue emerged late and is still marginal for Latin Americans.

Although North Africa shaped the earliest Christian theology of the first centuries, Islam superseded Christianity in North Africa in the seventh century, and only pockets of ancient African Christianity continue in the Coptic tradition from Egypt to Ethiopia and the southern Sudan.[9] Catholic missionaries arrived in the sixteenth century, but there was little impact on the interior of Africa until the mid-nineteenth century. At that time Catholic and Protestant missionaries flooded Africa, closely connected with the colonizing nations.

In the 1884-85 Berlin Conference, the European nations partitioned Africa among themselves, the British taking much of East Africa from Egypt to the Cape, as well as Ghana and Nigeria in West Africa, while the French carved out most of West Africa. The Belgians took the huge center of the Congo, and the Portuguese and Germans occupied large areas to the east and west in Southern Africa. The Italians, who held Libya, made a short-lived grab for Ethiopia in 1936. The European partitioning of Africa drew the borders of modern African states, and Europeans brought the languages and cultures that shaped the colonial institutions of church, education, and government.

Although some European missionaries belatedly began to appreciate African culture, the primary impact of missionary education was to treat Africans as people with a totally worthless and evil culture that had to be expunged in order to be Christianized and incorporated into the culture of the colonizers. This negative view of African culture was mingled with racism toward the African person. European cultural colonialism of Africans moved ambiguously between "uplift"—to become like Europeans— and proletarianization—to be made into workers in mines and plantations, with the assumption that higher professions were beyond their capabilities.

African women received a double version of these negative views, shaped by a combined European racism and sexism. The African woman was seen as highly sexed and needing to be "tamed," while at the same time she was viewed as oppressed, by working in the fields or by practices such as polygamy and clitoridectomy, and needing to be protected. For European missionaries this double view meant the African woman needed to be domesticated: washed, clothed in garments that concealed her body, trained to work in the kitchen and become a housemaid in the European manner.[10] But the higher education extended to an African male elite was usually assumed to be beyond her reach.

Europeans not only divided Africa politically and culturally, but they also reshaped its internal society and economy by taking all the best land for themselves for export agribusiness, either marginalizing African farmers on poor land, or incorporating them into these farms as low-wage labor. African families were often broken up as women became maids in white households, while men became workers in fields and mines. The old, the young, and the sick were often sent to marginal zones reserved for Africans.[11] This distortion of the African socio-economic structure remains to a large extent today, creating extremes of wealth and poverty and skewing development in the neocolonial era.

Missionary churches were slow to hand over control of their structures to Africans and even slower to make higher theological education and ordination available to African women, even when this was happening in their home churches in Europe or America. At the end of the nineteenth century, breakaway movements occurred in which African men shaped independent churches under their own leadership, drawing on the polity and liturgical tradition of the denominations from which they had come. There was no change in the patriarchal leadership patterns in these churches. These churches often took the name "Ethiopian" in order to claim a relation to the ancient African or Coptic Christianity that remains today in Ethiopia.[12]

In the 1920s and continuing until today a more radical movement of African independent churches has grown, often referred to as Spirit, Prophet, or Aladura (praying) churches. These churches draw on the religious patterns of healing, spirit-possession, and prophecy of the African traditional religions, as well as their cultural styles of music, dress, and organization—although often understanding themselves as transcending the power of the "demonic" spirits of African religions by being filled with the "Holy Spirit" that comes from the "true God" of Christianity.[13]

Women generally have larger roles in these Spirit or Prophet churches than in either mission or Ethiopian churches, and some of these churches have been founded and led by women. But these churches are far from egalitarian in gender roles. Women, while playing roles in ministry, are usually not in the top leadership or administration, but are located on the lower levels of the church hierarchy. They are, for the most part, relegated to those roles having to do with charismatic gifts to discern the causes and heal the spiritual and physical maladies that afflict those who come to them for help, a role similar to the traditional shaman/healers in African culture.[14]

These Spirit churches, which arise mostly from poorer and urbanized sectors of society, primarily provide spiritual and physical means of survival, rebuilding community, and identity for those uprooted and disoriented in the new Africa. They have generally not been leaders in movements of liberation, in the sense of transforming social structures.[15] Since some of these churches also carry on African customs, such as polygamy and pollution taboos, their usefulness for African feminist theology is questionable, although they are highly significant as examples of women's ministerial roles and a new "folk" amalgamation of Christianity and African tradition.[16]

From 1958 to 1965 the French, the British, and the Belgians departed from their colonies in Africa, seeking to put African male elites in power who would be amenable to European neocolonial control over the resources of the area. Some Europeans, particularly where there was a significant settler population, hung on to power, forcing prolonged wars of liberation in countries such as Zimbabwe, followed by destructive civil wars, as in the cases of the former Portuguese territories of Mozambique and Angola.[17]

South Africa, with the largest and most entrenched white settler population, is a special case. There the whites attempted a rigid system of separate development for whites and blacks (apartheid). Only a prolonged struggle, led by the African National Congress for more than eighty years, finally succeeded in dismantling the legal-political expressions of apartheid in the 1990s. But the legacy of this racist system lives on in skewed land tenure and the gap between a wealthy white elite, who own most of the resources, and the impoverished African majority (despite an emerging African middle class).

In the postcolonial period in Africa since the 1960s, there have emerged two major expressions of African Christian theology: African theology, and black theology. African theology was founded by religious anthropologists, such as John Mbiti[18] and E. Bolaji Idowu.[19] Later, African theology developed under the rubrics of "indigenization" or "inculturation" of Christian theology into African culture. These scholars did careful research to reclaim distinctive African religious-cultural world views as exemplified in distinct cultural groups. They sought to rescue these cultures from the heritage of vilification by Western missionaries and show that they contained coherent and positive spiritual values, in many cases strikingly similar to those found in the Bible (particularly the Hebrew Scriptures). Once these cultures were accorded their due respect, it would be possible for Africans to shape an integral inculturation of Christian theological themes into the African cultural world view and traditional ritual practices.[20]

Black theology was developed in South Africa during the heat of the anti-apartheid struggle, sparked by the Black Consciousness movement of the 1970s, as well as the influence of black theology in the United States, specifically the theological work of James Cone. This theological movement understood itself as calling for liberation, not inculturation. Liberation meant throwing off the racist system of apartheid and creating a nonracial, just democratic society in South Africa. Black Christian leaders, such as Allan Boesak, Desmond Tutu, and Itumeleng Mosala, were leaders of the Black Theology movement.[21]

As leaders of these two movements met in international gatherings, each criticized what they saw as the limitations of the other. Black theologians attacked African theology for viewing African culture as a static heritage of the past into which Christianity is to be incorporated, without recognizing the ongoing evolution of this culture and the need for the liberating transformation of unjust cultural and social patterns, both from African society and from Western colonialism.[22] Some African theologians, particularly John Mbiti, attacked black theology as an American import inappropriate in Africa.[23] Neither group paid much attention to women or to gender injustice.[24]

Among a new generation of African theologians, including women theologians, this dispute is being resolved by a recognition that both inculturation and liberation are necessary.[25] There is a need to incarnate Christian theology into African culture. But there is also a need to transform that culture to overcome its oppressive aspects, while moving to a new cultural and sociopolitical liberative future, freed from the heritage of racism, poverty, and gender inequity inherited by African societies across their history. Africans cannot afford to split this agenda into segregated and warring pieces, rather they need to create an African liberation theology that can embrace all of its aspects, even if some thinkers may choose to concentrate on cultural and others on socio-economic issues.

African feminist theologians are very much at the heart of this new union of theologies of inculturation and liberation, seeking to look at both aspects through the focus on African women's oppression and liberation. A significant and growing community of African women theologians is emerging, led by Ghanaian theologian and church leader Mercy Amba Oduyoye, together with many sisters, such as Rosemary Edet, Daisy Nwachuku, Teresa Okure, R. Modupe Owanikin, and Bette Ekeya (Nigeria); Anne Nasimiyu-Wasike, Musimbi Kanyoro, Judith Mbula Bahemuka, and Teresia Hinga (Kenya); Isabel Phiri and Anne Nachisale Musopole (Malawi); Elizabeth Amoah (Ghana); and Bernadette Mbuy Beya (Congo), among others.[26]

These African women theologians and sociologists cross denominational lives. They are Catholics and mainline Protestants for the most part, and belong to a new educated professional class. Most have gotten their doctoral degrees in Europe or the United States, but many find their major base for work in Africa in religious studies departments of universities, rather than as ministers in the churches or faculties of seminaries that train those going into ordained ministry, although this may be changing in the late 1990s. Secular modern Africa, represented by university departments, seems to be more open to what they are doing than the institutions of the churches in Africa, although the international church supports their work. Mercy Oduyoye has been Deputy General Secretary of the World Council of Churches, while Musimbi Kanyoro has been Executive Secretary for Women in Church and Society of the Lutheran World Federation, also based in Geneva. (Presently she is head of the World YWCA.)

In the two major books, *The Will to Arise: Women, Tradition and the Church in Africa,* edited by Mercy Oduyoye and Musimbi Kanyoro, and Oduyoye's book, *Daughters of Anowa: African Women and Patriarchy,*[27] as well as numerous articles in journals and symposia, these women are shaping their critique of culture and Christianity and their vision of gender liberation and equity in an African context. This work of cultural critique has only begun. Much more investigation into the many cultures of Africa, from women's perspectives, is needed. Women's reconstruction of theological symbols, as well as religiocultural practices, is still largely in the future.

African feminist liberation theologians claim the sovereign right to evaluate all the cultural patterns they have received, from traditional African cultures, from Christianity, and from Western secularism, in terms of how they promote or impede women's development.[28] They further claim the right to be the primary arbiters of what promotes or impedes women's development. It is not for African men to tell them that all African culture is sacrosanct or that to critique any of it is to betray African tradition; nor is it for Western men or women to judge these cultures from outside.

Only African women can determine which cultural patterns have debilitated them and which have been life-enhancing for them. African men must be willing to listen and learn from African women, rather than to dictate on these matters, if the goal is to be enhanced mutuality for African women and men together. This does not mean that all African women will agree on what is good or bad about such practices as polygamy, menstrual taboos, and the like. But the conversation must begin by granting primacy to African women's judgment, based on their experiences as African women in their distinct contexts.

African women theologians find some things that are debilitating to them as women in traditional African cultural practices. Many of these practices are shaped by an underlying assumption that women are both powerful and dangerous. Under this assumption their lives must be severely restricted and shaped to be servants of African men in all aspects of work, sexuality, reproduction, and family life, not independent persons in their own right. The impact of the pervasive African belief in evil spirits, acting through witches who cause all misfortunes, falls predominantly on women. African women often find themselves blamed and subjected to hostile mental and physical treatment based on the assumptions that misfortunes affecting others in the community, including their relatives, husbands, and children, are due to their evil thoughts or practices.[29]

For example, when a woman is pregnant, there is general rejoicing and many rituals of support, since it is in giving birth that the African woman is seen as fulfilling her primary function. But if the birth process goes badly, it may be assumed that she had done something wrong. She may be interrogated as to whether she has been unfaithful, on the assumption that this is causing her difficulties.[30]

Traditional widowhood rituals have been particularly negative for African women. The underlying assumption is that the widow is somehow responsible for her husband's death and must exculpate herself. In some Nigerian societies the widow is confined to her house for a long period, while being subjected to hostile treatment by her husband's relatives. She must loosen her hair, wear an old, dirty dress, refrain from washing, eat little, and cry out aloud three times a day. Her children may be taken from her, but neglected, and she is not allowed to care for them. After this prolonged mourning, which exacerbates the mental and physical pains of her widowhood, she often faces penury, since she is allowed no inheritance from her husband.[31]

African women theologians are not the only African women dealing with these negative customs toward women. National Councils for Women's Development have been established by many African governments. In Ghana the International Federation of Women Lawyers has been active in promoting new legislation that curtails these widowhood rituals and provides for inheritance for the wife.[32] But it is the task of women theologians to investigate the underlying religious views that support negative customs and to ask how these might be transformed by a world view that is more life-enhancing for women in partnership relations with men.

But women theologians are also reclaiming African traditions that are empowering for women. These include stories of female life-promoting and protecting deities and of powerful women ancestresses and leaders of the community. They include patterns of binary leadership of women and men, and traditions of women's prophetic and healing powers, often emphasized in Spirit churches. They also include the positive roles of women as mothers, economic producers, farmers, creators of market associations and women's cooperatives, by which African women have provided the means of life for their families. These traditions, however, need to be freed from exploitation that gives the African women twice as much work as men, but without decision-making power.[33]

Christianity, together with Western colonialism, has often claimed to have liberated African women from oppression by traditional African culture. But African women are rejecting this claim. For the most part colonial powers removed African women from the political and economic roles they had earlier enjoyed, to shape more patriarchal as well as racist societies. The Christian churches mostly operated to sacralize this more patriarchal pattern brought by the West, claiming that this reflected Biblical teaching and the will of God.[34]

The Bible thus became an additional authority to justify blood taboos and the removal of women from social and religious leadership. The churches also repressed sexual initiation practices that gave women some control over their sexuality and child-bearing and made them more vulnerable in their sexual and reproductive functions.[35] Finally, it justified passive acceptance of suffering by reference to shouldering the cross of Christ.[36]

While African Christian women theologians are vehemently questioning these ways Christianity reinforced and worsened patriarchy, they nevertheless draw a primary mandate for social change from Christian theology. The belief that women as much as men are created in the image of God and therefore are of equal worth,[37] that Jesus came to liberate all, with particular concern for those most oppressed, these are continually cited as mandates for criticizing both

African and Christian forms of patriarchy. Christ is set in tension with Christianity and aligned with the struggle and hope for African women's liberation.[38]

The God who speaks through Christ is One who calls Africans to create societies of justice and well-being for all, overcoming cultural and social patterns which mandate white or male domination at the expense of African women. The faith of African women that Christ is on their side against all forms of oppression that have come to them from African traditional culture, the church, and the West seems unshakable. But the Christ reference can be fluid, embracing the story of the historical Jesus as well as stories of African women's suffering and salvific risk on behalf of their communities.[39] Thus the relation of Christ to the redemption of African society from sexism and all injustice is open-ended, pointing forward to expanding future hopes, rather than confined to static African or Christian pasts. This is the dynamic promise of emerging African women's theologies.

Notes

1. Gustavo Gutiérrez, *A Theology of Liberation,* fifteenth anniversary edition (Maryknoll, N.Y.: Orbis Books, 1988).

2. See Prologue by Mary John Mananzan, in *Women Resisting Violence: Spirituality for Life,* ed. Mary John Mananzan, et al. (Maryknoll, N.Y.: Orbis Books, 1996), 1.

3. This account is taken from my personal remembrance of these events as a delegate to this conference.

4. For a history of the EATWOT process and the emergence of Third World feminist theology within it to 1993 from her experience, see Virginia Fabella, *Beyond Bonding: A Third World Women's Theological Journey* (Manila, Philippines: Institute of Women's Studies, 1993).

5. Major papers and statements from the intercontinental conference, as well as continental conferences, are found in *With Passion and Compassion: Third World Women Doing Theology,* ed. Virginia Fabella and Mercy Amba Oduyoye (Maryknoll, N.Y.: Orbis Books, 1988).

6. Major papers that emerged from this conference are found in the book, *Women Resisting Violence.*

7. White Western people tend to assume the term "Third World" is a put-down that implies third-down on some hierarchical scale. However, in her book, *Beyond Bonding,* Virginia Fabella recalls that this term had a different meaning for the EATWOT movement, suggesting a parallel to the French revolutionary term "third estate," meaning a whole new group that is emerging beyond the dominant hierarchy and reshaping a new majority; see 3-4.

8. The volume, *The Will to Arise: Women, Tradition and the Church in Africa,* ed. Mercy Amba Oduyoye and Musimbi Kanyoro (Maryknoll, N.Y.: Orbis Books, 1992) is the first publication of the Biennial Institutes of African Women in Religion and Culture, a project of the Circle of Concerned African Women Theologians. See Teresia M. Hinga, "Between Colonialism and Inculturation: Feminist Theologies in Africa," in *The Power of Naming,* Elisabeth Schüssler Fiorenza, ed., (Maryknoll, N.Y.: Orbis Books, 1996), 36-44.

9. In 1996, Orthodox, mostly Coptic, Christians in Africa numbered 30 million out of a total number of Christians of 351.8 million. *World Almanac* (Mahwah, N.J.: Funk and Wagnalls, 1996), 646.

10. See Tumani Mutasa Nyajeka, "The Meeting of Two Female Worlds: American Women Missionaries and Shona Women at Old Mutare and the Founding of Rukwadzano" (Ph.D. diss., Northwestern University, 1996).

11. Family breakup was particularly bad in South Africa. See Jacklyn Cock, *Madams and Maids: Domestic Workers Under Apartheid* (1980). For general economic distortion due to colonization, see Walter Rodney, *How Europe Underdeveloped Africa* (Nairobi: Heinemann, 1972).

12. See Adrian Hastings, *A History of African Christianity, 1950-1975* (Cambridge: Cambridge University Press, 1979), 67-85.

13. See H. W. Turner, *African Independent Church* (Oxford: Oxford University Press, 1967), 2 vols. Also J. Akinyele Omoyajowo, *Cherubim and Seraphim: The History of an African Independent Church* (New York: NOK Publishers, 1982).

14. See Rosalind Hackett, "Women as Leaders and Participants in Spiritual Churches," in *New Religious Movements in Nigeria,* ed. R. Hackett (Lewiston, N.Y.: Edwin Mellen Press, 1987), 191-208; also Helen Callaway, "Women in Yoruba Tradition and in the Cherubim and Seraphim Society," in *The History of Christianity in West Africa,* ed. O.U. Kalu (London: Longmanns, 1980), pp. 321- 332, and Cynthia Hoehler-Fatton, *Women of Fire and Spirit: History, Faith and Gender in Roho Religion in West Kenya* (New York: Oxford University Press, 1996).

15. J. Akinyele Omoyajowo, *The Cherubim and Seraphim in Relation to Church and State* (Ibadan: Claveriarum Press, 1975)

16. See Mercy Amba Oduyoye, *Daughters of Anowa: African Women and Patriarchy* (Maryknoll, N.Y.: Orbis Books, 1995), 123-30; see also Brigid Maa Sackey, "Women, Spiritual Churches and Politics in Ghana," (Ph.D. diss., Temple University, 1996).

17. David Birmingham, *The Decolonization of Africa* (Athens, Ohio: Ohio University Press, 1995).

18. John Mbiti, *African Religion and Philosophy* (London: Heinemann, 1969).

19. E. Bolaji Idowu, *Olodumare: God in Yoruba Belief* (London: Longmans, 1962).

20. Emmanuel Martey, *African Theology: Inculturation and Liberation* (Maryknoll, NY: Orbis Books, 1993), 63-85.

21. Ibid., 95-114.

22. Allan Boesak, *Farewell to Innocence: A Socio-Ethical Study of Black Theology and Power* (Maryknoll, N.Y.: Orbis Books, 1977); see also Jean-Marc Ela, *African Cry* (Maryknoll, N.Y.: Orbis Books, 1986).

23. See John Mbiti, "An African Views American Black Theology." See also Desmond M. Tutu, "Black Theology/African Theology: Soul Mates or Antagonists?" in *Black Theology: A Documentary History, vol. 1, 1966-79,* ed. James H. Cone and Gayraud S. Wilmore (Maryknoll, N.Y.: Orbis Books, 1993), 379-92.

24. For an example of a paternalistic view of African women in traditional religion, see John Mbiti, "Flowers in the Garden: Women in African Religion," in *African Traditional Religion in Contemporary Society,* ed. Jacob K. Olupona (New York: Paragon House, 1991). See the critique of Mbiti by Mercy Amba Oduyoye, in Jacob K. Olupona and Sulayman S. Nyanga, eds. *Religious Plurality in Africa* (New York: Mouten de Gruyter, 1993), 341-65.

25. See Martey, *African Theology,* 121-36.

26. The writings of these African women theologians are found particularly in the book, *The Will to Arise*; also the section on Africa in *With Passion and Compassion*, as well as in collections of African theology, Third World theology and Third World women's theology; see, for example, Mercy Amba Oduyoye's article, "Liberation and Development of Theology in Africa," in *The Ecumenical Movement Tomorrow*, ed. Marc Reuver, et al. (Kampen: Kok, 1993), 203-10.

27. See notes 8 and 16 of this essay.

28. This principle is stated or assumed throughout *The Will to Arise*; see also Mercy Amba Oduyoye, "The Spirituality of Resistance and Reconstruction," in *Women Resisting Violence*, 166-70.

29. Mercy Amba Oduyoye, *Daughters of Anowa*, 40-42, 120-23; also Elizabeth Amoah, "Femaleness: Akan Concepts and Practices" in *Women, Religion and Sexuality: The Impact of Religious Teachings on Women*, ed. Jeanne Becker (Geneva: World Council of Churches, 1990), 129-53.

30. Mercy Amba Oduyoye, "Women and Ritual in Africa" in *The Will to Arise*, 14.

31. See Rosemary Edet, "Christianity and African Women's Rituals," in *The Will to Arise*, 31-32.

32. Oduyoye, "The Spirituality of Resistance and Reconstruction," in *Women Resisting Violence*, 167.

33. See, for example, Anne Nachisale Musopole's article, "Sexuality and Religion in a Matriarchal Society" in *The Will to Arise*, where Malawean matrilineal societies are described as both empowering and overworking women:

> In the villages, both men and women wake up early in the morning and go to the farm to till the ground. At daybreak both men and women come home, but the woman carries a bundle of firewood on her head. She carries two hoes in her hand and a baby at her back. The man just walks home with nothing in his hands. When they reach home, the man sits down to rest, while the woman makes fires and cooks food for the day. After eating, the man either sleeps or goes to drink beer at the nearby village. The woman never rests, but looks for food for the rest of the day. The men do not give the women money to buy the food. The woman is the primary source of nourishment and nurture. (196)

34. Mercy Amba Oduyoye, *Daughters of Anowa*, 183.

35. Ephraim Mosothoane, of the Department of Religion and Biblical Studies of the University of the Transkei (UNITTA), Umtata, South Africa, told me when I visited there in 1990 that the African traditional initiation rites taught girls how to do sexual play without penetration and impregnation. The missionaries repressed these initiation rites, with the result that teenage pregnancy became common.

36. Mercy Amba Oduyoye, "Spirituality of Resistance and Reconstruction," in *Women Resisting Violence*, 167-68.

37. Ibid., 170.

38. See Therese Souga, "The Christ Event from the Viewpoint of African Women: A Catholic Perspective," and Louise Tappa, "A Protestant Perspective," in *With Passion and Compassion*, 22-46.

39. See Elizabeth Amoah and Mercy Oduyoye, "The Christ for African Women," in *With Passion and Compassion*, 47-59, and Teresia Hinga, "Jesus Christ and the Liberation of Women in Africa," in *The Will to Arise*, 183-94.

14

Emancipatory Christianity

LINDA E. THOMAS

The dynamism and influence of James H. Cone's *Black Theology and Black Power* leaves a legacy that demands that the black church globally cultivate an emancipatory Christianity. In honor of Cone's life and work as well as to draw a direct link between liberatory movements by grassroots black Christian women from a cross-cultural perspective, I would like to engage in a critical conversation between emancipatory Afro-Christian leadership in South Africa and the United States by comparing and contrasting the womanist life works of Christinah Mokotuli Nku, signifying a black South African pioneer who founded her own church, which has become the second largest independent black denomination in the Republic of South Africa, and those of Fannie Lou Hamer, representing a leader in the American Civil Rights movement of the 1960s. To achieve such a critical interchange, I present one interpretation of each woman's liberatory life works; examine how religion influenced each woman's contribution to emancipatory struggles in her respective context; offer an assessment of each figure; and then suggest some lessons by integrating their strengths.

Fannie Lou Hamer's Womanist Works

Fannie Lou Hamer, the twentieth child of sharecroppers named Ella and Jim Townsend, was born in 1917, in the predominately black Mississippi Delta, the most impoverished sector of the poorest state in the Union, where cotton was grown as an economic base.

Hamer lived during a period of extreme racial division in the United States. Ten years before her birth, in 1907, eighty-six people were lynched by white Mississippians: eighty-three black men, two white men, and one black woman. In the year of her birth, 1917, a white minority controlled the politics and wealth of the state. In 1920, when Hamer was only three years old, Mississippi had thirteen lynchings, surpassed only by Georgia, which had fourteen (*Contemporary Black Leaders* 1970:115). The state's economy was bolstered by federal government agricultural allotments administered by Mississippi's U.S. senator James O. Eastman. Dispersing the money without checks or balances, Eastman kept the wages of blacks at a subsistence level, causing generations to be negatively affected by an economic schema that disadvantaged their families. Finally, during the early years of Hamer's life, Jim and Jane Crow codes kept black people in subservient roles.

When she was forty-five, Hamer heard Reverend James Bevel of the Southern Christian Leadership Conference (SCLC) preach on Matthew 16:3, "discerning the signs of the time," relating the text to black people in Mississippi having the right to vote. During the same service, James Forman of the Student Nonviolent Coordinating Committee (SNCC) informed the congregation that as Americans they had a constitutional right to vote. Before the service concluded, a call was issued for volunteers to travel to the Sunflower County courthouse in Indianola to register to vote the next day. Hamer was one of eighteen people who volunteered, and her life was forever transformed as a result of this decision.

However, in order to exercise the franchise, a literacy test was required; all eighteen volunteers copied sections of the Constitution and interpreted it, while white men with rifles walked in and out of the testing room all day. Although all of the volunteers failed the exam, they journeyed home feeling satisfied with their efforts. The repercussions for breaking Jim Crow codes by attempting to register to vote were felt immediately, as police harassed the weary travelers by stopping their bus and fining the driver $100 because his vehicle too closely resembled the color of a school bus. Moreover, Hamer was harassed by the plantation owner for whom she had worked for eighteen years; he ordered her to disavow her attempt to register to vote or to leave his land. Hamer left her family that night to stay with the Tucker family in Ruleville, Miss. Harassment followed Hamer everywhere, as snipers fired sixteen bullets into the Tuckers' house ten days later. Furthermore, Hamer's family suffered. While the plantation owner encouraged Hamer's husband to stay on the plantation until the end of the harvest season and promised that he could take all of his possessions with him at the end of the season, this is not what happened. At the end of harvest, Perry Hamer was summarily dismissed and not allowed to take the family's belongings, including a car for which he'd been paying for ten years.

Yet these events did not deter Hamer as she became more strident in her conviction to claim her lawful right to vote. In December 1962 she returned to Indianola to register to vote. Upon learning that she failed the test, she told the clerk to expect to see her every thirty days.

Thirty days later in January 1963, she passed the exam and began to work as a SNCC supervisor tutoring blacks for the literacy exam. Being intimately linked to the liberationist struggle as advocated by SNCC and the SCLC, Hamer's womanist action was to promote other blacks to become registered. Moreover, she launched her career as a Civil Rights fieldworker by putting nonviolent resistance techniques into action immediately following a training session she attended in South Carolina. Hamer and others challenged whites-only privileges at a Trailways bus station by sitting at a lunch counter, using bathrooms designated only for whites, and sitting at the front of the bus. The police met the bus when it stopped in Winona and arrested Hamer and the others. While in jail, black prisoners, who were ordered by white guards, beat Hamer with brass knuckles. Her body was permanently injured, but her spirit became even more determined in its fight for freedom.

Moreover, Hamer demonstrated her determined womanist spirit by her leadership in initiating the Mississippi Freedom Democratic Party (MFDP) in 1964 as an alternative to the state's whites-only Democratic Party. As elected vice-chair of the delegation, Hamer testified on television before the national credentials committee about the restrictive atmosphere in which blacks lived in Mississippi and argued that the white delegation from the Democratic Party had been seated through a fraudulent process. The MFDP asked the credentials committee to not seat the Democratic Party's all-white delegation, but rather the biracial MFDP delegation, as the representatives of Mississippi. Hamer used her womanist voice on national television and also exposed and "talked back" to black and white patriarchs in her midst who protected northern liberal democrats. In an interview, Hamer disclosed that Roy Wilkins, the executive secretary of the NAACP, said to her, "You people have put your point across. You don't know anything, you're ignorant, you don't know anything about politics. I've been in the business over twenty years. You people have put your point across, now why don't you pack up and go home?" (*Southern Exposure* 1993:71). The MFDP's lawyer, Joseph Rauh, reported to Hamer that their actions could jeopardize Hubert Humphrey's chances of being nominated for vice-president of the United States. Upon meeting Mr. Humphrey, Hamer said, "Well, Mr. Humphrey, do you mean to tell me that your position is more important to you than 400,000 black lives?" (*Southern Exposure* 1993:71). Hamer continued to fight for seats for the MFDP at the national convention. When a long-time friend conceded to Hamer that perhaps the MFDP would have to listen to leaders in the Democratic Party, Hamer indicated that the leaders of SNCC were her role models, and as for other leaders she asserted boldly, "Don't go telling me about anybody that ain't been in Mississippi two weeks and don't know nothing about the problem because they're not leading us" (*Southern Exposure* 1993:71). After the 1964 national Democratic Party convention in Atlantic City concluded, Hamer continued her battle to register voters in Mississippi. She summed up her experiences and articulated her womanist voice saying, "You see, this is not Mississippi's problem, it is America's problem. All of it is America's problem" (*Contemporary Black Leaders* 1970:127).

Hamer and Black Religion

While the white American South worked earnestly to break the back and spirit of Mrs. Hamer and others, the religion of the black church provided a message that she was made in God's image and was therefore a splendid creation. Reflecting on her decision to volunteer to register to vote, Hamer explained, "When they asked for those to raise their hands who'd go down to the courthouse the next day, I raised mine. Had it up as high as I could get it. I guess if I'd had any sense I'd a-been a little scared, but what was the point to being scared. The only thing they whites could do was kill me and it seemed like they'd been trying to do that a little bit at a time since I could remember" ("To Praise Our Bridges" in *Mississippi Writers*:324).

The call to which Hamer responded that night was a rallying cry for blacks to fight for justice; its message was not only biblically based, it was proclaimed in the midst of a beloved community which struggled daily to have a decent life. The harassment, beatings, and hardships that Hamer encountered during the fight for freedom were tempered by a spiritual essence cultivated in the black church. Reflecting on the life of Jesus and her role in the Civil Rights movement, she articulated the following: "Christ was a revolutionary person, out there where it was happening. That's what God is all about, and that's where I get my strength" (King 1982:20). Moreover, Hamer had a gift of synthesizing biblical themes with allusions to the civil rights struggle in song. These compositions were the essence of a bold theology of civil rights. For instance, she took the familiar song, "Go Tell It on the Mountain," and synthesized it with "Go Down Moses":

> Go tell it on the mountain
> over the hills and everywhere
> go tell it on the mountain
> that Jesus Christ is born.

In the next verse she sang,

> When Israel was in Egypt's land, let my people go
> oppressed so hard they could not stand, let my people go
> Go down Moses, way down in Egypt's land;
> Tell old Pharaoh, let my people go.

She followed this verse with several others:

> Paul and Silas was bound in jail, let my people go
> Had no money for to go their bail, let my people go.
>
> Paul and Silas began to shout, let my people go.
> Jail doors open and they walked out, let my people go.
>
> Who's that yonder dressed in red? Let my people go.
> Must be the children that Moses led, let my people go.
>
> Who's that yonder dressed in black? Let my people go.
> Must be the hypocrites turning back, let my people go.
>
> Who's that yonder dressed in blue? Let my people go.
> Must be the children now passing through, let my people go.

> I had a little book he gave to me, let my people go.
> And every page spelled victory, let my people go.

She concluded with a final verse:

> Go tell it on the mountain, over the hills and everywhere
> Go tell it on the mountain, let my people go!

Mrs. Hamer's womanist voice proclaimed in song the necessity for the birth of Christ and the declaration of the Israelites' struggle for freedom from Pharaoh to be reported everywhere. Her own personal life commitment to Christ was to be affirmed by her works as she stood up to the Pharaohs of her own time (Marsh 1996:16).

Christinah Nku's Womanist Works

Mokotuli Nku, the daughter of Enock Lethamaha and Magdalene Serati, was born in the Transvaal region of South Africa[1] in 1894, baptized during her childhood, and given the Christian name Christinah. Her life spanned nine decades; hence, from birth to old age, she experienced the multilayered and complex history of her native land, South Africa. Consequently, as an African woman, she lived with the devastating effects of segregation administrated by local authorities in Johannesburg and formal apartheid as executed by the Nationalists in 1948.

When she was thirty years old, Nku had a dream about a large brick church with twelve doors, and she heard a voice telling her to build a church for God. The voice told her that her children would help to build the church, and that her son John would one day be the chief priest of all of the churches emerging from the original church with twelve doors. This dream gave Nku the conviction to establish her own church, whose primary ministry was for the healing of the sick.

Mother Nku's healing treatments were initially administered to people who lived in African townships on the Witwatersrand.[2] During the period from 1913 to 1940, black people who lived in townships on the Witwatersrand were proletarians from various social locations. Many were migrants who worked in mines and lived in single-sex hostels, others were "*amakumsha* or *abaphakathi*," people who lived betwixt and between, some lived on the margins because they had neither an economic base in rural areas nor wage work, and finally many were forced to relinquish their land and establish life in the city (Koch 1983:151).

During and after World War I, the African population on the Witwatersrand soared because the effects of the 1913 Land Act caused entire families to enter a proletarian status (Koch 1983:152). Manufacturing and commercial businesses like the mining industry paid wages that were based on the subsistence needs of an individual worker. These industries refused to add capital to public housing for workers. Moreover, Africans were impacted by the coalition between local capitalists and white workers who insisted on a policy of residential segregation that became public policy, as formulated by the Stallard Commission and enacted in the 1923 Urban Areas Act. This policy enshrined the white suprema-cist belief that "natives—men, women and children—should only be permitted within municipal areas in so far and for so long as their presence is demanded by the wants of the white population."[3] While an act of the Supreme Court in 1926 made the 1923 Urban Areas act void because alternative housing was not avail-able for Africans, white landowners cashed in on this ruling by building shanty towns in the city and charging excessive rents (Koch 1983:153). White residents moved out of the areas occupied by black renters and "old 'fashionable' sub-urbs were transformed into highly crowded slumyard areas" (Koch 1983:154). Slumyards grew all over Johannesburg and included areas such as Doorn-fontein, Vrededorp, and Prospect Township, all of which were in close proxim-ity to the healing ministry of Mother Nku.

The wilderness that black people experienced daily is highlighted in a report published by the Johannesburg "Joint Council of Europeans and Natives" in 1921. The wages paid by Johannesburg industry were woefully inadequate since they were based on the "industrial male worker" who was not related to his family. The report claims that:

> the native engaged in town work looks for quarters of his own and per-haps brings his family with him. Under these altered circumstances it is impossible for the wages received ... to meet the requirements of town dwellers.[4]

Children were forced to move to the city to look for employment because of the extreme poverty in rural areas, but jobs were not always available. This resulted in high unemployment and social deterioration in urban areas occupied by Africans. In 1924, J. D. Rheinhallt Jones, a liberal, wrote about the social situa-tion of some African workers who "have become aged, crippled or otherwise incapacitated from earning a livelihood ... the living conditions under which some of them exist and eke out a precarious living are deplorable."[5] Another report written by the Director of Native Labour in 1937 indicated that one hun-dred thousand children, women, and men were unemployed on the Witwaters-rand. In the same year, Councillor A. Immink reported that ninety-three thousand people in the same area did not have the means to live decently as "they live by their wits, sleep with their friends at night and are not included in the census."[6] The conditions of life, the squalor, lack of sanitation, high rents, and overcrowding produced a horrific situation for Africans. These factors also contributed to the genocide of Africans, as the infant mortality rate for black children was double that of whites for the period between 1923 and 1936 (Phillips 1938:110).

Mother Nku practiced her ministry in these areas where social and economic conditions were oppressive. Thousands of desolate and forlorn people gathered daily at her two-room Prospect Township home for prayer and healing services which were held daily at 5 A.M., 9 A.M., 3 P.M., and 7 P.M. (August n.d.:2).

If the vicious and inhuman white supremacist policies that formed the sociopolitical environment for black life in South Africa constituted the context for Christinah Nku's life, and healing rituals were the agency through which she willfully and vigorously gave witness to her profound religious faith and dedication to her community, then prophecy gave Nku a commitment to her life's work that reflected theological urgency and "oppositional engagement"[7] against the suffering of African people.

Nku's singular focus in life was listening to messages from God. As a result, she was not a political activist in the usual sense of the term. She did not attend political meetings, nor did she belong to a political party.[8] Nku believed herself to be an agent of God on earth. God told her what to do, and she resolutely carried out her assignments. This life of pure devotion and unyielding attention to God led her to create healing rituals which liberated the oppressed to such an extent that they were empowered to believe that they were worthy of and entitled to food, shelter, and clothing.

As the Union of South Africa became an apartheid state and the genocide of black people more overt, Nku's church grew rapidly, and congregations spread all over South Africa and its borders. Nku's ministry expanded, while her church grew, through the establishment of schools for children and programs for youth and adults. People's lives were transformed and this directly benefited the community. Nku's ministry was subversive in that it functioned as a "hidden transcript"[9] which was a response to systems that dominated the poor. According to Ramphele, "apartheid" as a system "affect[ed] people's sense of well being along a continuum" (Ramphele: August 12, 1992, personal communication). Though there were a variety of responses to apartheid, the ministry of Nku was the medium through which poor people disempowered by a brutal state system "talked back."[10] The bodies of black people afflicted with manifold illnesses, undoubtedly rooted in the stressful social situations in which they lived, were resurrected from the death-dealing system of racial discrimination through the healing rituals and the community that Mother Nku provided.

Assessments of Hamer and Nku

The strength of Fannie Lou Hamer was the reality that though she was born into poverty, poverty was not in her vision, determination, or emotional constitution. She did not allow an abject circumstantial social location to limit her commitment to the fight for justice. Quite the contrary, her acute destitution within the political economy of the United States tied her intimately to the hardships of others who shared the pain and challenges of being black, poor, and (for women, the added layer of) female. For instance, four years before her death in 1977, Hamer testified on behalf of several young black women in a lawsuit concerning the denial of their employment at a local Mississippi school district because they were single mothers. Hamer recontextualized the debate from the immorality of single mothers (the argument advanced by the opposing attorney) into a theological realm when she eloquently stated:

> We still love these children. And after these babies are born we are not going to disband these children from their families. . . . God breathed life into them just like he did into us. And I think these children have a right to live. And I think that these mothers have a right to support them in a decent way. . . What would have happened to Virgin Mary if she walked into that school, what would have happened if Christ had been born into that school? . . . We are dealing with human beings. (Derr 1994:22)

In her own fashion, Hamer embodied a practical liberation theology from below, that is, from the situation of all marginalized peoples and especially poor folk. Her clarity about the christological dimension of poverty, in the above case as it related to black women, marks her as a precursor of contemporary womanist and black theologies. With fearlessness and forthrightness, she talked back to mainstream established authority figures and sacrosanct institutions. She persisted in positing Jesus as the result of an unwed mother who lacked capital to stay in housing and, therefore, gave birth to the savior and liberator of humanity on a barn floor amidst a crowd of dumb beasts huddled in animal dung. In contrast, if Jesus arrived on today's scene, he would feel accepted and right at home with unwed, poor, black mothers struggling to make ends meet for their children while suffering the stings of racist arrows from dominating powers too callous to distinguish privilege and profits from people and personhood.

Furthermore, Hamer was able to live out daily her Christian commitment for the full humanity of all of God's creation. A faith grounded in the full spiritual and material humanity of the least in society—a theology from below—mandated a witnessing in the public domain about what side the Lord was on, thereby clarifying the side for Christian practice. Such a public posture of Christian faith required risking not only her voice in talking back, it, moreover, necessitated risking her physical being to the point of actual death. And Hamer bore the scars of right-wing racist beatings on her broken body until her death. For her, to "go tell it on the mountain" meant more than symbolic and metaphorical discourse or the persuasive styles of alliterative linguistics. Though her oratorical skills gave evidence of her astute handling of talking back, she lived out a belief in a God of freedom and a Jesus who dwelled among the poor. And these sacred faith principles gave life to both her talking and walking in the shadow of literal bodily harm and death's sordid grasp.

Even though Hamer was "sick and tired of being sick and tired," at the same time, she never tired of singing, "This little light of mine, I'm gonna let it shine." Indeed, Hamer struggled among many such apparently paradoxical juxtapositions. She recognized the tension and stress faced by the Christian warrior and the inevitable suffering from battle fatigue, but she compensated for such dangers by her emboldened faith and courageous acts, as signified in inspirational lyrics to let her and other poor folks' lights shine. One could justifiably claim that Hamer employed lyrics and songs of struggle and joy as rituals of renewal amid conditions deleterious to her physical and mental health. She had to say she was sick of being tired to ventilate the frustrations of an apparently overwhelming opposition; yet the hope of light shining channeled that frustration into an uplifting moment surrounding other civil rights freedom fighters. Thus the ritual of singing served as positive negotiations of harmful feelings and as spiritual armor for colleagues attempting to make a way out of the no way of segregation.

Mother Christinah Nku listened to the voice of God and deployed a very basic resource available to all people—water—as an all-encompassing remedy for spiritual and material illness among poor black South Africans. Unlike Hamer who took on the larger macroconfigurations of segregation's economic, political, and racial attacks, Nku situated her survival and resistance ministry at the micro-local level of individual healing. For her the weapons of faith were the rituals of healing. Rituals of healing took on a strict regimen of purifications and spiritual discipline for black South African shack dwellers. Every day of the week she held Christian healing services. Members of the church and surrounding communities seeking relief from polluted environments (whether polluted by the material effects of apartheid or by the lack of spiritual connections to one's ancestors, family, or community) came to her St. John's Apostolic Faith Mission Church to undergo the rigorous regimen of water prescriptions in the form of drinking, bathing, vomiting, and enemas. Spiritual and regularized rituals became cornerstones of Christian manifestations of faith.

However, Nku's Christianity was not merely a carbon copy or epiphenomenon of white missionary doctrine and principles. On the contrary, she understood the necessity of poor black people indigenizing the gospel in their native cultures. That is why she combined a reinterpreted missionary Christianity from whites with the cultural contours of African sensibilities. For instance, Nku synthesized the prophetic role of the Hebrew scriptures with the diviner's hermeneutic found in African cultures and religion. Hence propheting became a central ritual whereby the church pastor spoke truth by telling congregants about the causes of their sickness and instructing them about what types of sacrifices to ancestors were required. At the same time, propheting could entail advising church members to pursue traditional biomedicine prescriptions.

An additional manifestation of embracing Christianity within the cultural particularities of poor black folk is shown in the combination of the worshiping of Jesus and the veneration of African ancestors. Jesus is viewed as an ancestor, that is, one whose spirit is present and alive beyond the expiration of the body. At the same time the doctrine of the Trinity is not of central importance because children are not equal to their parents in most African cultures. Thus, Jesus could not possibly be equal to God. Just as Jesus assumed a central place within the belief, cosmology, and adoration rituals of Mother Nku's Christianity, so did veneration of African ancestors. The latter had passed over into the spirit realm and were, thus, closer to and in more direct communication with God. The living Christian did not forget obligations or ritual symbolizations owed the ancestors, because those recently dead acted as intercessors with Jehovah or *Thixo*, the indigenous name for the Christian God, on behalf of the living. Therefore Jesus and the ancestors located themselves within a Christian and indigenous pantheon, which proved essential to the rituals of healing and conversations between God and humanity.

In addition Nku created successful practical strategies for survival for non-elites suffering within a world that classified them as bestial servants for white supremacist privileges. St. John's Church became a shelter for the homeless, even though homes were no more than shacks which barely withstood the cold wet winds, especially in areas such as Cape Town. Community members from far away literally interpreted St. John's as a hospital for healing, and many sought sanctuary there from sicknesses before and after visiting mainstream doctors. In fact, in my years of fieldwork at St. John's, not one person interviewed ever stated that the church's rituals of healing ever failed them. The unemployed also gravitated to the church, because those without a livelihood perceived St. John's as a rock in a weary land comprised of an always welcoming extended family atmosphere. Likewise black South Africans traveling from rural to urban areas utilized the church as a loving and familiar way station, a beacon of refuge and hope.

Finally Mother Nku exhibited and embodied in her syncretized African Christianity the power of female spirituality and faith—a testament to the reality that poor black women not only hold up half the sky, they, at least in the realm of Nku, provide a spiritual paradigm of leadership, innovation, and consistent conviction. Though her husband, Archbishop John Nku, became the head of the initial church due to the strictures of a patriarchal system existing within Christian and African indigenous discourses, nonetheless Mother Nku had the vision from God to inaugurate St. John's Apostolic Faith Mission Church; and therefore she proved to be the medium for the Holy Spirit's presence in a church which today numbers more than two million.

Integrated Lessons for Today

Despite poverty and all other circumstances and all kinds of unsavory social conditions, poor black women on both sides of the Atlantic teach us that the Christian faith and witness empower us to assert our voices and struggle for personal, communal, spiritual, and material well-being. To be accountable to our calling before the leadership of Jesus and our ever-present ancestors, we rejoice in the moment; because the future which is promised to us includes those departed, the salvation and liberation way of Jesus, and the brightness of that which is to come with our unborn.

In the pain and the pleasure, the hope and the promise, we are called to believe that being born in poverty does not necessitate allowing the dregs of poverty to be in us. Furthermore, a practical liberation theology has to embrace a prominent role for healing of the broken-hearted through the implementation of ritualized acts of spiritual discipline. To heal ourselves is fundamentally a spiritual exercise upon our real bodies. Similarly, our struggle to be full human beings at every level of this world and the next denotes the power of singing in the throes of despair and formidable circumstances. Though trouble may seem to last always, we sing because we know that joy comes in the morning. And culture, black culture (that is, African and African American) assumes an important role in Christian ministry and practice. What good is religion if the culture of the poor is not evident in the feel, rhythm, language, and smells of faith?

Practical strategies manifested in lived-out Christian commitments complete the challenging lessons presented to us by Fannie Lou Hamer and Mother Christinah Nku. One was a warrior who chose to step out in her belief in the civil rights of blacks as God-given grace. It cost her a permanently broken body. The other stepped out on a vision from God to go build a church grounded in the healing power of water. Both point to the powerful potential and realized authenticity of poor black women doing God's work through recognizing, accepting, risking, and implementing gifts of divine grace from on high to rebuild a new world on earth down here. In the saying of black South African women, "When you have touched the woman, you have struck a rock." And likewise in the mother to daughter wisdom of African American women, we learn "If you put at least two black women together, they can hit a straight lick with a crooked stick and make the impossible possible."

Bibliography

August, Lydia. "How St. John's Apostolic Faith Mission Came into Being." Family unpublished records. Evaton, Transvaal, Republic of South Africa, n.d.

Collum, Danny. "Stepping Out into Freedom." *Sojourners Magazine*, vol. 11, no. 11 (Dec. 1982): 3-4, 10-21.

Derr, Mary Krane. "Letting Everyone's Light Shine: The Life and Work of Fannie Low Hamer (1912-1977)." *Daughters of Sarah*, vol. 20, no. 4 (Fall 1994): 21.

Fox, Elton C., ed. "Fannie Lou Hamer." In *Contemporary Black Leaders*. New York: Dodd, Mead, and Co., 1970, 114-30.

Hamer, Fannie Lou. "To Praise Our Bridges." *Mississippi Writers: Reflections of Childhood and Youth*, vol. 2. Ed. Dorothy Abbot. Jackson: University Press of Mississippi, 1986, 321-30.

hooks, bell. *Talking Back: Thinking Feminist, Thinking Black*. Boston: South End Press, 1988.

King, Edwin. "A Prophet from the Delta." *Sojourners Magazine*, vol. 11, no. 11 (Dec. 1982): 18.

Koch, Eddie. "'Without Visible Means of Subsistence': Slumyard Culture in Johannesburg 1918-1940." In *Town and Countryside in the Transvaal*. Ed. Belinda Bozzoli. Johannesburg: Ravan Press, 1983, 151-75.

Marsh, Charles. "The Self for Others in Lived Experience: Questions to Bonhoeffer from the American Civil Rights Movement." Unpublished paper presented at the Bonhoeffer Congress, University of Cape Town, January 1996.

Martin, Clarice. "The Miry Bog, the Desolate Pit, a New Song in My Mouth." *A Troubling in My Soul: Womanist Perspectives on Evil and Suffering*. Ed. Emilie M. Townes. Maryknoll, N.Y.: Orbis Books, 1993: 13-36.

"Mississippi Freedom Democratic Party," *Southern Exposure,* vol. 21, no. 1-2 (Spring 1993): 71.

Phillips, Ray E. *The Bantu in the City: A Study of Cultural Adjustment on the Witwatersrand.* Lovedale: The Lovedale Press, 1938.

Scott, James C. *Domination and the Arts of Resistance: Hidden Transcripts.* New Haven: Yale University Press, 1990.

Notes

1. This region is now called "Gauteng."

2. The Witwatersrand is a geographic area in Johannesburg.

3. Report of the Local Government Commission of Enquiry (Stallard), TP 1, 1922, 241.

4. Johannesburg Joint Council of Europeans and Natives, Report of the Wages Committee, 1921, 1.

5. Rheinhallt Jones, Memorandum, "Home for Destitute Native Children," 31 January 1934.

6. *The Star*, October 22, 1937.

7. Clarice Martin (1993:21) uses this term for Maria Stewart's biblical commitment and spiritual determination for African Americans to have racial equality in the nineteenth century.

8. While Mother Nku saw her role as a visionary totally committed to God's work and healing, her husband Lazarus and their daughter, Lydia, were members of the African National Congress (ANC) and extremely active in the resistance movement.

9. See James C. Scott's, *Domination and the Arts of Resistance: Hidden Transcripts* (1990) for a detailed cross-cultural presentation about subalterns' response to power and domination.

10. See bell hooks's *Talking Back* (1988) for more detail about the ways that subordinates are empowered when they speak truth to authority.

15

Black Latin American Theology

A New Way to Sense, to Feel, and to Speak of God

SILVIA REGINA DE LIMA SILVA

The day will come when we will not need to leave our blackness to be Christians.

D. Jose Maria Pires, Brazil

The black community makes up a significant part of the Latin American population. That assertion becomes more relevant if we recognize their important role in the economic and cultural development of this continent. In our past, the labor of black men and women in the large plantations of coffee, bananas, and sugar cane, as well as their work in the mines and the metallurgic industry, has been fundamental for the economic development of the Latin American countries, where they were sold as slaves.

Nevertheless, today as yesterday we find that the great majority of the black population forms part of those groups that are excluded from participating in and appropriating the fruits of technical and economic development. The struggle to have access to basic needs such as housing, food, education, and health care, along with the struggle to see the recovery of and respect for their history and culture, continues to be a challenge at this end of the century.

This reality makes us black Latin Americans ask about God, and it poses questions about the spirituality that has nourished the black community in times of Calvary and the experiences of Easter that they have been able to celebrate in different moments of history. We cannot omit the great question about the face of God that sometimes is hidden and manifested in the Afro-Latin American experience.

The reflections presented in this essay seek to share that which has been gathered in the thinking about God from the experience of the black community in Latin America. First, we recover the memories of pain as a form of denouncement of what the Christian experience meant for our ancestors. These recollections of oppression are pages that cannot be erased from our history. Secondly, the black experience has become more complete with the discovery of new faces of God that had been covered over by an ethnocentric theology turned back on itself. This made the churches incapable of recognizing and dialoguing with the distinct ways of experiencing and thinking about God present in the continent.

We invite you to start to walk on the path of the blackening of theology and to discover a new way to sense, to feel, and to speak about God.

A Theology of Racism

The history of the black community is marked by different forms of racism. We understand racism as a belief that assumes that the observable physical differences between groups of individuals are of a qualitative significance that has to do with levels of intelligence, emotions, moral conduct, and inclinations toward certain activities or artistic forms and experiences.[1] Latin American racism as an ideology has its roots in slavery and finds one of its origins in theology.[2] Thus, the theological foundation of black slavery is an expression of that theology.

In the case of Brazil, theological formulations which tried to legitimate slavery had three principal authors: Antonio Vieira, Jorge Benci, and Andre João Antonil. The discourse of these three authors along with other theological developments of this era shaped the theology of slavery. It was used above all in sermons that were directed either toward slaves or their owners. What was the content of these sermons? What follows is an investigation into this question.

Theology Directed toward Slaves

In the discourse directed to the slaves, we find two principal themes: a theology of transmigration and a theology of retribution. The theology of *transmigration* was based on the assertion that the black community needed to pass through successive migrations as a process of purification in order to obtain the salvation of their souls. Among the texts used was Genesis 9:18-27, the curse against Ham. The way this text was taught identified the Africans as descendants of Ham, cursed by Noah, which meant that they were perpetually condemned to slavery. According to Vieira, one of the representatives of this theology, the departure of the blacks from Africa to the Americas was a first transmigration. The second would be from the Americas to heaven. In this way, slavery was a necessary step as part of God's plan of salvation for this people. This bondage benefited the blacks because it provided them with the possibility to have an encounter with the Christian faith. Still, in the theology of slavery, the body was captive but the soul was free after having been liberated from the power of the devil that reigned in Africa.[3]

The Portuguese conquered western Ethiopia and today are fulfilling their obligation, better and more than in any part of the world, in the Americas, where having brought the same Ethiopians in such a great number, all kneeling on the earth, and arms raised to heaven, [they] believe, confess and worship in the rosary of Our Lady all the mysteries of the incarnation, death and resurrection of our Creator and Redeemer of the world, as the true Son of God and of the Virgin Mary.[4]

In this theology, baptism was the sign of rescue and redemption for the blacks: rescue of their souls which were enslaved in Africa and redemption from the original sins that they brought. The first sin was for being the son of Adam, and the second was for being the son of Ham. There were three places reserved for black slaves: Africa as hell where the body and soul were held captive, Brazil as purgatory where only the body was held captive, and heaven where they could finally enjoy freedom.[5]

The second approach to theological reflection was the theology of *retribution*. This theology taught the black slaves patience and submission in the suffering that they experienced because of their condition. The practice of these virtues, they were told, made them like Christ; and through this suffering they would obtain eternal happiness.

What you must do is to conserve these examples: suffer with patience the work of your station; be very grateful to God for the moderation of your captivity to which He brought you; and above all avail yourself to Him to obtain freedom and happiness in the other life that does not pass but will endure forever.[6]

Theology Directed toward the Slave Owners

The task of teaching and initiating the slaves into the Christian life was a key element in the theological discourse dictated toward the owners of slaves. Antonil tells us:

The masters say that the slaves do not have the capacity to learn to confess nor to ask pardon from God, nor to pray the rosary, nor to know the Ten Commandments; all because of lack of teaching and because you do not believe that the slaves are accountable to God. . . . Nor do you obligate them to hear mass on All Saints' Days, you keep them busy so that they do not have time for that; neither do you give the chaplain additional salary to teach them.[7]

Another element present in the preaching to the masters was to ask them to not exaggerate the application of corporal punishment. When punishing their human property, slave owners were admonished to observe what the Bible says:

Punishments should be given in moderation. The number of lashes should follow the biblical instruction with care. God commanded in the old law that if someone commits a crime for which the delinquent deserves to be whipped, the judges will give the order and the quantity will depend upon the quality of guilt, the lashes being no more than forty. The reason to limit this number is given by God himself: So that your brother will not be degraded and indignantly mistreated, and you see him cruelly wounded and afflicted (Deut. 25:23). . . . From this you will understand the reason why the Hebrews desiring so anxiously to drink the blood of Saint Paul and condemning him at times to lashes, the Apostle himself affirms in the Second Epistle to the Corinthians (2 Cor. 11:24) that he never received forty lashes, they always gave him less.[8]

Slave women were also victims of mistreatment; they were not even respected when they were pregnant. However, the slave owners' attitude toward slave women appeared to have a certain sensibility in relation to women. But, in fact, their perspective and practice were based in economic interests.

One should not permit that the administrators kick pregnant women mainly in the stomach, nor hit them with a rod because one does not calculate a blow in anger and they could mortally injure the head of a borrowed slave that is worth a lot of money.[9]

Here we are faced with a manipulation of theological discourse, one that has been repeated in different moments of history. The fundamentalist and distorted reading of the Bible expresses what was and is part of the misappropriation of the Bible by groups that hold power.[10] As we will see, this theology left its marks and consequences.

Theology and Black Resistance

Parallel to this slave theology of transmigration and retribution, we find a black religious practice that, on the one hand, looked for a way to maintain the African roots and, on the other hand, outwardly assumed Catholicism as a form of survival. In other words, the original African religion, condemned by the church and society, was practiced in secret. These hidden religious rituals and ways of life were carried out at great risks. In fact, black women or men who were caught practicing indigenous African religion were severely punished, some even with death sentences. In relation to this theme, a grandmother tells us the story of old Andre.

The great fame of the Blacks is to be a witch doctor. True or not, it was seen as such. True or not the Black Andre, with his hair now white and body bent over because of his years, was condemned. A child on the plantation was sick. Truly, she was dying. Her whole body was swollen. The doctor couldn't do anything to cure her. Black Andre came with his *mezinhas*[11] prepared with the herbs of the jungle that only the Blacks and Indigenous knew. The old man prepared the tea, bathed the child, and gave her some tea. He also lit a candle in the jungle and another beside the child's bed. He threw out the tea leaves that he had prepared and cleaned up well the room where the child was. After seven days the child could stand up, she was now healed.

That is all. The Black's destiny was already known. Condemned to death. In that plantation in Recife[12] a Black who acted as a sorcerer or witch doctor was cast into fire. Andre could not escape. The master decided to give him a different kind of death. He said to everyone: "I want to see a witch doctor cooking just like he cooked the leaves to make his spell." He ordered a huge pot to be heated with oil. On a night with a full moon he called everyone to attend the biggest spell ever cast. The Blacks looked and everyone was afraid and could imagine what was going to happen. When the oil was boiling he ordered for Andre to be put in the pot and cooked until he was transformed into tea to be served to anyone from time on, who might cast a spell. He ordered it and it was done.[13]

The strong repression and violence against the African religion led the black community to be creative in order to resist and to preserve their traditional beliefs. For instance, religious parallelism, which some classify as syncretism, was a form of black resistance. This parallelism is characterized by the essential elements of Christian and African faiths living side by side. Behind the veneration of a particular saint or an aspect of the Christian religious universe, was the worship by blacks of those elements in their own tradition. This is not to be understood as a mixing of both traditions. In other cases, we find a double religious practice. There were two distinct worlds that intertwined, coming closer and drawing apart in a movement that was dictated by the spiritual forces themselves. We can say that this understanding, accompanied by the prophetic force of those who insisted on their traditional practices, made possible the endurance of the black spiritual richness up until now.

In spite of black determination and resistance, what remained at the level of black and white relationships and in the official history and theology was the theology of slavery. Indeed, these brief reflections have shown a theology that served the ideological apparatus to justify slavery. Furthermore, the explicit racism in the examples we have presented could lead us to believe that we are looking at a theology of the past, historically distant and now overcome.

But before beginning the theme of black theology today in Latin America, we would like to present a small, but more contemporary, illustration. This indicates how the racism, as we have defined it at the beginning of this work, and the theology of racism have left their mark on theological language, liturgies, hymns, and other expressions of Christian faith. Who in Latin America does not remember the black heart and the white heart used in Sunday schools and catechism classes to symbolize the sinful heart and the pure heart where Jesus lives? An example from a 1956 hymn book depicts exactly what we have just argued.

"My Name Is There"

Chorus:
Oh, the precious Book

of your eternal Reign!
I am always happy
if my name is there.

My sins are many,
like the sand of the sea,
but thy precious blood
will wash them away.
Because thou hast promised
Oh, blessed Emmanuel!
If your sins are black
I will make them white.[14]

Even today, sin continues to be black and salvation white. For black children, who hear this from the time they are little in catechism classes or Sunday school, it is difficult to convince them of the worthiness of their culture and their value as a people.[15] We could continue on this theme with other examples.

Black theology was born in Latin America because of these and other forms of racism in the churches, theology, and society. Black theology is a movement that searches, through theological reflection, questioning, and recreating within theology the symbolic universe of the Christian churches, for a place for black culture. Consequently, the discovery of a God that takes on their pain, their culture, and their history has made possible the recovery of the black community's self-esteem.

What, then, is Latin American black theology? Its objectives and methodology will be the themes of the analysis that follows.

Toward a Latin American Black Theology[16]
A Black Way of Doing Theology Is Born[17]

Latin American black theology is a part of the theologies of liberation.[18] It is a communal theology that has come out of the process of re-establishing black identity and culture. We believe that black theology, in the broadest sense, has been present since the arrival of the blacks, with their experience of God, to this Latin American continent. This experience is transmitted in codes different from that of Western theology. It is a religious system where oral tradition is the basic principle for the initiation and the transmission of knowledge. For that reason, there is no sacred book, thesis, or written doctrine. It will not be possible in the space of this essay to go deeper into the complex nature and meaning of this dynamic. But we believe it is important to mention it, not only because there existed an original African religion, but also because this process remains a part of Latin American black theology as one of the sources that feeds today's theological reflection. We will return to this point later on.

The process of systematizing Latin American black theology is recent. We cannot speak of its exact origin in a certain place because there have been works being done on this theme in different parts of the continent for a while now. But we can take, as a point of reference, the Consultation on Black Culture and Theology organized by the Ecumenical Association of Third World Theologians in 1985.[19] Indeed, this was the first occasion of sharing the different works and experiences, of blackness and theologizing, from different countries. Here too at this gathering, participants began to perceive common elements and diversities that characterized black theological reflection.

In a related manner, the theme of gender has been present from the beginning. In the Latin American context, grassroots theological groups have usually had a majority of women. But if we were to speak of their roles in the theological academy, there are very few women who participate. In addition to the examples of reflection carried on in co-ed groups, we create specific women's groups to be able to reflect on our own interests. The systematization and written works follow these reflections. Still, it is a challenge to make black feminist theology known.

One of the characteristics of Latin American black theological work is its communitarian nature. From the beginning, the groups focusing on black theology had an important place in the reflection and systematization of the theology. Methodologies were developed that made it possible to begin a process of collective work, encouraging the participants of groups and communities to write down their ideas and experiences.[20]

Body, Identity, and Theology

Collective experiences of the pain of racism and the presence of God within the struggles of resistance for dignity and life are the starting points for black theological reflection. Suffering and resistance are meeting places between God and the black community. More specifically, black reflection and consciousness groups begin with the experience of black women's and men's bodies, reserving their first meetings to recount their stories.[21] From their personal stories they go on to the reconstruction of the collective memory. This bringing together of the past and the present gives liberating and politically transforming significance to life. Thus, to recover the historical memory is an important step in the rediscovery of the black body in the search for identity and in the self-reconstruction as a people.

The discovery and the strengthening of black history and identity bring about a significant change in the lives of black men and women. In the context of racial discrimination, where the prevalence of values are white and Western, where the patterns of behavior, beauty, and theological production are determined by this dominant culture, to discover and accept the black identity is to re-encounter oneself and the black community. Moreover, it is a step that motivates and nourishes the doing of theology. It means a re-encounter with God or a re-encounter with a different way of thinking about God. This new existential framework leads to an attitude of permanent suspicion toward the religious values imposed by white Western Christianity. Now, a desire/need arises to rethink God, to discover a new language, a new way to speak of the religious experience characteristic of the black community.

Presence in the Ecclesial Body

In itself, the discovery of the black community and God implies a new ecclesial presence. The presence and participation of black women and men in the churches in Latin America present a challenge and, at the same time, provide a permanent richness. And black theology has been an important space that systematizes, questions, and brings about this relationship.

A first challenge to the churches was to recognize the reality of black men and women within the church. The first challenge was to the blacks themselves, in the sense of recognizing their own identity, history, and culture. This remains true, because, as we affirmed earlier, to be black in a racist society means a constant exercise in the affirmation of identity. The challenge is also directed toward the congregations, that is, to discover ethnic-racial diversity as part of their situation. Underneath the discourse of equality within the church, diversity was hidden and continues to be hidden. Even more than hidden, diversity is denied by those who make up the ecclesial community. The church lives under a racist totalizing, hegemonic culture that has been confused with the Christian faith.

The second step was to recognize the racism present in ecclesial practice. For some sectors of the churches, it was possible to recognize racist attitudes in the past or as a social sin, but not as a present reality in ecclesial institutions. When blacks and black theology began to point out racial oppression within the church, they were interpreted as being racist. Moreover, they were seen as those who wanted to be different, encouraging feelings of revolt and provoking divisions within the community. But the churches, who are touched by God's Spirit present in the cry and song of the black community, little by little overcome their prejudices and begin participating in the newness that blackness brings.

One more step is the recognition that blacks renounce racism but at the same time bring good news that enriches church life. The first and most visible contribution can be seen in liturgical life. In Brazil and other countries of Latin America and the Caribbean, where there is a black presence, there emerge new ways to celebrate that are more participatory, more incarnational, alive, corporal, symbolic, and committed to memory and history. Such a theological reflection accompanies the liturgy and gives it consistency and brings together the challenges that arise. Thus the liturgical renewal comes out of the questions presented by black theology. As in liturgical life, the movement of a popular rereading of the Bible has also been enriched and is permanently challenged by the theme of blackness. This black rereading is another expression of the blackening of the faith in Latin America.[22]

In this way, we can conclude that black theology has a place in ecclesial life; but at the same time it is a critical presence that does not fit within the limits of traditional churches.

Drinking from Our Own Wells[23]

From its beginning, the experience of black theology on the Latin American continent has been diversified. It would be better to speak of black theologies.

We would like to comment on one of these theologies. This is a theological proposal that is found within the recovery of the original African religions, one of the sources that nourishes the doing of black theology. Mae menininha do Cantois, one of the most well known and important Holy Mothers of Condomble in Bahia,[24] Brazil, has said:

> God? I don't know if everyone thinks like I do, But He is the Supreme being. Besides Him, there is no one. I have a lot of respect and a lot of faith. The God of the church is the same God of Condomblé (. . .) Africa knows our God as well as we know God, with a different name, but it is the same God, with the name Olorum. God's dwelling is there above and ours is here below. It is in my belief in Him that in all these years as a Holy Mother, I have never thought of leaving my position.[25]

This double religious reality for black men and women, as we mentioned earlier, is a practice that continues today. Not surprisingly, we find many different views about this theme of dual religious encounters, perspectives from the churches as well as those from black religions and organizations. Within these different faith communities, however, are those who share both religious traditions, the black and the Christian, and experience no feelings of contradiction.

The re-encounter with the ancestral religion has meant, for many Christians, an encounter with a part of themselves that they had lost or forgotten. It is as if our hearts feel strange, the God as taught by Christianity seems lacking. Yes and no—it is something more. In this sense, and without abandoning the Christian faith, the encounter with the ancestral religions has meant an encounter with this extra something. We feel strengthened and protected as if we have returned to the embrace of our mother or father.

This experience has permitted us to find a new face for God, which has enriched our lives and has opened us up to a new spirituality. The first characteristic of this spirituality is its ecumenical nature. The black experience as well as the indigenous experience in Latin America has led us to broaden the concept of ecumenism. We blacks press the frontiers of official ecumenism so that we are taken into account. The ecumenical experience is an existential reality when we discover that God is more than that experience of God we received from the religious denomination to which we belong. Instead, black theology points toward an ecumenism that does not unite denominations and religious expressions only around the good that they have in common, but an ecumenism that respects and welcomes the differences of the various religious identities. Through the ancestral religions, we re-encounter a God who permanently takes care of life. In the history of the black community, this God has always accompanied us, and has always invented ways, each day, to demonstrate that, yes, God has been present. In the Afro religions, we perceive that this means a preoccupation with concrete life, as expressed in a special way with care for the body and with the basic conditions of life. We feel God's care through the Holy Mother who cares for the health of her sons and daughters. The teas and the herbal baths are an expression of this attention and care.

Being an ancestral religion (i.e., the Afro or African religions), the idea and maintenance of community has a very important place. Specifically, the structure of the community is like a family—a very large family in which the mother, father, aunts, uncles, sons, and daughters all take part. In addition, their ancestors, who have passed on but remain in a different form, manifest themselves and dwell among their loved ones. In this perspective and practice of the community, the woman has a special place and role. She, above all, is entrusted with the secret of the divine. She is the priestess, par excellence, who transmits the Axé,[26] that is to say, energy or vital force. Another aspect is in the value given to elderly men and women. They are the carriers and guardians of wisdom, memory, and the mysteries of God and nature. Basically, this authority is recognized because of their years of service and dedication. And finally, the elderly women, carriers of the blessing, are in charge of training and initiating the young.

Becoming acquainted with this source of our religious experience has given us the possibility of a liberating relationship with our own bodies. The God of our mothers and fathers is manifested through the body. This God dances, sings, caresses, and embraces, is joyful in celebration, and likes the beautiful colors and the sound of drums. This can be seen in worship and in other expressions of the religion.

In addition to the theological significance of the body, harmony with nature opens us to communion with the cosmos. Trees are important, also stones, rivers, the seas, the earth; all have a place, a function. They are a word, a memory of God.

To speak about this theme is to open the heart and let loose precious memories and experiences of God. We have limited ourselves to only a few, even though the richness of the theme could lead us to others. We think it is important to reaffirm that we are not dealing with distinct experiences of faith, or better said, they are distinct but not exclusive. In this, it seems to us, there is something new that is worthwhile investigating and deepening further, though that is not possible to do in this essay.

Conclusion: Black Latin American Theology or Spirituality?

The objective of this essay has been to show some elements that underscore the process of black Latin American theological production. The limited space has meant that we have highlighted only some aspects. There are other dimensions and experiences that we could share. Maybe a way of concluding would be to revisit the meaning of the word "theology" within the reflection of black theology.

One of the issues that frequently came up during the initial reflections on black theology in Latin America was in relation to the form of identification, or what to call black theological production. Some identified it as black liberation theology due to its relation, at the methodological level, to liberation theology, and, for similar reasons, because it emerged as a part of liberation theology. Others, preoccupied with a larger emphasis on African roots within the Latin American reality, preferred to call it Afro-Latin American and Caribbean theology. But, in our case, we are not interested so much in the terminologies used by one or another group that refer to the identification of black expression. The question that is before us today is how to take it up as theology. We experienced an enormous newness when we started to deepen our reflection on black religious-spiritual experience, as we have noted. We often feel that the concept of theology seems too narrow, Western, and incapable of embracing the totality of the experiences of which we have been speaking. More than that, at times the notion of theology puts us in a straitjacket which we have to make fit. Because of this, such a restricting term runs the risk of sacrificing or caricaturizing aspects of the practice and reflection that are precious to us. An easier and shorter way would be to use the expression "black spirituality," which would give us more freedom and perhaps would be more comfortable.

But, we prefer to insist on the concept of theology. This means taking on the terminology and forcing its limits; in other words, recreating it. As there was a theology of slavery ideologically responsible for the sacrifice and death of our ancestors and, in large part, for the marginalization and prejudice that we descendants of Africa still suffer in Latin America, we believe it is urgent to proclaim a black Latin American theology that announces a new day, and proclaims in a loud voice: "There is fragrance of the gospel in the life of the black community."[27]

Notes

1. Quince Duncan, "*Racismo: apuntes para una teoría general del racismo,*" in *Cultura negra y teología* (San José: DEI, 1998), 54.

2. Ibid., 58.

3. Eduardo Hoornaert, "*La leitura de la Biblia en relação a escravidão negra no Brasi-colônia (um inventario),*" in *Estudos biblicos* 17 (Petrópolis: Ed. Vozes, 1988), 11-29.

4. Antônio Soares Amora, ed. *Obras completas do Padre Antônio Vieira—Sermones*, vol. 4 (São Paulo: Ed. Cultrix, 1981), 299.

5. Eduardo Hoornaert, "*La leitura de la Biblia,*" 24.

6. Antônio Soares Amora, ed. *Obras completas do Padre Antônio Vieira—Sermones*, 363.

7. André João Antonil, "*Como se ha de haver o senhor de engenho com seus escravos,*" in *Escravidão de indios e negros no Brasil*, Decio Freitas, ed. (Puerto Alegre: EST-ICP, 1980), 146.

8. Jorge Bensi, *Economia cristã dos senhores de escravos* (São Paulo: Ed. Grijalbo, 1977), 162-63.

9. Eduardo Hoornaert, "*La leitura de la Biblia,*" 17.

10. Pablo Richard, "*Lectura popular de la Bíblia en América Latina,*" in *Revista de Interpretación Bíblica Latinoamericano* 1 (1988), pp. 41-42.

11. An herbal tea.

12. A city in northeast Brazil.

13. Joana dos Anjos, *Ovindo histórias na senzala* (São Paulo: Ed. Paulinas, 1987), 39-40.

14. Pedro Grado, "*Mi nombre está allí,*" in Vicente Mendonza, *Himnos Selectos*, 11th ed. (Mexico: Casa Unida de Publicaciones, 1956), 102.

15. In the majority of the Latin American countries, groups of the black movement have insisted on reserving the term "black" to refer to the descendants of Africa. In the dictionaries and in common language, however, people continue using the word "black" for the bad, dirty, or negative.

16. The reference to Latin America does not exclude the Caribbean because of the common elements that join us. We recognize the richness of the work that is being done in the region. See, for example, *Los rostros de Dios. Ensayos sobre cultura y religion afrocaribeña* (Quito: Ed. CLAI, 1998).

17. See the reflections of Antônio Aparecido da Silva, "*Reflexiones teológicas a partir de las comunidades negras de Brasil*" in *Vida y Pensamiento* 17/2 (San José: UBL, 1997); and José Geraldo Rocha, *Teologia e Negretude: Um Estudo dos Agentes de Pastoral Negros* (Santa Maria: Gráfica Editora Pallotti, 1998).

18. Antônio Aparecido da Silva, "Reflexiones teológicas," 56.

19. The consultation took place in Rio de Janeiro, Brazil, with thirty-three people representing eight different countries of Latin America and the Caribbean.

20. José Geraldo Rocha, ed., *Amadurece uma esperanca: Cadernos de Teologia negra 1., Groupos de Teologia Negra* (Rio de Janeiro: Gráfica SB Ltda., 1993).

21. Marcos Rodriguez da Silva, *Teología Afro-latinoamericana: Primer ensayo Ecuménico para una Teología Negra de la Liberación* (Quito: Edic. Afro-América y Centro Cultural Ecuatoriano, 1990).

22. *Revista de Interpretación Bíblica Latinoamerica* 19 (San José: DEI, 1994).

23. To study this theme in depth, see Heitor Frisotti, *Passos no diálogo: Igreja Católica e religiões afro-brasileiras* (São Paulo: Ed. Paulus, 1996).

24. Holy Mother (Madre de Santo) is the expression used to refer to a religious leader, the priestess of Candomblé, which is one of the Afro-Brazilian religious expressions.

25. "*Ialorixá nasceu em 1894*," in *A Tribuna da Bahia 3* (Bahia, Brazil, February 1, 1994), 1.

26. "*O ecumenismo das comunidades de fe negras*," in *Teologia Afro-Americana —II Consulta Ecuménica de Teologia e Culturas Afro-Americana e Caribenha*, ATABAQUE-ASETT (São Paulo: Ed. Paulus, 1997), 164.

27. Phrase of Heitor Frisotti, friend of the black cause.

Part V

Black Faith,
James H. Cone,
and
the Future of
Black Theology

Race and Civil Society

A Democratic Conversation

JEAN BETHKE ELSHTAIN
and CHRISTOPHER BEEM

We've all seen them—the World War II films in which the airplane crew or the platoon has a group of guys—all GIs and proud of it—with names like LaRosa, O'Brien, Goldberg, Chavez, Olafsen, Mickweicz. They're Americans to the man, and they are making a point—we're different from the people we are fighting.[1] America is open to all comers. You don't have to be of a particular race, or adhere to a given religion, or bear an identifiable ethnic name from one of a handful of accepted groups to be one of us. But the picture is by no means perfect. You don't see an African American or a Japanese American in the group.[2] The armed services were segregated until after World War II, and Japanese Americans fought in a separate *nisei* regiment. But the point could be taken nonetheless: America was different because it enabled people who were "different" to nevertheless hold something in common: their identity as citizens, their aspirations as free men and women, their determination to make life better for their children. That seems rather a long time ago—a frozen tableau from another time and place; a time when we were innocent, perhaps, or naive, or just "didn't get it."

A "reading" of the "text" of a World War II war film, in today's jargon, would probably go something like this: Men from various ethnic groups were unwittingly coopted to conform to the model of the hegemonic, phallogocentric, dominant Anglo-Saxon Protestant male, save for those the society implacably refused to normalize—namely, blacks and, in this era, Japanese Americans. Having encoded this dominance more generally, such men, already oppressors in their own households by virtue of their superior standing in patriarchal society, became even more eager embodiments of the normative standards of a racist, sexist, imperialist society. End of story.

We exaggerate a bit—for comedic effect or shock value, depending on how familiar the reader is with the coinage of the academic marketplace—but not by much, for we are all now enjoined to see the past in harsh and dismissive terms: Christianity is nothing but the violent re-encoding in new guise of the violent Jewish God; the U.S. Constitution is nothing but the writing into law of the privileges of a dominant, male class; Abraham Lincoln, as one mightily exercised soul shouted after a lecture Elshtain had delivered, should never be quoted because he was nothing but a racist. The relentless drumbeat goes on. Harsh criticism—trashing, as it is called in the vernacular—has become an end in itself. But we worry about this willful contempt for the past, a contempt that stokes arrogance and fuels the flames of historicist prejudice. In short, we do not believe that the way we have "wised up" is so much a victory for wisdom as for cynicism. And that isn't so smart. A free society cannot long survive widespread cynicism among its citizens. Cynicism, the assumption that one's words and deeds always mask an ulterior and crassly self-interested motivation, breeds a politics of resentment. And resentment, finally, drains our normative institutions, including education and politics and even the family, of their ethical legitimacy and deters them from doing the tasks they are there to do.

The sad thing is that much of what we decry here is undertaken in the name of putting some things right, of correcting some wrongs, of celebrating what is called "multiculturalism." But in this area as in so many others, things are not necessarily what they claim to be. We propose that we take a closer look at this new multiculturalism. What do its proponents assume? What do they claim? What do they aim for? What are the effects of these aims and claims on relations between the races? What are their effects on citizenship and responsibility for a free society?

We want to begin to answer these and other questions by reminding us all, once again, of what is at stake. There are two false and dangerous stories about ethnic and racial diversity and American identity. The first is drawn from a historical era, now past; the second, from the present moment. We shall rehearse these two tales that pose or posed particular threats to the generous dream of democracy as the way free citizens come to know a good in common that they cannot know alone.

Our first cautionary tale is the story of a quest for unity and homogeneity that assaulted diversity in the process: a too strong and too overreaching homogeneous identity was deemed necessary as a prerequisite for citizenship and responsibility. We want to take the reader back to the World War I era, when the allure of an overreaching, collective civic purpose took a statist turn that seemed to be a cure for what ailed the republic, at least in the view of those who lamented an excessive diversity. Nationalizing progressives were disheartened at the cultural impact of both the rampant, unbridled industrialism of the Gilded Age and the messy, cacophonous sprawl brought on by wave after wave of immigrants. Desirous of finding some way to forge a unified national will and civic philosophy, these progressives saw the coming of World War I as a way to attain at long last a homogeneous, ordered, and rational society.[3]

Evincing the spirit of the times, John R. Commons, a progressive labor economist, maintained that national greatness required a new singularity of purpose and identity—one nation, one mind. Walter Lippmann likewise assailed the evils of localism and fretted that American diversity was too great and had become a block in the way of order, purpose, and discipline. Progressives like these saw World War I as the great engine of social progress. Conscription would serve, in historian David Kennedy's words, as an "effective homogenizing agent in what many regarded as a dangerously diverse society. Shared military service, one advocate colorfully argued, was the only way to 'yank the hyphen' out of Italian-Americans or Polish-Americans or other such imperfectly assimilated immigrants."[4]

President Woodrow Wilson, who had already proclaimed that "any man who carries a hyphen about him carries a dagger that he is ready to plunge into the vitals of the Republic,"[5] thundered, in words of unifying excess:

> There are citizens of the United States, I blush to admit, under our generous naturalization laws born under other flags but welcome to the full freedom and opportunity of America, who have poured the poison of disloyalty into the very arteries of our national life. . . . Such creatures of passion, disloyalty, and anarchy must be crushed out. . . . The hand of our power should close over them at once.[6]

"Americanization" became the goal, the watchword—but for some, the threat: one nation indivisible. To be sure, genuine regard for the welfare of immigrant groups lay at the base of much progressive sentiment, the fear that separatism and heterogeneity were synonymous with inequality and marginality. One must also acknowledge that this drive for national unity was in large measure born of pressing political demands. There was, after all, a war going on. For all this, progressive and liberal opinion proved particularly susceptible to the cry for unity because of its emphasis on the notion that the voice of America must speak as one. The temptation to forge a unity that is indistinguishable from stifling conformity is great. It invited figures from Woodrow Wilson down to trim the sails of free speech on the grounds that the war against dissent was a war against civic dismemberment, a war for great national aspirations, and an opportunity to forge a community that might encompass the entire continent. The coming of the first world war offered this particular progressive mind-set an optimistic set of "social possibilities."

Perhaps, then, the current practitioners of the "hermeneutics of suspicion" are right. Perhaps the entire thrust of American history has been to destroy our particular identities, even our dignity, in order to create some common identity, some homogenized product. There is a kernel of truth to such claims, but it is not the truth unadorned, for even in the midst of the rush to yank out the hyphens there were dissenting voices. One was that of Randolph Bourne, himself a member of the progressive crowd and a regular correspondent for *The New Republic* until he fell out with the publishers over their newfound war fervor. Bourne wrote a wonderful piece at the height of war suspicion and fanaticism and attacks on aliens and immigrants. Against the effort to cement a homogenized and decidedly WASPish American identity, he yearned for a politics of commonalities that cherished the bracing tonic of perspicuous contrasts. Bourne celebrated a cosmopolitan enterprise, a social world within which many voices were heard:

> America is coming to be, not a nationality but a trans-nationality, a weaving back and forth, with other lands, of many threads of all sizes and colors. Any movement which attempts to thwart this weaving or to dye the fabric any one color, or disentangle the threads of the strands, is false to this cosmopolitan vision.[7]

No "tight and jealous" nationalism for Bourne; he called for an experimental ideal in which each of us is left free to fashion our own ways of living. Yet, Bourne also believed in the possibility of politics. To be sure, politics requires a common set of terms, but Bourne believed those terms could not be wholly imposed from above. They must rather emerge organically through the vibrant interplay of cultures and individuals.

This Bournian ideal (or, perhaps, Bournian mean) is necessarily hostile to any overly robust proclamation of the American identity that demands a single, overarching collective unity, under the aegis of the state, to attain or to sustain its purpose. But his ideal also alerts us to a second false and dangerous story: the harsh particularism, now under way in American civic and scholarly life, in which we reduce ourselves to ethnic, racial, or gender categories, cynically dismissive of the possibility of an outsider understanding one's own group. In the name of diversity and multiculturalism, this rigidifying of difference pigeonholes people by racial, ethnic, gender, or sexual orientation categories and says in effect, that *these* are the differences that matter—not the quality of a person's intellect, the depth of a person's commitment to community, the scope of a person's understanding of the human condition, the dignity of a person's life, or the ill-dignity heaped on a person by an unjust social circumstance. Bourne's rich tapestry contrasts mightily with the multiculturalist's quilt, a collection of solid patches representing this color, this gender, and this or that identity, all kept separate and each threatening at any moment to detach itself. This second story is also a perversion of the dream of democracy and the civic life constitutive of it.

Rather than negotiating the complexity of public and private identities and embracing the notion of the "citizen" as the way we have to sustain a public identity not reducible to the terms of our private selves, more and more we are told that we must gain recognition exclusively along race, gender, or sexual preference lines. The public world becomes a world of many "I's" who form a "we" only with others like themselves in these prefixed categories. Of course, Democrats recognize in the demand for recognition a powerful concern. Some forms of equal recognition are surely not only possible in a democracy but form its very lifeblood. The question is: What sort of recognition? Recognition of what? For what? To claim "I am different. You must recognize me and honor my difference" tells us nothing that is interesting. Should you or I honor some-one, recognize her, simply because she is female or because she proclaims a par-ticular version of her sexual identity? This makes little sense. We may disagree with her about every current political issue we find important—from what American post–Cold War foreign policy ought to be, to what needs to be done to stem the tide of deterioration and despair in America's inner cities, to whether violence on television is a serious concern or just an easy target for riled and worried parents and educators.

Indeed, one could even insist that it is incorporation within a single civic body that makes meaningful diversity possible. Our differences must be recog-nized if they are to exist substantively at all. As political philosopher Charles Taylor writes, "My discovering my own identity doesn't mean that I work it out in isolation, but that I negotiate it through dialogue, partly overt, partly inter-nal, with others. . . . My own identity crucially depends on my dialogical rela-tions with others."[8] What this means is that we cannot be different all by ourselves. A political body that brings people together, creating a "we," but which enables these same persons to separate themselves and to recognize one another in and through their differences as well as their commonalities—that was the great challenge. Bourne's call for transnationality was thus a call for balance, a balance that is at the core of democratic life. The worst excesses of the multicultural movement are just as destructive to this balance as the pro-gressive's unbridled call for unity. Thus, in our time and our society, the great challenge remains.

A survey of the landscape of *fin-de-siècle* America makes it apparent that the drive for identity politics is merely one manifestation of our contemporary trou-bles. Although a dwindling band of pundits and apologists insist that Americans are suffering the pangs of dislocation en route to salutary change, even progress, such reassurances ring increasingly hollow. Experts and ordinary citizens lament the growth of a culture of mistrust, cynicism, and scandal. Our suspicion is that this broader cultural crisis is also properly characterized as a problem of imbalance. If this is so, then exploring this crisis affords us an opportunity to reconnect our discussion about race with these basic questions about American politics, society, and culture. We therefore want to focus for a moment on another source for, and manifestation of, this cultural pathology—namely, the overall weakening of that world known as democratic civil society.

By any standard of objective evidence, our society has experienced serious growth of corrosive forms of isolation, boredom, and despair, and declining lev-els of involvement in politics and community life—from simple acts like voting and exchanging pleasantries with a neighbor, to more demanding participation in political parties and in local and other civic associations. Collectively, these myriad opportunities for social interaction and civic engagement constitute democratic society, for that is where Americans forge the bonds of social and political trusts and competence. Yet in our contemporary social world, these opportunities are increasingly passed over, and American society clearly shows the unhappy results. Social scientists who have researched the matter argue for a causal relationship: This sharp decline in participation has led to a notable decline in social trust. Ultimately, the evaporation of American civil society points to nothing less than a crisis in "social capital formation." Just like identity politics, the decline of civil society at once manifests and reinforces the increasing inability of American society to pursue a good that is common.

Historically, democratic theorists have either taken for granted the web of mediating institutions, vibrant informal and formal civic associations, or they have pointed specifically to those institutions as the means by which a society maintains the relationship between democracy and the everyday actions and spirit of a people. In the latter group, the most famous thinker is Alexis de Tocqueville. Democracy requires laws, constitutions, and authoritative institutions, but Tocqueville also insisted that it depends on democratic dispositions. These include the preparedness to work with others for shared ends; a combination of often strong convictions coupled with a readiness to compromise, in the recognition that one cannot always get everything one wants; a sense of individuality; and commitment to civic goods that are not the possession of one person or of one small group alone. The world that nourished and sustained such democratic dispositions was a thickly interwoven social fabric.[9] The tale here is a story of the unraveling of the institutions of civil society and hence the dramatic upsurge in all forms of social mistrust and generalized fearfulness and cynicism.

The pernicious effects of the resultant mistrust, privatization, and anomie are many. For example, there is empirical support for the popularly held view that where neighborhoods are intact—that is, where there is a strong sense of common interest and a fairly strong moral consensus—drug, alcohol abuse, crime, and truancy among the young diminish. Because neighborhoods are less and less likely to be intact, all forms of socially destructive behavior are on the rise. Children, in particular, have borne the brunt of negative social trends. All one has to do is look at any American newspaper any day of the week to learn about the devastating effects on the young. The stories paint a picture of continuing downward spiral—what Elshtain has called a spiral of delegitimation. The decline in neighborhoods leads to a further strain on families and child rearing. Family breakdown generates unparented children who attend schools that increasingly resemble detention homes rather than centers of enduring training and discipline; and declining levels of education and training contribute further to out-of-wedlock births and violence at unprecedented levels.

This cultural crisis and its various causes—the fact that we are hunkered down into bristling "identity groups," isolated and fearful, expecting the worst from each other—helps to explain the quaint, faraway feeling that is likely to be evoked by the platoon full of GIs. But perhaps there is still something to be learned from them. Consider the social world that those GIs are supposed to symbolize. If those men are indeed representative, then it is clear that the earlier effort of Wilson, Croly, Lippmann, and others to yank out the hyphens was at best only partially successful. Twenty years or so after strict immigration quotas were imposed, the men portrayed in these movies likely lived in neighborhoods and towns where theirs was the dominant ethnic group. Strong lines of demarcation separated these neighborhoods, and they were often crossed only with impunity. They likely went to church, and that church probably would have reflected a strong ethnic and cultural heritage. They were not members of the Lutheran church, they went to the Norwegian Lutheran Church; they didn't belong to a Catholic parish, they belonged to Santa Lucia's or Saint Patrick's. Some of these men came to know members of other ethnic groups through the public school, or later, through the workplace; for many World War II veterans their cultural experience was a singularly hyphenated one, and their first and most significant exposure to other cultures, other ideas about what it means to be an American, took place during the war itself. In other words, those war movies celebrated a shared sense of identity and community for which the war itself was largely responsible.

Yet this does not mean that their message was pure propaganda. Indeed, social scientists concerned about civil society argue that these experiences within a very cohesive neighborhood enabled that commonality to happen. The mediating institutions of civil society—like family, neighborhood, and church—bridge the gap between the individual group and the nation. At their best, they inculcate a shared sense of national identity and solidarity even as they express and reinforce a specific and unique ethnic identity. If this is true, then it is precisely their strong and unique identities, and ultimately their strong ethnic neighborhoods, that enabled or at least facilitated their coming together. It also means that, willy-nilly, something like Bourne's vision triumphed in World War II America. Americans maintained their separate identities even as they were able to come together in pursuit of a common cause.

But again, the movie scene is notable for what is left out—most relevant here, African Americans. Lest we forget, the war had a remarkable impact in this respect as well. The shameful reality of segregation, in light of the notable heroism and sacrifice of Negro units, helped accelerate the black migration to the North, as well as Truman's first fitful steps toward civil rights. Yet the exclusion of African Americans in the movie is representative only of society at large. All the ethnic enclaves of the 1940s were notable in their ability to inculcate a strong sense of ethnic identity and civic virtue; thereafter, they also became notably united in their desire to keep blacks out.

As the Civil Rights movement came alive, the idea of segregation—whether manifested at drinking fountains, in movie houses, or in neighborhoods—was rejected as an inherently illegitimate structural impediment to full citizenship and full humanity. A new ideal of a color-blind society was put forward, and desegregation was championed as the indispensable means for achieving this end. In his famous speech at Howard University in 1965, President Lyndon Johnson noted that the "deep, corrosive, obstinate differences" between "Negro poverty" and "white poverty" were "simply and solely the consequence of ancient brutality, past injustice, and present prejudice." He therefore "dedicated the expanding efforts of the Johnson administration" to addressing the differences, so that the nation might someday "reach the time when the only differences between Negroes and whites is the color of their skin."[10]

Surveying the sorry state of race relations and civil society at the end of the century, we can see that Johnson's hopeful exhortations seem like a long time ago. To be sure, it is easy to forget or belittle the remarkable achievements of this era, but it is nevertheless the case that thirty years after these words were spoken, fifty years after World War II, most interaction between whites and blacks takes place where it always has: in the schools, in the workplace, and in the military. Integrated neighborhoods are more common, but they remain a rare commodity, and even when they exist in fact, it is even more unlikely that they manifest the kind of ethical cohesion that characterized neighborhoods past. As for the idea that our commonality might someday be limited only by our pigmentation, even the goal seems a far-off memory.

Historical hindsight allows us to suspect that, in this case, our faraway feeling is born of the fact that while President Johnson's intentions might have been wholly benign, his goals were not. In the end, the goal of desegregation as Johnson outlines it bears a striking similarity to the Progressives' idea of national community. Johnson too sought to yank the hyphen out of the American experience, and he wanted to use the power of the national government to further that end. To be sure, both movements were hopeful and even noble ideals, born of the best intentions, seeking to address serious problems. Wilson and Johnson might have put forward a different understanding of the evils of localism, but both described it as evil. And at least in the later case, one must be clear about the successes. The Civil Rights movement brought down the social ethos of Jim Crow. Indeed, in some large measure it achieved the goals outlined by Croly and Lippmann. Scenes of fire hoses, attack dogs, and blown-up churches instigated a national mandate, a national moral consensus, that ultimately crushed the localism of the old South. But just like the Progressive movement, desegregation sought community at an unsustainable level—the nation—even as it compromised the viability of community-sustaining institutions at the local level. It also sought to redress the wrongs of prejudice by slowly extinguishing ethnic identity and cultural difference. From a contemporary perspective, it appears that for all their noble intentions, both movements failed in their ultimate objectives because both goals were misguided from the start.

There is a similar connection on the reverse side as well. Notice that a kind of ethnic isolation attaches both to identity politics and to the neighborhoods of World War II America. Whatever good this isolation might achieve in either case—a point that is surely debatable—there is clearly an intolerant and isolated quality to both which undermines a commitment to the common, transethnic group good. There are clear differences between the two. The America of the 1940s was for the most part able to achieve a common good, but it was a racially constricted conception. The identity politics associated with contemporary America seeks to identify and reject that conception, but in doing so it makes the search for a common good not more possible but more distant, and tends, disastrously, to see "culture" as an outgrowth of "race." In both cases, commitment to the group undermines and invalidates the search for a common good that is truly shared.

This long and unhappy jaunt through twentieth-century American history reveals that there is, finally, a shared dimension to the problem of race and the problem of civil society. Living in the aftermath of Wilson and Johnson has shown us that real, sustainable community is local and that a national community is at best a temporary reality. Desegregation can address serious historical injustices, and a strong national government may be able to ameliorate the inequities of unbridled capitalism, but neither can create community and neither can legitimately or profitably seek to homogenize the American experience.

Nevertheless, in both instances, a serious problem remains. On the one hand, we want to reinvigorate the institutions of civic culture, the virtue-building neighborhoods of two generations ago, and we guardedly question whether such neighborhoods do not depend on or at least thrive on a kind of ethnic identity that sustains long-standing prejudices. On the other hand, we want to ameliorate, and finally eliminate, the remaining vestiges of a racist culture, and that requires a commitment to a specific conception of fairness and justice that is almost universal and that surely transcends the insular ethos of an ethnic community. There are, of course, always voices that represent either the overly strenuous vision of a unified (if not homogenized) single national community, or alternatively, that preach a version of separatism. One by-now classic work that cautions blacks against nearly any form of association with white Americans is James Cone's *Black Theology and Black Power*.[11] Cone's rough language sets blacks apart from whites. The possibilities for dialogue, for Cone, are simply not present or are present in the most tenuous and anemic ways. He has a "word to Whitey," and that word is that the structures of what he calls "white society" are a nigh demonic force. Of course, Cone's anger is all too understandable. But Christianity *and*, it must be said, the liberalism Cone spends a good bit of time berating, all turn on the possibility that we might move beyond resentment *even* in situations of oppression. This is, to say the least, an extraordinarily challenging and demanding regimen and Cone really doesn't want any part of it. Politics, for him, is war by other means—or the possibility of other means, as he leaves the door open to the use of violence *if* blacks deem it necessary. "There is no neutral position in war,"[12] he claims. Now the problem with such a stance is its absolutism, its demand for absolute surrender or total victory. That is not the way of democratic politics, which is always a frustrating business, a series of half-advances, half-retreats because one is obliged to deal again and again with people who differ and who dissent from whatever it is one is endorsing.

The difficulty with Cone's position is that it leaves "whitey" very little room in which to make gestures of friendship and solidarity with black Americans. One is, so to speak, condemned for doing nothing or condemned for doing something. Cone approaches Martin Luther King, Jr., rather condescendingly, claiming that most whites "loved" him because his "approach was the least threatening to the white power structure,"[13] not because of his attempt to free his people. H. Richard Niebuhr is taken to task for praising the historic example of blacks and whites worshiping together. For Cone this form of integration was a way to prevent blacks from controlling their own churches; integration, so to speak, was a way to keep track of blacks.[14] But this runs counter to our experience and that of thousands of others. Elshtain, for example, recalls her sisters returning from a Lutheran Youth Leadership Conference in Chicago in

1956 declaiming about Martin Luther King, Jr., who had addressed the group, and about the plight of African Americans in America's southland. For those of us living in small towns in northern Colorado this was a startling and troubling revelation. We began to agitate about it in our school and our church. One of my sisters and I were part of the first protest ever (at least according to the local paper) in front of the federal post office in Fort Collins, Colorado, at the time of the Birmingham sit-ins. It seemed as if there *was* something we could do and we were obliged to do it.

Now this is no doubt small potatoes. But, as Camus and others have noted (we think here of Dietrich Bonhoeffer) you can't be universal anywhere save in your own backyard. It is vital to take the decent action one can and to be able to see oneself as a citizen contributing to a wider sense of what a fair, just, and free America could look like. Cone really undermines this possibility for "whitey," and that is consistent with his counsel of division, if not outright separatism. If white society is a "racist Antichrist," indeed, why should black Americans want anything to do with it.[15] If "black theology counsels all black people to be sus-picious of all white people," the upshot is that we stand and bleat at one another across a vast distance rather than engaging, sometimes angrily and militantly but engaging nonetheless, as free citizens or would-be free citizens.[16] Suggest-ing that burning down seminaries with Molotov cocktails cannot be ruled out doesn't seem a way to build the necessary political bridges to achieve enduring political ends.[17] This, then, leads us to endorse Martin Luther King, Jr.'s vision, not because it is easy but precisely because it is hard. It demands a generosity of spirit (rather than inviting bitter withdrawal) that is difficult for people to muster consistently. But muster this spirit we must, King insists, embracing as we go a complex notion of freedom composed of a number of critical registers.

A modulated politics whose practitioners open their hands in gestures of anticipated fellowship to all persons of good will, white or black, rich or poor, offends those who want a totalistic politics. But hate is easy; arousing the regres-sive urges of one's fellow men and women requires little more than a capacity for spite. What is difficult is to fight the allure of hate, particularly when it comes to us in the name of revolution. Martin Luther King, Jr., knew well what an experience of "the political" was and how it rested uneasily within the con-fines of a politics of mere proceduralism, yet stood as an alternative to a politics of revolutionary violence. The historian Richard King talks of the "repertory of freedom" embraced by the Civil Rights movement. He observed that freedom in Western political thinking involves at least four basis meanings: legal freedom, freedom as autonomy, participatory freedom, and freedom as collective deliver-ance from a subjugated condition. The tens of thousands of ordinary folks who found within themselves the courage to act for each "I" and in so doing sought to create a "we" are the result of a generous vision of democratic possibility. Rooted in hope, the action of a free citizen marks new beginnings and generates possibilities that once seemed foreclosed. To see the goals of the Civil Rights movement, namely, the "liquidation of racial segregation and black disenfran-chisement" and the solidaristic vision of freedom and self-transformation con-

stitutive of it, as somehow peripheral or even a kind of sell-out is to lose the ethical power and historic complexity of this movement.[18] In a culture brimming
with cynicism and despair it no doubt sounds as if we want to have our cake and
eat it too, but what we want is a Bournian ideal for race relations. Fortunately,
that ideal has already found an able advocate, and we therefore close by turning
to the words of Martin Luther King, Jr.

King championed much of Johnson's program—indeed, he repeatedly noted
that desegregation, and the dismantling of Jim Crow laws, was a good in and of
itself. King acknowledged that while these changes "may not change the heart"
they could "restrain the heartless."[19] Nevertheless, King was equally adamant
that desegregation was not enough. "Our ultimate goal," King said, "is integration." King argued that desegregation was merely a physical description and
"only a first step on the road to a good society."[20] True integration was a spiritual reality. It reflected the belief in the sacredness of all persons and required
nothing less than a change of heart.

It is true that King's rhetoric often reflected the tone of the time. His writings
sometimes echo Johnson's strategy of bringing all races together by eliminating
cultural differences. King also used terms that are reminiscent of the Progressives, even talking about "a national community." But these words are not
the whole story. Because true integration is a spiritual goal, and because it
respected the status of all persons, King would not allow that race or ethnicity
could or should be yanked out of a person's identity. In short, true integration
did not constitute homogenization. His words are worth quoting at length:

> The Negro is the child of two cultures—Africa and America. The problem
> is that in the search for wholeness all too many Negroes seek to embrace
> only one side of their natures. Some, seeking to reject their heritage, are
> ashamed of their color, ashamed of black art and music, and determine
> what is beautiful and good by the standards of white society. They end up
> frustrated and without cultural roots. Others seek to reject everything
> American and to identify totally with Africa, even to the point of wearing
> African clothes. But this approach also leads to frustration because the
> American Negro is not an African. . . . The American Negro is neither
> totally African nor totally Western. He is Afro-American, a true hybrid, a
> combination of two cultures.[21]

In short, Martin Luther King, Jr., believed that the spiritual ideal of integration requires that equality and commonality coexist with racial and ethnic
pride, cultural diversity, and spirited, challenging exchange. So understood,
King's objectives for race relations echo Bourne's objectives for American culture. Uncannily, they independently appeal to the phrase "the beloved community" to describe what a truly integrated America would be like. Here, too,
King's use of the term has a more deeply spiritual dimension; he is finally talking
about the Eschaton. But in both cases, their entreaties reveal that what is
required is an uneasy yet charitable and deeply principled balancing act—

between unity and diversity, between pluralism and consensus.

We know that in our jaded age, King's religious exhortations are cloying to many. More to the point, we have made no effort to connect these exhortations to specific policy suggestions. Many who are concerned with these issues may well fear that questions about neighborhood cohesion are nothing more than yet another elaborate strategy for maintaining segregation. These are formidable questions, and we do not want to minimize their importance, but race relations in the United States have not only reached an impasse in recent years, they have soured gravely. There is new and recurrent talk of a gigantic and insoluble fissure in the American body politic. If this is so, then perhaps it is enough to suggest that we take another look at exactly what we want to achieve. If such a reinvestigation allows us to integrate our hopes for race relations with our more general concerns about American culture, so much the better.

Notes

1. We draw here on a lecture Jean Bethke Elshtain delivered in 1992 under the auspices of the Andrew Cecil Lectures for a Free Society at the University of Dallas.

2. Exclusion of African Americans in this depiction of the military melting pot was common but not complete. The movie *Bataan* (1943) is probably the most important counterexample. See Larry May, "Making the American Consensus: The Narrative of Conversion and Subversion in World War II Films," in *The War in American Culture: Society and Consciousness During World War II*, ed. Lewis A. Erenberg and Susan E. Hirsch (Chicago: University of Chicago Press, 1996), 76-77.

3. The longer story can be found in Elshtain's *Women and War* (New York: Basic Books, 1987).

4. David M. Kennedy, *Over Here: The First World War and American Society* (New York: Oxford University Press, 1980), 17.

5. Quoted in ibid., 87.

6. Quoted in ibid., 24.

7. Randolph Bourne, "Trans-national America," in *The Radical Will: Randolph Bourne, Selected Writings, 1911-1918*, ed. Christopher Lasch (New York: Urizen Books, 1977), 262.

8. Charles Taylor, *Multiculturalism and the Politics of Recognition* (Princeton: Princeton University Press, 1992), 34.

9. Alexis de Tocqueville, *Democracy in America*, trans. George Lawrence, ed. J. P. Mayer (New York: Anchor Books, 1969), esp. vol. 2.

10. Lyndon B. Johnson, "The Howard University Address," in *The American Reader*, ed. Diane Ravitch (New York: HarperCollins, 1990), 341-42.

11. James H. Cone, *Black Theology and Black Power* (Maryknoll, N.Y.: Orbis Books, 1997). Published originally in 1969.

12. Ibid., 67. Here it must be noted that Cone draws Albert Camus in as support for an "all or nothing" position when this is a view Camus explicitly *denies*. Camus associates this view with the metaphysical rebellion and most Marxist-inspired forms of historical rebellion he rejects. Camus insists that the rebel, in contrast to the revolutionary, always affirms solidarity with others even in revolt. The point of the rebel is that he or she must recognize a limit. The rebel aspires only to the relative, for Camus;

and the rebel affirms ongoingly that there are limits in rebellion itself. See Camus, *The Rebel* (New York: Knopf, 1956), 14, 290; and contrast with Cone's comments about Camus, especially on page 7.

13. Ibid., 56.

14. Ibid., 77.

15. Ibid., 135.

16. Ibid., 145

17. Ibid., 131. Another problem is Cone's insistence on speaking of "white culture." But we have no idea what "white culture" is. White isn't a coherent category. Is "white culture" the plays of Eugene O'Neill? The films of John Ford? The writing of Herman Melville? The pragmatism of William James? The social activism of Jane Addams? The pacifist militancy of Dorothy Day? There is so much variation and disagreement and fundamental difference in ordering visions that to speak of a monolith called "white culture" is really incoherent. There *is* an *American* culture and that culture is unthinkable without the contributions of African Americans.

18. Richard H. King, *Civil Rights and the Idea of Freedom* (Oxford, England: Oxford University Press, 1992), 28.

19. Martin Luther King, Jr., "An Address Before the National Press Club," in *A Testament of Hope: The Essential Writings and Speeches of Martin Luther King, Jr.*, ed. James M. Washington (San Francisco: HarperCollins, 1986), 100.

20. Martin Luther King, Jr., "A Public Address Before a Nashville Church Conference" (December 27, 1962), in *Testament of Hope*, 118.

21. Martin Luther King, Jr., "Where Do We Go from Here: Chaos or Community?" in *Testament of Hope*, 588.

17

Comparing the Public Theologies of James H. Cone and Martin Luther King, Jr.

PETER J. PARIS

The publication of James H. Cone's *Black Theology and Black Power* three decades ago marked the author's rise to international recognition as the progenitor of a major critique of the thought and practice of the white and black churches in the United States as well as the entire theological academy. In presenting itself as a theological justification for many of the basic principles of the nascent black consciousness movement symbolized by the slogan *Black Power,* Cone's theology was either ignored or rejected by most white theologians and church leaders as a spurious guise for the political ideology of an angry black theologian.

While most black church leaders were not privy to the internal life of the theological academy, those who were tended to express either their ambivalence or a tentative affirmation of some revised version of this intriguing new phenomenon.[1] The president of the National Baptist Convention, USA, Inc. (the largest black denomination in the world, then claiming a membership of more than seven million) issued a strident denunciation of Cone's entire project. Yet, there was a relatively small number of black clergy, religious scholars, and students who welcomed Cone's theological thought with enthusiasm. A couple of years earlier, several of these had joined with Adam Clayton Powell, Jr., pastor of Abyssinian Baptist Church in Harlem and a U.S. congressman, as signatories on a full-page ad in the *New York Times* supporting Black Power.[2] Most of these later formed the nucleus of the National Conference of Black Churchmen (NCBC) later renamed the National Conference of Black Christians. Many of them were black clergy and church administrators in predominantly white denominations who were bent on directing the latter to channel funds and other resources into empowerment programs in the black community. Clearly, most black seminary students and doctoral candidates celebrated the rise of black theology, which gave them a theological rationale and a methodology for pursuing what was for them a meaningful and relevant academic agenda. This event was a novel occurrence in theological education. Never before had it been possible for black seminarians and doctoral students to study and undertake research on the black religious experience using a methodology developed by a black theologian: a methodology that claimed to be adequate for its subject matter since its point of departure was the black religious experience and its goal was to enhance the understanding and practice of that experience.

Since there were very few African Americans in theological education at the time when Cone's first book was published, and since the Eurocentric American Academy of Religion (AAR) and the Society of Biblical Literature (SBL) provided very little space for black religious scholars to carry on sufficient discourse among themselves about black theology, the Society for the Study of Black Religion (SSBR) was organized in 1970[3] for the purpose of reviewing and critiquing one another's work, celebrating and encouraging academic publications among its members, and promoting the use of the black theological perspective throughout the various disciplines of theological study. In the early years, the agenda included both interdisciplinary discussions and separate disciplinary workshops.

It is important to note that the SSBR never intended to be a substitute for either the AAR or the SBL. Rather, it viewed itself as a necessary external auxiliary to enable African American religious scholars to achieve academic excellence in this new field of inquiry. To date three of its founding members have risen to the presidency of the AAR, and several of its members sit on its standing committees. At the time of this writing, an African American female doctoral candidate is serving as an elected student representative on the AAR's board of directors. Similar trends have been occurring in the SBL even though that body has not yet elected an African American to its presidency. Both associations have standing committees on the status of racial and ethnic minorities chaired by African American religious scholars. These committees have advocated and directed various types of reform in their respective organizations. In my judgment, all of these developments are by-products of the Black Theology movement.

In the early eighties, a significant reform measure occurred within black theology. Interestingly, its primary locus was Union Theological Seminary, where James Cone has taught for three decades, and three of its leading proponents were African American female doctoral students in theology and ethics, namely, professors Katie Cannon, Jacquelyn Grant, and Delores Williams. These women, while still students, allied themselves with colleagues around the country to demonstrate *in their own voice*[4] their desire to affirm the major principles of both black theology and feminist theology. They were all painfully aware that the experiences and voices of African American women were wholly absent from the theological discourse in both camps. In their search for a name for this corrective they adopted a term first used and definitively explained by the novelist, Alice Walker, namely, w*omanist*. Thus, womanist theology was born as a constructive alternative to both black theology and feminist theology. It soon became abundantly clear that these womanist theologians would be friendly to both without being coopted by either. It is to James Cone's enduring credit that he quickly recognized the important deficiency in black theology that the womanist theologians had identified, namely, the claim of the former to speak for the whole of the African American Christian community solely through the voices of African American men. Accordingly, he affirmed the new movement and has remained one of its strongest male supporters. Yet, let me hasten to add that the civility and communal spirit of the womanist theologians coupled with Cone's gracious response to them served then and now to preserve and enhance communal harmony throughout the African American theological academy.

The many and varied contributions of black theology to both the churches and the academy have been significant both within the United States and beyond. Though Cone was not the first person to use the term "black theology," he was the first to lay the groundwork for a coherent approach to the subject with a prolegomenon set forth in his first book published thirty years ago. Yet, his theological contributions cannot be fully understood apart from the context in which he wrote and taught. In 1969, the African American context was almost wholly shaped by the assassination of Dr. Martin Luther King, Jr., on April 4, 1968, an event that angered virtually every part of the African American religious community, anger that often alternated between deep mourning and near despair.

Since King's theology exemplified the black Christian tradition[5] par excellence, it had been readily embraced by the black churches even though his advocacy of nonviolent direct confrontation had not been as widely accepted. In contrast, Cone's thought appeared to be racially chauvinistic and, hence, a threat to the traditional thought and practice of the black churches. Consequently, he was sharply criticized by most of them that were at the time still debating the value of using the appellation "black Americans" as a substitute for the traditional names, "Negro" and "colored." Cone's attempt to give ontological status to the term "black" by equating it with God further exasperated the black churches. In short, both his rhetoric and his strident tone placed his theology at odds with their traditional conciliatory style. They had always striven to effect the redemption of the nation rather than that of African Americans alone. Suffice it to say, Cone's theology placed virtually no emphasis whatsoever on such prominent concepts in the black Christian tradition as love, forgiveness, redemption, or reconciliation. Rather, his thought gave pre-eminence to such principles as justice, power, audacious resistance to oppression, strong affirmation of blackness, and a definite devaluation of nonviolent resistance as a way of life. All of these features were made vividly explicit in Cone's first book, *Black Theology and Black Power*.

Similarities and Differences between Cone and King

In my judgment, Martin Luther King, Jr., and James H. Cone are the two major American theologians of the twentieth century, black or white. The most significant similarity between the two is their respective understandings of the relation of the Christian gospel to the struggle for racial justice in the United States. In fact, each viewed ecclesiology as the proper subject matter of theological inquiry. That is to say, they considered the tasks of theology to be that of explicating the nature of Christian praxis in order to enable people to become faithful in their discipleship by practicing the faith in all dimensions of their common life. Thus, Cone wrote:

> The mission of the church is to announce and to act out the gospel it has-received. . . . It is the job of theology to remind her what the true Church is, for theology is that discipline which has the responsibility of continually examining the proclamation of the church in the light of Jesus Christ.[6]

Similarly, King believed implicitly in the integral relationship between the Christian gospel and the societal needs of human beings. Admitting the early influence of the Social Gospel movement, he wrote:

> It has been my conviction ever since reading Rauschenbusch that any religion which professes to be concerned about the souls of men [sic] and is not concerned about the social and economic conditions that scar the soul is a spiritually moribund religion only waiting for the day to be buried. It well has been said: "A religion that ends with the individual ends."[7]

Clearly, neither King nor Cone engaged in speculative theology concerning the nature of God nor did they participate in much academic discourse about classical doctrines of faith. Rather, their theologies served the practical purpose of effecting racial justice. Each believed that the truth of the gospel is evidenced in its capacity to restore wholeness to a broken community. Hence, it was imperative for them that theology be integrally related to the concrete issues of social injustice in general and to the pursuit of racial justice in particular. Each viewed theology as necessarily prophetic because Jesus was a prophet who had summoned his followers to prophetic discipleship. This viewpoint is exemplified in Cone's contention that "it is impossible to respond creatively and prophetically to the life-situational problems of society without identifying with the problems of the disinherited and unwanted in society."[8]

More specifically, King viewed any alliance of Christians with racial segregation as a betrayal of Christianity and a blasphemy against God. Thus, he wrote:

> I understand that there are Christians among you who try to find biblical bases to justify segregation and argue that the Negro is inferior by nature. Oh, my friends, this is blasphemy and against everything that the Christian religion stands for. . . . Segregation is a blatant denial of the unity which we have in Christ. It substitutes an "I-It" relationship for the "I-Thou" relationship, and relegates persons to the status of things. It scars the soul and degrades the personality. It inflicts the segregated with a false sense of inferiority, while confirming the segregator in a false estimate of his own superiority. It destroys community and makes brotherhood

impossible. The underlying philosophy of Christianity is diametrically opposed to the underlying philosophy of racial segregation.[9]

Both King and Cone viewed the Exodus tradition as the paramount biblical paradigm for depicting God's relation to the human condition, and they saw the incarnation as continuous with that tradition. In other words, they believed that God's initiative in effecting the freedom of the oppressed Israelites constituted the mission of Jesus and characterizes the way God relates to all peoples. By joining with the oppressed against their oppressors, God's righteousness in history is revealed, and that alone liberates all concerned: the oppressed from their suffering and the oppressors from their inhumanity. This understanding of God's relation to history implies a theological dimension in the immoral activity of oppressing human beings. Diminishing and/or denying the humanity of others blasphemes against God because it contradicts God's purpose in creation. Most importantly, each claimed that Christians who justify such activities and/or participate in them practice heresy. It is this very contention that is at the center of the prophetic judgments both King and Cone leveled against all who directly or indirectly support societal structures of racial injustice.

Like the ancient Hebrew prophets, they both called America to turn away from its apostasy and practice the Christian gospel by joining in solidarity with all efforts to effect racial justice. Thus Cone wrote,

> If the church is to remain faithful to its Lord, it must make a decisive break with the structures of this society by launching a vehement attack on the evils of racism in all forms. It must become prophetic, demanding a radical change in the interlocking structures of this society.[10]

Both Cone and King believed unequivocally that the political activity of establishing racial justice was a moral obligation implied by the Christian gospel. Moreover, King believed beyond a doubt that God was present in the Montgomery struggle.

> God is using Montgomery as His proving ground. . . . Remember, if I am stopped, this movement will not stop because God is with the movement. . . . But amid all of this we have kept going with the faith that as we struggle, God struggles with us, and that the arc of the moral universe, although long, is bending toward justice.[11]

Cone has always insisted that there is very little substantive difference between his theology and that of Martin Luther King, Jr. In 1985 he wrote: "I see very little difference between the King of 1966-68 and my current perspective on black theology."[12]

We should not overlook the fact that both Cone and King readily acknowledged their reliance on the thought of several major Western theologians in constructing their respective theologies. In his first book, Cone drew heavily from the thought of both Karl Barth and Paul Tillich in support of his prophetic understandings. Similarly, in King's first book he spoke of his indebtedness to the Social Gospel movement and the Personalist school of theology, as well as Reinhold Niebuhr, Henry Nelson Wieman, and Paul Tillich. Thus, each drew upon those elements in Western theological thought that supported his prophetic thought. Clearly, both gave primacy to the importance of relating the gospel to the social issues of the day.

In his first book, Cone discussed at length his attraction to Karl Barth's thought. He argued that Barth's deep commitment to the task of relating the gospel to the pressing social issues of his day accounted for his early identification with the Social Gospel movement as well as his later change to a transcendental perspective that was occasioned by the rise of a new political order which based its legitimacy on a natural theology.[13] In his later writings Cone emphasized the social basis of all theology and accordingly, argued that black theology differed radically from both European and Euro-American theologies because their respective social locations were so different. More importantly, Cone's thinking led him to see clearly that thinking about God from the perspective of one's experience conditioned the types of questions one asked of the gospel and that those questions, in turn, conditioned the form the answers assumed. That rather Tillichian approach was expressed thusly by Cone: "One's social and historical context decides not only the questions we address to God but also the mode or form of the answers given to the questions."[14]

Cone's elaboration of the social basis of theology leads to the main methodological difference between him and King. My thesis, however, is that their thought is not contradictory but complementary. When Cone argued that "Black theology must uncover the structure and forms of the black experience, because the categories of interpretation must arise out of the thought forms of the black experience itself,"[15] he was making the kind of methodological move in theological thinking that King did not make in the same way. Yet, I contend that there was no major conflict between the two because Cone never departed from his neo-orthodox position of relating contextual experience dialectically to God's activity. "Truth is divine action entering into our lives and creating the human action of liberation."[16] More specifically, Cone discussed his commitment to the transcendence of the gospel in considerable detail in a later book when he wrote: "Despite what some persons might think, I still believe in the transcendent foundation of the church."[17] In other words, Cone never reduced the Christian gospel to cultural history because that would have been contrary to the black church experience which always viewed the struggle for liberation as commensurate with a transcendent gospel. Contrary to the views of all those who claimed that Cone's thought was basically political and not theological, Cone reiterated time and again that the validity of the liberation struggle as the starting point for theology lies not in the culture of the oppressed but in the nature of God, who initiated the activity of liberating Israel. The interdependent relationship between Christ the Liberator and the black struggle for liberation is a guiding motif for Cone's thought, which he considered the essence of black religion.

Even a casual observer of King and Cone would quickly discern that their theologies can not be abstracted from the practical goals of freedom and liberation. Each viewed theology as a servant of the freedom/liberation struggle, and the goal of the latter determined the shape of the former. In other words, their theologies were prophetic in both form and substance.

Clearly, King's style of discourse encouraged the broadest possible public participation of all peoples of good will. The goal he sought was not for blacks alone but, rather, the creation of a wider community. In addition, he taught that the quality of the means (i.e., both the agents and their style of action) should be commensurate with the quality of the goal itself. Thus, we can easily see the difficulty King would have with the "black power" slogan because it presented a problem in semantics. Since King believed that language constitutes reality, and since the "black power" slogan implied many unfortunate connotations, he thought its use was both imprudent and misleading. Thus, he wrote:

> Why not use the slogan "black consciousness" or "black equality"? These phrases would be less vulnerable and would more accurately describe what we are about. The words "black" and "power" together give the impression that we are talking about black domination rather than black equality.[18]

In contrast, Cone's theological focus centered on the agential dimension of the liberation struggle and the way human agency is allied with God's activity in sociopolitical transformation. His focus on agency implied rigorous historical analysis and, more specifically, a critical analytical description of the experience of oppression as suffered by African Americans, along with their many and varied activities aimed at liberation. Cone's claim that God was acting in solidarity with the black liberation struggle implied that all authentic Christian discipleship was obligated to do likewise. That constituted a virtual revolutionary claim both in the academy and the churches. Making blackness (hitherto a concept of opprobrium for most whites and many blacks) a theological symbol with profound moral and political implications had both psychological and cultural effects on all concerned. Thus, we can see why the slogans "black power" and "freedom now" resulted in such immense conflict between Stokely Carmichael and Martin Luther King, Jr., during the second stage of the Meredith Mississippi Freedom March. Stokely Carmichael and his supporters emphasized black agency as the sole agent for effecting social change while King emphasized a racially integrated approach. The rise of black power marked the beginning of a changed strategy bent on giving primacy to black agency in a context that had become characterized by widespread frustration and disappointment. The slogan "freedom now" had come to typify King's commitment to nonviolent direct resistance exercised by a racially integrated vanguard of disciplined and courageous demonstrators. Cone's theology aimed at providing a theological justification for black power while King's aimed at demonstrating how the principle of divine love could be manifested in effective nonviolent direct resistance in search for a society of interracial harmony.

Certainly, the styles of the two men differed greatly. From the beginning, Cone's rhetoric exhibited a threatening, aggressive, judgmental, acrimonious tone aimed at militantly confronting the evil practice of racism and its countless deceptions. By contrast, King's rhetorical style consistently expressed a message of hope and redemption to all who had ears to hear. Cone's theology established a cosmic polarization between the oppressed and the oppressors while King's theology aimed at describing justice as a cosmic principle of unity for all peoples. Yet, in spite of these differences of style, I contend that their theologies complement rather than contradict each other.

Cone's insistence that his theology is built on the foundations of King's thought and practice can be understood best by seeing the two as related to each other as human agency is related to its objective goal. On the one hand, Cone's contextual orientation implied an emphasis on material conditions and the particularity of agency. On the other hand, King's universalist orientation implied an emphasis on the ideal form of the desired goal (i.e., the beloved community) as the normative criterion for evaluating the character and practice of the agents in their efforts to realize that goal.

Cone's emphasis on black agency struggling to liberate itself from oppression implied that the oppressed alone were fully justified in determining the effective means for achieving their purpose. In response to the question of violence versus nonviolence, Cone has consistently maintained that the oppressed alone must decide that question, and no one else has the right to judge what the right answer should be. Clearly, Cone's position is rooted in a contextual ethic, which, by definition, can never provide an absolute answer to any moral question. In contrast, King's answer was idealist in that it was based on the principle of divine love and, like all idealists, his task was to seek adequate ways to apply that principle to historical situations. His discovery of a praxis adequate to that ideal was the result of a long intellectual and moral pilgrimage that culminated in the Montgomery bus boycott, which he described in his first book, *Stride Toward Freedom: The Montgomery Story.*

As we have said above, King's emphasis on the form and goal of the struggle implied that the being of the agent must be brought into conformity with the end sought. In other words, a community of peace and justice must be sought by similar means (i.e., nonviolent direct resistance), the doing of which inevitably results in men and women becoming morally peaceful and just in the process. In King's perspective the habitual practice of nonviolence was a necessary condition for authentic community. Thus, he repeatedly reminded his followers that nonviolence was not merely a philosophical principle but a way of life. Finally, on the question of violence or nonviolence as a strategy for effecting liberation, it seems to me that one might conclude that Cone and King are related to each other as Christian just-war theorists are related to Christian pacifists. Both are fundamentally committed to peace as the authentic Christian norm. The one believes that absolute obedience to nonviolence is the only appropriate response to that norm, while the other argues for flexibility in light of a careful weighing of particular circumstances and prospective consequences.

Although Cone has been accused of reducing theology to ideology, calling for violence, advocating racial separation, opposing reconciliation, and flaunting racial chauvinism, none of these accusations can be proved by appeal to his writings. In fact, he has answered all of his critics with the kind of candor, insight, and knowledge that have characterized his work throughout his career.

Cone's theology focuses more on the human response to the gospel than on any attempt to set forth fixed universal principles of Christian thought. This leaves him vulnerable to many of the above attacks but not defeated by those attacks, because they usually fail to discuss the issues in dialogue with Cone's actual arguments. Although Cone's discussion of dialogue is very helpful as a method for avoiding ideology, one does not find in his thought any imperative calling one liberation movement to join in coalition with other liberation movements. This is due, in large part, to the limitation implicit in his method, namely, doing theology from the perspective of one group, namely, African Americans. Yet, other oppressed peoples have been helped by Cone's thought. In fact, South African black theologians are deeply indebted to Cone and his method of approaching the gospel from the perspective of the oppressed. As praiseworthy as that may be, however, it is no answer to the question of whether black theology itself motivates its adherents to go out to expand and enhance the quality of the human community at large. Thus, as with all contextual thought, I conclude that an endemic parochialism attends the black theology project.

Martin Luther King, Jr., exhibits the opposite problem. Deeply focused on the universal principles of love and justice, coupled with his full commitment to the application of the gospel to the problems of racial and economic justice both in the United States and beyond, King's methodology did not lead him to reflect theologically on the religious history of African Americans. Consequently, that which Cone thematizes is almost totally absent in King's thought. Although for him much of the black religious experience functions implicitly and explicitly in the various forms the movement utilized (i.e., preaching, music, song, testimony, prayer, leadership style, institutional locus, etc.) he gave little attention to any extended explication of its virtues and contributions. Accordingly, Cone rightly concludes:

> Thus much of King's writings reflect theological and philosophical discourse that had little to do with his actual creative thinking and acting. The source of the latter is not Gandhi or Bostonian personalism, despite his implied claims to the contrary. King's creative thought and power in the struggle of freedom were found in his black Church heritage. This was the heritage that brought him face to face with agony and despair but also hope and joy that somewhere in the bosom of God's eternity, justice would become a reality "in the land of the free and the home of the brave." This was the source of King's dream and his anticipation that "trouble won't last always."[19]

King devoted a great amount of energy throughout his addresses and writings to analyses of the pathological dimensions of racial discrimination and segregation and their corresponding effects as evidenced by blacks internalizing notions of inferiority and self-disrespect. In that respect, King's theology can be criticized for describing the pathological aspects of black history at the expense

of the positive, healthy elements that contributed importantly to the race's survival and its quest for freedom and equality. Thus, the weaknesses of each of
these theologians are compensated for by the strengths of the other. This
accounts for the ambiguity King manifests in his discussion of black power and
black consciousness, as well as that which Cone manifests when discussing
racial integration and reconciliation. It is important to note at this point that
although the nascent womanist theology bears many noticeable marks of the
influence of black theology, its deep concern for community between the races
and the sexes reveals the strong influence of Martin Luther King, Jr., and the
black church tradition he represented.

We must not neglect to speak about the different associational contexts from
which King and Cone thought, wrote, and spoke. On the one hand, King has
been immortalized in our lifetime as a person who led a major social movement
aimed at effecting a moral transformation in our body politic. During his entire
public career he was at the helm of this movement, inspiring its supporters and
persuading others both spiritually and morally. When we think of King, we
think of public speeches, sermons, and nonviolent marches in the service of
racial justice, never understood in a parochial way but always bent on creating
the conditions that would enable a wider humanity to flourish. Consequently,
the limited goals of the Montgomery bus boycott soon gave way to the task of
dismantling racial discrimination and segregation throughout the South under
the aegis of the Southern Christian Leadership Conference. Following the Civil
Rights bills of 1964 and 1965 King turned his attention to the northern city of
Chicago and merged his organization with the Coalition of Chicago Community
Organizations to form the Chicago Freedom movement, which launched an
attack on segregated housing patterns in that city. In 1968, he joined in solidarity with the peace movement in denouncing the war in Vietnam, and he was
assassinated while supporting the garbage workers' strike in Memphis as part of
his aim to bring together the nation's poor in the quest for economic justice. All
of King's thinking, speaking, acting, and suffering occurred in contexts characterized by a praxis oriented toward the expansion of human community through
eradicating racial segregation and discrimination, stopping an unfair war, and
eliminating poverty. All of this inevitably made him acutely aware of the need to
maximize political power via coalition building, alliances with legislative and
judicial agencies, churches, and the media. Further, as his writings clearly reveal,
he was keenly aware of the various social, economic, and political conditions
that either favored or threatened his program. Attention to these forces led him
to discern definite alliances among them and especially to see the interrelated-
ness of racism, poverty, and militarism as dehumanizing societal systems.

James Cone, on the other hand, is well known nationally and internationally as a professional theologian at Union Theological Seminary in New York
City. His prolific writings have been translated into many languages and are
catalogued in most of the theological libraries of the world. Throughout his
career he has aimed at effecting a radical transformation in theological studies
by attempting to stand the Euro-American tradition of theology on its head
with the introduction of a new theological method, namely, that of doing theol-

ogy from the perspective of oppressed peoples rather than from the viewpoint of the ruling classes. Clearly, his transformational objective within the academy has had some important results. Although his work began as an assignment from a group of black church leaders seeking to make a theological response to the debate over the "black power" slogan, he soon found himself isolated in the American theological academy, pioneering a new genre of theological thought by himself. Yet, in various places in the so-called Third World, Cone's works were eagerly read as significant theological guides for liberation struggles. This was especially true in South Africa where his thought became the impetus for the development of the influential Institute for Contextual Theology (ICT). Thus, Cone's principal contribution has been to the theological academy, with major implications for the nation, the church, and its ministry; while King's principal contribution was to the nation, the church, and its ministry, with important implications for the theological academy. Once again, the complementary relation of the two is evident.

Although the scope of this paper does not permit a full discussion, it is important to note that the experience of black Americans spans a range of political responses extending along a continuum from racial integration to racial separatism. These political responses have had their corresponding theological supporters, and King and Cone represent the two most prominent examples in the latter half of the twentieth century. Their mutual quest for racial justice holds both of them together. Hence, Cone wrote:

> From the foregoing analysis of violence and nonviolence, it is obvious that I do not share Martin Luther King, Jr.'s explication of this issue, although I agree with much of the actual programmatic thrust of his leadership. His dependence on the analysis of love found in liberal theology and his confidence that "the universe is on the side of justice" seem not to take seriously white violence in America. I disagreed with his conceptual analysis of violence verses nonviolence, because his distinctions between those terms did not appear to face head-on the historical and sociological complexities of human existence in a racist society. . . . The idea that hope is created in the context of despair and oppression is what made King such a creative activist and a great preacher. It is also what makes my theology very similar to King's, despite our apparent difference on violence and nonviolence. For we both recognize that a fight is on and black survival and liberation are at stake. Therefore, we do not need to debate the relative merits of certain academic distinctions between violence and force and force or violence and non-violence. The task is what King demonstrated so well in his life and thought, to try to replace inhumanity with humanity.[20]

Therefore, the theologies of Martin Luther King, Jr., and James H. Cone are related to each other as racial self-respect is related to first-class American citizenship or as parts are related to larger wholes.

Conclusion

It should be obvious to all that the theologies of both King and Cone are political theologies. Each emerged from the context of racial strife and each endeavored to provide theological justification for the struggle to resist racial oppression in all dimensions of human life, namely, the political, economical, social, and psychological. While King was called to lead a social movement aimed at societal transformation, Cone was called to help black church leaders develop a constructive theological approach to the progressive forces in the post–Civil Rights era of the black liberation struggle. King aimed his prophetic challenge at white America's racial dilemma between its ideals and its practices. Cone aimed his prophetic challenge at the black "quietist" churches, the racist practices of the white churches, and the theological methodologies of white seminaries. The impact King made on the nation is now clear but more study is needed to assess Cone's precise impact on his chosen targets. Yet, Cone's impact on theological studies in America and abroad has been considerable as evidenced in the number of courses presently offered in African American religious studies as compared with virtually none offered three decades ago. In my judgment, one of the principal achievements of the black theology movement was its systematic explication of the theology of the black churches and its success in gaining legitimation for it in the curricula of theological education. As indicated above, its most decisive impact on the practical life of the churches occurred not in this country but in South Africa, where Christian opposition to apartheid desperately needed theological categories other than those provided by their oppressors, categories that would enable them to rebut the theological justification of apartheid as provided by the Dutch Reformed Church. Accordingly, black theology enabled black and so-called colored South African theologians to construct a contextual theology with which to proclaim a prophetic message of liberation within the context of Christian devotion, biblical exegesis, and courageous action to overthrow a racist constitution.

It should be noted, however, that Cone's black theology differed from that of Martin Luther King, Jr., and the tradition of the black churches by the primacy it gives to the principles of racial identity, self-respect, independence, self-determination, and African heritage. In short, black theology maximizes the values implied by the distinctiveness of the African race and vigorously denies the accusation that it represents reverse racism. One of its principal aims has always been that of liberating the race from every vestige of inferiority bequeathed to it by white racism. In fact, black theology implies a politics of self-determination either racially separate from or racially allied with whites.

Along with the black church tradition and its pre-eminent exemplar, Martin Luther King, Jr., Cone's theology also aims at enriching the public realm by promoting issues of social justice relative to public responsibility and citizenship rights and by publicly exposing all forms of racial hypocrisy and injustice.

Finally, I contend that a major issue faces theological education in present-day America, namely, the problem of racial injustice which is evidenced primarily in the many inadequacies of theological education. Thus, in my view, neither blacks nor whites are being trained adequately for the demands of ministry in our day, because the methods for training ministers have long been obsolete. Business, medical, and legal education all face many similar problems. Like them, theological education will need to launch some bold and innovative pedagogical approaches or choose to become anomalous. Sociological, political, and economic forces continue to reshape institutions, urbanization processes, and human personality in ways undreamed of even a generation ago. Churches of every race and class face a cultural environment that differs radically from that which gave rise to our theological pattern of education a century or more ago. The thought of both King and Cone could be important sources for reshaping theological education. It is undoubtedly true that the type of comparative study of King and Cone we have undertaken in this essay evokes very high interest among both black and white students because they are able to see its immediate relevance for contemporary ministry. Now, this fact should not be devalued.

For too long students in training for ministry have been mainly pursuing certification goals rather than actual training for ministry. This fact may be a major contributing factor in the high rate of burnout among young ministers. Hence, we are concerned about the total educational process, which cannot be addressed merely by adding new courses to the curriculum. Rather, a radical change in the style and substance of theological education is required.

In our discussion of Cone and King we noted that both were primarily concerned with relating the Christian faith to the pressing issues of the day. In fact, we saw that the theology of each was thought of as serving that practical task which, in turn, generated its own questions for theological inquiry. One major conclusion we draw from this study is the importance of having the theological curriculum informed by and responsive to this and other problems in our social order. The challenge of a new curriculum would be that of exploring how the Christian faith should be related to contemporary social and cultural problems.

An adequate theological method of inquiry would necessitate focus on agency, form, and desired goal in addition to the material conditions relative to both the maintenance of the problem and its solution. As with every social problem and every inquiry methodologies of knowing and acting must attend to the relevant dimensions of particularity and generalization. We have seen that the weaknesses implicit in the contextual method of Cone and in the idealist method of King are complemented by the strengths of each. That implies a mutuality of perspectives. Therefore, one should not choose one or the other, but, rather, affirm both in order to gain a comprehensive perspective.

For certain, affirming these theologies does not imply a radical turn away from the knowledge and wisdom of the Western theological tradition. On the contrary, a critical investigation of that tradition relative to the historical contexts of its theologians, churches, and society is necessary. Regaining the historicity of the faith must constitute the purpose of a new curriculum. In other words, theological education must become problem-centered throughout. The importance of historical studies must be seen in their capacity to illuminate the contemporary situation. Both pedagogy and learning must center on problem-solving inquiries which necessarily involve relevant social analyses, historical, biblical, and theological study, and adequate practical experience. All must be completely integrated throughout the whole program. Thus, the combined theological enterprise of Cone and King should be moved to a place of primacy in theological education in order to save it from its current crisis.

Notes

1. This position was developed by J. Deotis Roberts in his rejoinder to Cone's book, *Liberation and Reconciliation: A Black Theology* (1971; Maryknoll, N.Y.: Orbis Books, 1994).

2. See the *New York Times*, July 31, 1966.

3. For a full discussion of the emergence of this organization, see Charles Shelby Rooks, *Revolution in Zion: Reshaping African American Ministry, 1960–1974* (New York: Pilgrim Press, 1990).

4. See one of the early essays on this subject by Delores S. Williams in which the title itself carries the message, namely, "The Color of Feminism: Or Speaking the Black Woman's Tongue," in *The Journal of Religious Thought,* vol. 43, no. 1 (Spring–Summer 1986):42-58.

5. In my book, *The Social Teaching of the Black Churches* (Philadelphia: Fortress, 1995), 10-20, I described the black Christian tradition in accordance with the biblical principle exemplified in the expression *the parenthood of God and the kinship of all peoples.*

6. James H. Cone, *Black Theology and Black Power* (New York: The Seabury Press, 1969), 83-84. Current edition published by Orbis Books (Maryknoll, N.Y.: 1997).

7. Martin Luther King, Jr., *Stride Toward Freedom: The Montgomery Story* (New York: Harper and Row, 1964), 73.

8. James H. Cone, *Black Theology and Black Power,* 85.

9. See "Paul's Letter to American Christians," in Martin Luther King, Jr., *Strength to Love* (Philadelphia: Fortress Press, 1981), 142.

10. James H. Cone, *Black Theology and Black Power,* 2.

11. John J. Ansbro, *Martin Luther King, Jr.: The Making of a Mind* (Maryknoll, N.Y.: Orbis Books, 1982), 37.

12. James H. Cone, "Martin Luther King, Jr., Black Theology and the Black Church," in *The Drew Gateway* (Madison, NJ: Drew University Theological School, Winter 1985), 9.

13. James H. Cone, *Black Theology and Black Power,* 87.

14. James H. Cone, *God of the Oppressed* (New York: The Seabury Press, 1975), 15. Revised edition published by Orbis Books (Maryknoll, N.Y.: 1997).

15. Ibid., 18.

16. Ibid., 30.

17. James H. Cone, *Speaking the Truth: Ecumenism, Liberation and Black Theology* (Grand Rapids, Mich.: William Eerdmans, 1986), 14ff.

18. Martin Luther King, Jr., *Where Do We Go From Here: Chaos or Community?"* (Boston: Beacon Press, 1968), 11.

19. James H. Cone, *God of the Oppressed,* 221-222.

20. Ibid.

Black Theology at the Turn of the Century

Some Unmet Needs and Challenges

GAYRAUD S. WILMORE

James Cone's *Black Theology and Black Power* and *A Black Theology of Liberation* together represent the first phase of his work. He says somewhere that the printer's ink had hardly dried on the first book before he was hard at work on the second. The original edition of *Black Theology and Black Power* came out in March 1969. The very next year Lippincott brought out his second volume. I remember wondering how Cone could have turned out another book-length manuscript so quickly with the terrific pressure that descended on him after his appointment as Union Theological Seminary's first black systematic theologian. He immediately became the target of shamelessly disdainful white theologians. But it may have been possible for him because these two books are actually companion pieces. In the language of the boxing ring, they belong together like the old "one-two," a left hook followed by a quick right cross.

The first book, *Black Theology and Black Power*, was a shout of anger against the spurious Christianity of white America, and it made the shocking announcement to the world that true and authentic "Christianity . . . *is* Black Power."[1] The second book, *A Black Theology of Liberation*, retained some of that angry tone, but under more control; it spoke in a calmer voice with the intention of reclaiming the essential message of the church by reinterpreting Christian doctrine more systematically. The first book was about black power; the second, about a theology of black liberation. The two themes are two sides of the same coin, but they are not exactly the same.

Of the two books, it is my opinion that *Black Theology and Black Power*, though more passionate and less profound, is the more significant. By relating his position to the radical concept of black power, by echoing with approval some of the most belligerent pronouncements of people like Malcolm X, Stokely Carmichael, Maulana Karenga, and LeRoi Jones, and by playing down the nonviolent love ethic of Martin Luther King, Jr. (which most whites were praising at the time), Jim deliberately separated himself from the majority of African American scholars, journeymen preachers, and church bureaucrats. I don't mean to imply that no other black person was thinking what he had the nerve to say out loud, but no one in 1969—except perhaps Al Cleage and James Forman—was as instantaneous and straightforward in putting it all together in one daring public jeremiad against mainstream Christianity. No other Christian thinker presented such an unambiguous *apologia* for the radical positions of the black cultural nationalists and urban revolutionaries of the 1960s.

Just how much Jim Cone strayed from the liberal, Social Gospel Christianity or the irenic neo-orthodoxy of most African American mainstream preachers and seminary professors is seen in a special project of the Theological Commission on the National Committee of Negro Churchmen (NCNC) that was launched the year before *Black Theology and Black Power* came out.

In 1967 the NCNC Theological Commission was chaired by Preston Williams, an ethics professor at the Boston University School of Theology. At the commission's 1967 meeting in Dallas, Professor Williams announced that the commission planned to recommend to NCNC, at some future time, a theological statement that could be used as a consensus document for in-house consultations among NCNC members and in the anticipated dialogues between us and white theologians. It was suggested that the commission's statement might be something like a black American "Barmen Declaration," which would pronounce a radical "No!" to any assumed connection between biblical faith and the oppressive, genocidal racism masquerading as historical Christianity.

In the summer of 1968, after I assumed the chairmanship of the Theological Commission, in order to implement the drafting of such a statement we mailed out a set of ten questions to twenty black religious leaders—about half of them seminary or college professors. Our purpose was to find out if any agreement existed about what might be considered the main outlines of a so-called "black theology."[2]

Most readers of this essay won't recognize these names, but for the sake of the record let me list them. We received fairly extensive replies from Grant Shockley, Edsel Ammons, G. Murray Branch, Henry Mitchell, James Hargett, C. Shelby Rooks, Lawrence E. Lucas, Frank T. Wilson, L. L. Haynes, John H. Satterwhite, Vincent Harding, Joseph R. Washington, and Lawrence A. Jones. I doubt that more than two or three of those men (I don't need to remind anyone how sexist we were thirty years ago!) had ever heard of a young professor at Adrian College named James Hal Cone. I'd also be willing to bet a small sum that Cone knew fewer than half of that list of black churchmen, except perhaps from their writings.

This is not the time to go into a detailed analysis of the responses we received from these nationally recognized black ministers and scholars, but I have preserved a copy of the summary report the Theological Commission made to NCNC in the fall of 1968. Let me share one or two paragraphs of that interesting report.

What conclusions can be drawn from these reactions, taken as a whole? Are there unities or patterns here which may suggest currents of black scholarship . . . and offer guidance to the theological development of NCNC and the black caucuses of several denominations?

One thing . . . seems clear. It is the lively interest and enthusiasm black academicians and pastors have for breaking into what has obviously been a quiescent, almost sterile theological orthodoxy among black churches of all denomination. . . . There is a sneaking suspicion . . . that there is a kind of "black theology" aborning, equal to the budding renaissance in arts and letters . . . [going on today] in Harlem and other black communities across the nation.

Reading that report today, I can't help but notice that after coming to the conclusion in the two paragraphs above, found on page 17, on the last page of the report, page 18, I waffled, qualifying what I had just written by the following words:

As stated above, there is great interest in, but some uncertainty about the unique and distinctive qualities of black religion. . . . Even if, as with most of the writers in this project, there is talk of the "gospel of Blackness" or "soul theology," no radical changes from what may be thought of as mainline Reformation theology and ethics are suggested . . . in these papers. . . . None of the respondents go as far, for example, as Dr. Albert Cleage, in a radical redefinition of the Christian faith. With few exceptions they reach back for a purer version of "the faith once delivered to the Apostles," but corrupted by the culture religion of both blacks and whites. . . . By far the most noteworthy characteristic of these papers is the emphasis upon the church as a social institution dedicated to the pursuit of freedom, justice, and material well-being for oppressed peoples.[3]

Those words were written in the fall of 1968. I believe they support a contention that I want to make today: that what James H. Cone did in *Black Theology and Black Power* produced a historic and unprecedented turning point in African American theological thought.

It was not until June 13, 1969, three months *after* the publication of *Black Theology and Black Power*, that African American theologians and church leaders, following Cone, were able to define a point of view that broke decisively with the mainstream of white American theology. It was on June 13, 1969, with Jim Cone playing a central role, that the Theological Commission of NCBC (by that time we had changed our name to the National Committee of *Black* Churchmen) was finally able to draft a consensus document declaring those now famous words:

Black Theology is a theology of black liberation. It seeks to plumb the black condition in the light of God's revelation in Jesus Christ, so that the black community can see that the gospel is commensurate with the achievement of black humanity.[4]

That is why it is appropriate for the Christian theological community, both black and white, to celebrate the publication of *Black Theology and Black Power*. It is the pivotal work in the modern history of African American religious thought. This small book inaugurated a new tradition among black Christian scholars, seminary students, pastors, and church leaders, including many intelligent and literate folks in the pews of black churches. First, it brought about a way of doing theology that closed the gap, at least temporarily, between African American religion and African American political and social thought. Secondly, it opened the way for the black church, in the words of Dwight N. Hopkins, "to deepen further its reliance on indigenous resources in the African American church and community, thereby demanding black theology to cut loose its stammering tongue."[5] And most of us who tried to speak in those days had been stammering as we sought a middle ground between political militancy and conventional Christianity. Thirdly, it was *Black Theology and Black Power*, for all its exclusive language and neglect of African American women as contributors to the church and its religious thought, that tied the theme of liberation so firmly to black folk culture, that African American women, who had always been the primary preservers of our culture, could not fail to see where and how they entered the struggle.

In years to come there will be many attempts to analyze the reasons why black theology, as influenced by the writings of James Cone, did not reach its full potential in the last half of the twentieth century. In 1990 I put my own two-cents worth into that discussion in an essay written for the twentieth anniversary edition of Cone's second book, *A Black Theology of Liberation*.[6] If I may briefly recall some of the substance of that essay, my reasons for the movement's decline were these: (1) its lack of an infrastructure that could sustain a long-range mobilization and mount an educational program among the masses of church folk; (2) the rise in the 1970s and 1980s of a regressive form of black religiosity that mimicked the evangelistic technique and style of conservative, charismatic, white televangelists and fundamentalists like Jerry Falwell, Jimmy Swaggert, and Pat Robertson; (3) the death of the Honorable Elijah Muhammad in 1975, which effectively removed the old Nation of Islam from the scene as a source of radical ideological and theological competition with the mainstream black church; and finally, (4) the Nixon administration's purge of black radicals and his theory of "benign neglect" and "black capitalism," which betrayed the urban revolt of the masses and cut the ground out from under black theology and black power as viable topics for public discourse.

Today I would add a fifth reason for the decline of the movement potential of black theology: namely, the eventually sincere though half-hearted embrace of the white academy which, while helpfully accrediting black theology for seminary and university teaching, flattered and then distracted black theologians and scholars of religion from dealing more directly with the urgent problems of the poor and disinherited black people who needed them the most.

The unspoken question hovering over this conference[7] on the thirtieth anniversary of the publication of Cone's seminal work is whether or not black theology ought not to be pronounced dead at the Divinity School of the University of Chicago and given a decent burial back at Union Theological Seminary in New York City and at the Interdenominational Theological Center (ITC) in Atlanta where it was first acclaimed. I don't believe that black theology is ready for any such burial. I don't believe that Jim Cone or Dwight Hopkins thinks so either. And I don't think that Robert Franklin, the new president of the ITC, has any intention of permitting an interment to take place on his watch.

But let us lay aside our rose-colored glasses for the moment. What indeed is the future of this way of doing theology in the United States? Is there any hope that the ideas that *Black Theology and Black Power* introduced to the church, the academy, and the public in 1969 have enough staying power, in this vastly different ideological and socio-economic climate in both the black and the white communities, to carry over beyond the turn of the century and give renewed impetus and meaning to the struggle for human liberation?

What I'd like to do now is focus on what I perceive to be three unmet needs that face those of us who are still convinced of the cogency of black power and black theology for the future of African American religious thought and praxis. I suspect that many people who respect and honor the work that Jim Cone has done have many questions about its continuation. We honor Cone, but we also want to ask whether black theology has a further role to play in helping our churches—and perhaps even the white church—to confront the racism, sexism, homophobia, and classism that continue to exercise dominating power in this society. If I'm correct in that assumption, the question that still must be addressed by the scholarly community and the black church, as they consider the possibility of public discourse about black theology, is, what in fact needs to be done now? It is rather late to be asking that question of the black church and its scholars—for much water that should have been harnessed for energy has already passed over the dam—but perhaps not too late.

I have never believed, even at the height of NCBC's effectiveness, that black theology would produce a real mass movement. The social gospel didn't do that; nor did the crisis theology of Barth, Brunner, and Bonhoeffer; nor did the death of God theology. Those movements were basically intellectual, and while they had a significant impact on the academy and on some middle-class church members, mainly white, they were never able to become mass movements. On the other hand, among blacks, Garveyism was a mass movement; King's nonviolent campaign produced a mass movement; the War on Poverty and Saul Alinsky's Industrial Areas Foundation produced something close to a mass movement; and the Million Man March in October 1995 had the marks of a mass movement, although they show signs of rapid evaporation despite efforts to revive the spiritual dynamic of the original gathering.

But black theology, it seems, was not destined to become a mass movement in any of these senses. It involved too many middle-class blacks who, at the time, were too satisfied with their own self-worth and view of reality to be really committed to a radically new body of theological doctrine that would break with orthodoxy; who were too well-placed in their own niches and too obsessed with their own personal advancement in the church and community; and who were not characteristically "true believers," those who, as C. Eric Lincoln reminds us, "are prepared to exchange their individuality for a corporate identity."[8] If all this is true, what other options for corporate identity and action does black theology have today?

Instead of a true mass movement, I believe that black theology can still be a center of contagion, administered by a small contingent of theologians and scholars, that could infect larger institutions, structures, and various ad hoc organizations by creating an educational program and ethos that make it okay—even if one doesn't use the term "black theology"—to talk about power, nationalism, African-centeredness, the black church as an agency of radical socioreligious political change, and the black Messiah, Jesus, as the fulfillment of God's promise that those who are marginalized and oppressed will be liberated.

Such a school of black thought and action does not require mobilizing masses of shouting, fist-clenching people at rallies, marches, or polling places. But it does require extrapolating political, economic, and cultural positions from theological assumptions, and making those positions available to diverse groups of influential people. It means articulating ideas that others can, without too much difficulty, translate into practical political programs that can influence friends and keep enemies at bay.

That potential was realized to some extent in the Black Manifesto crisis, the defense of Angela Davis' right to a fair trial, and the part black churches and religious groups played in popularizing and supporting the South African liberation movements, but not nearly enough to have made the theological, political, and cultural implications of black theology matters of public discourse. The dissolution of the National Committee of Black Churchmen, the black theology project of "Theology in the Americas," and the increasing tendency of the Society for the Study of Black Religion to become an academic guild rather than an intellectual think-tank for religious activists mean that black theologians have no place to stand when they identify issues that the black electorate can respond to, or shape public policy in the way that Jesse Jackson and Louis Farrakhan have been somewhat able to do in recent years.

This was partly because James Cone, J. Deotis Roberts, Delores Williams, Jacquelyn Grant, and other black and womanist theologians are all tenured academics who have neither the interests nor the gifts of public movers and shakers. But this brings us to the conclusion that one of the most serious unmet needs of the black theology and womanist movements (and I am inclined to put them together in this context) is a clear policy base and action program that could resource those who deal with the most pressing issues of the race and the nation.

This situation is different from what we have seen in the past. Samuel

Cornish, Nathaniel Paul, Daniel Alexander Payne, Henry Highland Garnet, and J. W. C. Pennington, to mention only five nineteenth-century churchmen, were all able religious thinkers. But they were also public activists—directly involved in the abolition of slavery, opposition to the American Colonization Society, protesting the Fugitive Slave Act of 1850, promoting the Liberty Party, politicking for the temperance movement, publishing crusading newspapers, petitioning for citizenship rights, and building public and private schools for Negro youth. They were, in other words, religious activists who shaped a theology that took serious account of biblical revelation and personal ethics, but also put the highest premium on *doing* theology in the public arena. Most of those men and women would have agreed with James Cone's statement that, "Theology, as Latin American liberation theologians have stressed, is the *second* step, a reflective action taken in response to the first act of a practical commitment in behalf of the poor."[9]

Today, comparable issues to the ones black religious leaders of the past were embroiled in are hunger and homelessness in the wealthiest nation in the world, the discouraging number of poor black women and children in a time of unprecedented prosperity, the so-far unsuccessful attempt to dismantle the Civil Rights acts of the 1960s, the disproportionate and demonstrably unjust incarceration of young black men, the infestation of black neighborhoods with guns and crack cocaine, whose source and distribution systems seem beyond our control, the unequal treatment of blacks by the police and the courts, the reduction of black voting power by Congressional redistricting, the shameful condition of our public schools, the proliferation of white supremacy hate groups, and the current attacks on both affirmative action and the idea that welfare is a necessary safety net for many deserving and unfortunate poor people.

It is precisely these so-called "secular" issues that black theology promised to deal with in the 1960s but has not effectively addressed in the 1990s. A mass movement would help, but a mass movement is not so much needed as the development of think-tanks, policy institutes, and publication outlets. In other words, black theology needs to establish a strategic presence at the places where political and economic decisions are made and—perhaps even more important—to indicate to blacks, whites, and other ethnic minorities, the points at which theological and spiritual questions intersect with public issues.

There was a period between 1968 and 1970 when leadership elements from the National Conference of Black Churchmen, the Southern Christian Leadership Council, the Student Nonviolent Coordinating Committee, and the Black Panther party were on the verge of forming a national coalition around theological and political ideas stimulated by the interaction between black power advocates and black theologians—particularly the work of James Cone. The slow dissolution of NCBC notwithstanding, that possibility still existed as late as the summer of 1977, when church folk, urban guerrillas, street people, community organizers, and academics, all came to Atlanta under the auspices of the Black Theology Project. Already in 1976 the Theological Commission of NCBC had drafted a document on the state of black theology that declared:

Black Theology is a political theology. The encounter of Black people with God takes in the arena of history and involves ethical judgments and decisions having to do with liberation from racism, poverty, cultural and political domination and economic exploitation. Black people see the hand of God not only in personal salvation but in social and political deliverance.[10]

Unfortunately, the cadres that were present in Oakland in 1969, when we first met with the Black Panthers and the Alamo Black Clergy, and in Atlanta in 1977, when Muhammad Kenyatta and Shawn Copeland brought out a sizable group of grassroots organizers and street people, are no longer in existence. Nor are, with the possible exception of Jesse Jackson, traditional black church activists readily available today. Most of us have become so old, middle-class, tenured, and disoriented by personal greed and the irresponsible use of power, that we have permitted the radical tradition in African American culture and religion to become weakened and trivialized.[11] Moreover, instead of the hopeful poor and powerless who occupied the central cities in the 1970s, we now have the hopeless, sick, and abandoned poor; the homeless and jobless young men and women who slouch along the downtown streets from one church soup kitchen in the morning to another in the evening, and who stand in line on wintry nights trying to get into a shelter.

The National Association for the Advancement of Colored People, the National Urban League, and the Congress of National Black Churches, are so fixated on image making at gala award banquets financed by white corporations and on jockeying for foundation grants that they have become paper tigers. Today a few notable churches may be involved in meaningful political and economic programs, but their influence is so localized and cut off from the levers of real power in the larger society, that the most they can do is produce isolated models that the rest of us, who lack the charisma of a J. Alfred Smith, a Floyd Flake, or a Jeremiah A. Wright, have difficulty replicating in other contexts.

A second area of unmet needs is in the field of catechesis, or more plainly, the instruction of children, high school students, college-age young people, and adults in the biblical and theological foundations of black religious thought and how what we say we believe impinges on our daily decision making and our economic, cultural, and political life. Much has been written in the last thirty years about the need to "blackenize" Christian education materials in our churches and Sunday schools, but there is still a great gulf between our professions as black Christians and the practical application of those beliefs to what we do. There have been attempts in recent years, mainly by the historic black Baptist and Methodist denominations, to redesign and revise curriculum material so that black children and adults can recognize their own life experiences, hopes, and aspirations in the life and message of Jesus Christ, the black Messiah.[12] But, on the whole, the quality of what is being produced is inadequate for translating black theology into the thought forms and idioms of the people and, unaccountably, few if any of our most highly qualified and creative theologians have been recruited for planning and designing such curricula. Black theology cannot hope to become public discourse among ordinary people until larger numbers of African American Christians have been immersed in what black theology, at its best, teaches; or until they are enabled to see the connections between its asseverations and the practical, day-to-day behaviors in which they must be engaged if we are to survive as individuals, develop our communities, and surmount the obstacles thrown up against us by a racist society.

How many of our children can speak intelligently about black theology? How many adult church study groups meet regularly to wrestle with the work of black scholars like Delores Williams, Dwight Hopkins, Marcia Y. Riggs, or Marsha Snulligan Haney? Anyone who has visited our Sunday schools, studied the materials they customarily use for instruction, or who has led adult classes in some of our more reputable congregations knows that for the most part, Christian education in the black church is sorely lacking in substantive content that comes anywhere near communicating a black theological and ethical perspective. It is true that our churches have seldom been loath to enter the political arena when called upon, but too frequently they are represented by publicity-seeking clergymen, rarely by informed lay people—particularly lay women—who have a good grasp of the issues resulting from the sound teaching of biblical and theological truth by black scholars of religion.

What should make African American Christian education different from and superior to white American and European-centered concepts of the Christian faith, which rarely reflect its relevance to the particular issues facing African Americans? In the past thirty years black scholars have given us a more precise understanding of the importance of the ancient Nile Valley civilizations for the shaping of early Judaism, Christianity, and Islam in Africa. We have learned more about the black presence in the Bible and the usefulness of African traditional religions for reappropriating the values of certain spiritual and ritual emphases of the Hebrew Bible. We have been instructed by black scholars in the spiritual and theological lessons to be learned from a more careful study of the history of slavery and racism in the United States.[13]

In a study document on black Christian education I have written something that suggests how both black religion and culture can be used by Christian education programs in African American churches and Sunday schools.

In Black religion and culture the symbol of Blackness refers to much more than skin color—although symbols partake of the concrete reality they represent. *Blackness* is often used instead of the term *African American* ... because it conveys an important sense of perseverance in the absence of falsely comforting, illusory light—an opaqueness, a hardness toward life that is necessary for survival. It has to do with a state of mind, a mode of consciousness: in Christian terms, an attitude or perspective that is hard toward life but humble toward God because the believer has experienced the slings and arrows of an outrageous fortune that was somehow both deserved and undeserved. Blackness has always meant a pride and fearlessness toward oppressors, as in South Africa and America, because Africans and African Americans knew their own worth and believed that God would ultimately bring them up out of slavery, colonization, and apartheid to be a great people.[14]

These considerations, and others, mentioned in contemporary literature written by black scholars, give us the beginning of a model and pattern for our study of the Bible and theology when it is crafted to the needs of African American congregations. Of course, these ideas and insights need further research, but nothing prevents us from starting now to carefully incorporate them in the curriculum planning processes of churches serving black constituencies. Along with this kind of content, we need to devise the special pedagogical methodologies that can help our urban congregations address and educate the depressed and abandoned masses that still populate the neighborhoods in which so many of our churches are found. Christian education is the form in which black theology must be communicated to African American Christians and is the indispensable foundation for any effective public discourse and action on black liberation in the twenty-first century.

A third unmet need has to do with the reality of the black world outside of the United States and its inevitable importance in the twenty-first century. If building a new institutional base for a politically astute black liberation theology on the home front is greatly needed today, a renewed contact and bonding with African, Caribbean, and black Latin American churches, mosques, intellectuals, and religious leaders is greatly needed on the overseas front. How can we continue to theologize about the revelatory significance and pragmatic efficacy of blackness and African-centeredness, and not be in collaboration with black Christians, Muslims, and traditional religionists in the Motherland and wherever a self-conscious, religiously oriented African Diaspora exists—including, incidentally, in England and the European continent, where what is perhaps the most potentially dynamic form of black pentecostalism exists today?

The reception received by the large African American delegation at the recent All-Africa Conference of Churches Assembly in Addis Ababa and the conversations our academics and seminarians had with the Abuna Paulus and Ethiopian Orthodox Church officials suggest that the time is ripe for our church people and theologians to forge new, mutually beneficial relationships with brothers and sisters abroad. This is particularly critical in view of the 1998 initiative of the Clinton Administration and Jesse Jackson to hold up beguiling visions of economic development and democracy before the eyes of Africans, who have been ignored since the end of the Cold War. African American scholars, pastors, and church people need to move in and make our own singular contribution to the discussions about Africa. We not only know more about dealing with white people than any black people on earth (my dear departed mother used to say,

"I've summered them and wintered them"), but we need to make sure that Africa in the twenty-first century remains the rich sources of the spiritual and humanizing power that slavery, colonialism, and neocolonialism almost wiped out in the past and—if Africa becomes the new target of American capitalism and racism—will surely destroy in the future.

All this may sound too grandiose for a people who, up to now, have been unable to deeply impact our own churches and leaders at home. But the globalization and pluralization of black theology in cooperation and collaboration with black Christians, Muslims, and other religionists abroad will not wait. It is an urgent unmet need. We live in a shrinking and intensely interdependent world. Tomorrow our grandchildren and great grandchildren will fly in substratospheric rocket planes that will permit them to do business in Accra on a Friday morning, have lunch in Johannesburg on Saturday, and attend a church in Addis Ababa on Sunday, and still be back in their offices in Chicago on Monday. Will our black theology help them to accommodate that intercontinental experience, to feel at home with rising black folks in the Motherland, or will our religion and culture remain so narrow, so exceptional to the North American situation and conditions, so trammeled by a rigid and overblown Christocentrism and denominationalism, that we cannot detect the voice of God in other places where black people will be struggling for a higher quality of life, a deeper experience of liberation and salvation?

That remarkable 1976 document of NCBC quoted earlier, still rings true and addresses our separation from Africa and brothers and sisters in the Diaspora:

> Black theology . . . seeks the reunion of all Black Christians, Protestant and Roman Catholic, in one Church encompassing the totality of the Black religious experience and the history and destiny of all Black people. All efforts to reunite and renew the Black Church serve the ultimate purpose of confirming the catholicity, apostolicity, and holiness of the whole Church of Jesus Christ . . . [black theology] asserts the operational unity of all Black Christians *as the first step toward a wider unity in which the restructuring of power relations in church and society and the liberation of the poor and oppressed will be recognized as the first priority of mission.*[15]

Given these realities and this commitment, what are we to do now? The most immediate challenge I see before us—who still draw from the wellsprings that were tapped by James Cone, J. Deotis Roberts, and early black feminist theologians like Pauli Murray, Theressa Hoover, Jamie Phelps, and Yvonne Delk—is a new institutional base that can accomplish some of the tasks we have outlined here. What should be the nature of that base and who will construct it?

I have been stimulated by some of the articles in Garth Kasimu Baker-Fletcher's book, *Black Religion after the Million Man March.*[16] These younger voices, who are heralding the significance of that October 16, 1995, event in Washington, D.C., have a vision of the future of black religious thought and its salience for public discourse and for action that opens up fresh possibilities. In one of his essays, "Keeping the Promises of the Million Man March," Garth

Baker-Fletcher discusses the nine pledges that Minister Farrakhan had everyone recite at the march and which Garth relates to the principles of the Nguza Saba. He then observes that the pledges go far beyond the march itself and create a space or communion that "calls the Cosmos to bear witness to our responsible cries for compassion, justice, and caring—for ourselves, our community, and the very dust underneath our feet."[17]

In the same book Cheryl J. Sanders writes on "Themes of Exile and Empowerment," urging the organizers of the march to bring the prophetic and ritual power of the D.C. experience into the Black Family Reunion program of the National Council of Negro Women and to join hands with the council and Marian Wright Edelman's Children's Defense Fund, to put political pressure on our lawmakers on behalf of children and youth.[18] In my mind, these recommendations from a younger generation of black theologians make a great deal of sense. They call for a new institutional base, something less than a mass movement, that will have strong spiritual and cultural dimensions, that will cut across gender lines, and at the same time, will amass sufficient political influence to force some changes upon the Congressional Black Caucus, black and white elected officials, the corporations, courts, and social welfare bureaucracies back in the states and cities where federal dollars will be spent in the future. That kind of base will also provide a launching pad for relating to the African Diaspora everywhere in the world.

At one time I had hoped that the Reverend Jesse Jackson would have given us the leadership we need to develop this kind of coalitional power, but he seems uninterested in black theology. Today I see more possibilities, as far as theological dialogue and networking are concerned, in the people who organized the Million Man and Million Woman's marches. I would look to theologians and church leaders like J. Alfred Smith, Delores Williams, Bishop John Bryan, Garth and Karen Baker-Fletcher, Susan Newman, Forrest Harris, and other grassroots leaders who have demonstrated the ability to think theologically, but who can also organize and move people. We have a wealth of talent, but it is dispersed and disengaged, pursuing narrow, personal albeit commendable goals, but goals that could be much more attainable if they could be brought into a structure that includes black Protestants, Catholics, Muslims, and secularists, all focused on developing a theology and praxis of pan-African liberation and elevation.

What I have described in this paper requires a willingness on our part to give up dogmatic commitments such as Islamic separatism, extreme Christocentrism, Christian and Muslim homophobia, and secular ideologies that tend to disrespect and marginalize church folks and religious scholars. A new African-centered ecumenism is called for that will severely test our commitment to democracy and religious pluralism, but as recent history in South Africa and on the mall in the nation's capital will attest, religiopolitical miracles do happen from time to time.

While I do not regard this development as a black separatism that eschews cooperation with the white church and community, I do believe that we ought finally to face the fact that the white liberal churches, by themselves, are unable to dismantle the structures of racism and economic injustice. If black theology can help to bring about a new coalition of religious and secular activists in our own ranks, and between us and white allies who are ready to join forces with us, the groundwork that was laid thirty years ago by this remarkable little book, *Black Theology and Black Power*, will not have been in vain. Then, perhaps, in the next century some of us will witness the power of black religious thought to liberate not only African Americans, but people of every race, color, class, gender, and religion in this country and even in other parts of the world.

Notes

1. *Black Theology and Black Power*, preface to the twentieth anniversary edition (New York: Harper & Row, 1989), ix. Current edition published by Orbis Books (Maryknoll, N.Y.: 1997).

2. 1It should be noted that in addition to the questionnaire, respondents were asked to react to four articles (three published and one soon to be published): Henry Mitchell's "Black Power and the Christian Church," in the *Baptist Journal of History and Theology*; Vincent Harding's "The Religion of Black Power," in Donald R. Cutler (ed.), *The Religious Situation*, 1968; Preston Williams's "The Black Church: Origin, History, Present Dilemmas," which I believe appeared in the *Journal of Religious Thought*; and my own, "The Case for a New Black Church Style," which came out in the fall of 1968 in *The Church Metropolis* magazine.

3. "The NCNC Theological Commission Project: A Summary Report," Fall, 1968, 17-18.

4. James H. Cone and Gayraud S. Wilmore, eds. *Black Theology: A Documentary History, vol. 1: 1966-1979* (Maryknoll, N.Y.: Orbis Books, 1993), 38.

5. Dwight N. Hopkins and George C. L. Cummings, eds. *Cut Loose Your Stammering Tongue: Black Theology in the Slave Narratives* (Maryknoll, N.Y.: Orbis Books, 1991), xv-xvi.

6. "A Revolution Unfulfilled, but Not Invalidated," in James H. Cone, *A Black Theology of Liberation*, twentieth anniversary edition (Maryknoll, N.Y.: Orbis Books, 1990), 145-69.

7. This essay was originally given as a presentation at the conference on "Black Theology as Public Discourse: From Retrospect to Prospect," hosted by the Divinity School of the University of Chicago, April 2-5, 1998. The conference, organized by Dwight N. Hopkins, anticipated the thirtieth anniversary of the publication of James H. Cone's *Black Theology and Black Power* (1969).

8. C. Eric Lincoln, *The Black Muslims in America* (Boston: Beacon Press, 1961), 100.

9. James H. Cone, *A Black Theology of Liberation*, xix.

10. "Black Theology in 1976," Statement by the National Conference of Black Christians, in Gayraud S. Wilmore and James H. Cone, eds., *Black Theology: A Documentary History*, 343.

11. A case in point is what happened with the leadership of the National Baptist Convention, Inc., despite the effort of a few ministers of proven integrity and a progressive orientation to turn the convention around before the election of Dr. Lyons.

12. See for example, the Faith Journey Series of the United Presbyterian Church, the curriculum of the National Baptist Convention of America, and the materials cur-

rently produced by the African American Christian Publishing and Communications Company of Urban Ministries, Inc., of Chicago.

13. It is not possible to suggest here an adequate bibliography for these three areas of black scholarly research, but for a beginning these few books are recommended as pathfinders for this kind of reconstruction of black Christian education: Charles B. Copher, *Black Biblical Studies: An Anthology of Charles B. Copher* (Chicago: Black Light Fellowship, 1993); Cheikh Anta Diop, *The African Origin of Civilization: Myth or Reality* (New York: Lawrence Hill & Co., 1974); Cain Hope Felder, *Troubling Biblical Waters: Race, Class, and Family* (Maryknoll, N.Y.: Orbis Books, 1989); Walter A. McCray, *The Black Presence in the Bible* (Chicago: Black Light Fellowship, 1989); Ivan Van Sertima, *Nile Valley Civilizations: Proceedings of the Nile Valley Conference* (Atlanta: Journal of African Civilization, 1985); Margaret W. Creel, *A Peculiar People: Slave Religion and Community Culture Among the Gullahs* (New York: New York University Press, 1988); Randall C. Bailey and Jacquelyn Grant, eds. *The Recovery of Black Presence: An Interdisciplinary Exploration. Essays in Honor of Charles B. Copher* (Nashville: Abingdon Press, 1995); Gayraud S. Wilmore, *Black Religion and Black Radicalism*, third revised edition (Maryknoll, N.Y.: Orbis Books, 1998); and Robert M. Franklin, *Another Day's Journey: Black Churches Confronting the American Crisis* (Minneapolis: Fortress Press, 1997).

14. Gayraud S. Wilmore, *The Nature and Task of Christian Education from an African American Perspective* (Louisville: Witherspoon Press, Presbyterian Church booklet, 1998), 10.

15. Gayraud S. Wilmore and James H. Cone, *Black Theology: A Documentary History*, 342. Italics mine.

16. Garth Kasimu Baker-Fletcher, ed. *Black Religion After the Million Man March* (Maryknoll, N.Y.: Orbis Books, 1998).

17. Ibid., 110.

18. Ibid., 118.

19

Looking Back,
Going Forward

Black Theology as Public Theology

JAMES H. CONE

This Black Theology Conference provides an opportunity for me to reflect on the origin and development of my theological perspective. When I think about my vocation, I go back to my childhood years in Bearden, Arkansas—a rural community of approximately 1,200 people. I do not remember Bearden for nostalgic reasons. In fact, I seldom return there in person, because of persistent racial tensions in my relations with the whites and lingering ambivalence in my feelings toward the blacks. I am not and do not wish to be Bearden's favorite son. My brother, Cecil, also a theologian and a preacher, has been bestowed that honor by the African American community, a distinction he gladly accepts and a role he fulfills quite well.

I remember Bearden because it is the place where I first discovered myself— as *black* and *Christian*. There, the meaning of black was defined primarily by the menacing presence of whites, which no African American could escape. I grew up during the age of Jim Crow (1940s and early 1950s). I attended segregated schools, drank water from colored fountains, went to movies in balconies, and—when absolutely necessary—greeted white adults at the back doors of their homes. I also observed the contempt and brutality that white law meted out to the blacks who transgressed their racial mores or who dared to question their authority. Bearden white people, like most southerners of that time, could be mean and vicious, and I, along with other blacks, avoided them whenever possible, as if they were poisonous snakes.

The Christian part of my identity was shaped primarily at Macedonia A.M.E. Church. Every Sunday and sometimes on weeknights, I encountered Jesus through rousing sermons, fervent prayers, spirited gospel songs, and the passionate testimonies of the people. Jesus was the dominant reality at

Macedonia and in black life in Bearden. The people walked with him and told him about their troubles as if he were a trusted friend who understood their trials and tribulations in this unfriendly world. They called Jesus "the lily of the valley and the bright and morning star," the "Rose of Sharon and the Lord of life," a "very present help in time of trouble." The people often shouted and danced, clapped their hands and stamped their feet as they bore witness to the power of Jesus' Spirit in their midst—"building them up where they are torn down and propping them up on every leaning side."

As he did for the people of Macedonia, Jesus became a significant presence in my life, too. I do not remember the exact date or time I "turned to Jesus," as the conversion experience was called. At home, church, and school, at play and at work, Jesus was always there, as the anchor of life, giving it meaning and purpose and bestowing hope and faith in the ultimate justice of things. Jesus was that reality who empowered black people to know that they were not the worthless human beings that white people said they were.

There were no atheists in the "Cotton Belt," as the "colored" section of Bearden was called—no proclaimers of Nietzsche's "God is dead" philosophy and none of the "cultured despisers" of religion that Friedrich Schleiermacher wrote to in 1799. The closest to Nietzsche's atheists and Schleiermacher's cultured despisers were the bluespeople who drank corn whiskey and boogied slowly and sensually to the deep guttural sound of the raunchy music at the juke joints every Friday and Saturday night. The sounds of Bessie Smith, Muddy Waters, and Howlin' Wolf took center stage as they belted out "I Used To Be Your Sweet Mama," "Hoochie Coochie Man," and "Somebody in My Home." Such music was called the "lowdown dirty blues."

Unlike the churchpeople, the bluespeople found the Sunday religion of Jesus inadequate for coping with their personal problems and the social contradictions they experienced during the week. As church people soothed their souls with the song, "Lord, I want to be a Christian in my heart," the people at the honky-tonk transcended their agony by facing it with stoic defiance or, as James Baldwin called it, "ironic tenacity"[1]: "I got the blues, but I'm too damned mean to cry."

Sometimes sharp tensions emerged between the celebrants of Saturday night and those of Sunday morning. But each group respected the other, because both knew that they were seeking, in their own way, to cope with the same troubles of life. Some people moved between the two groups during different periods of their lives, as my father did. But it was not possible to be a member in good standing in both groups at the same time, because the church demanded that an individual make a choice between the blues and the spirituals, between the "devil's music" and the "sweet melodies of Jesus." Baptist and Methodist churches, the only black denominations in Bearden, regularly accepted backsliders back into the fold, provided they repented of their wrongdoing and declared their intentions to lead a good and righteous life in service to the Lord. My father had a few lapses in faith, because he found it hard to cope with life's adversities without taking a nip of gin and hanging out with the bluespeople in

order to add a little spice to life not found at the church. But my mother moni-
tored him closely, and Macedonia readily received him back into the community of the faithful as often as he publicly repented.

During my childhood what puzzled me most about the religion of Jesus was
not the tension between Saturday night and Sunday morning in black life but
rather the conspicuous presence of the color bar in white churches. In Bearden,
like the rest of America, Sunday was the most segregated day of the week, and
11 A.M., the most segregated hour. Black and white Christians had virtually no
social or religious dealings with each other, even though both were Baptists and
Methodists—reading the same Bible, worshiping the same God, and reciting the
same confessions of faith in their congregations.

Although whites posted "Welcome" signs outside their churches, ostensibly
beckoning all visitors to join them in worship, blacks knew that the invitation
did not include them. "What kind of Christianity is it that preaches love and
practices segregation?" my brother Cecil and I, budding young theologians,
often asked each other. "How could whites exclude black people from their
churches and still claim Jesus as their Savior and the Bible as their holy book?"
We talked about testing the theological integrity of white faith by seeking to integrate one of their churches but felt that the risks of bodily harm were too great.

Despite the ever-present reality of white supremacy, I do not ever remember
experiencing a feeling of inferiority because of what whites said about me or
about other black people. One reason was the stellar example my father and
mother set before me. They were part of that cloud of black witnesses that
James Baldwin wrote about who "in the teeth of the most terrible odds,
achieved an unassailable and monumental dignity."[2] They taught me what
Baldwin told his nephew: "You can only be destroyed by believing that you
really are what the white world calls a *nigger*."[3]

My parents were strong and self-confident—exhibiting a determined opposition to white supremacy and creative leadership and great courage when they
and the black community faced adversity. Charlie and Lucy, as the people in
Bearden called them, were immensely intelligent, even though they had little
opportunity for formal education, having completed only the sixth and ninth
grades respectively. (With the support and encouragement of my father, my
mother went back and completed high school where her sons had graduated
earlier and also went on to finish her college degree four years later. She then
returned to teach in Bearden. I was struck by her determination.) Their education, they often told their sons, came from the "school of hard knocks"—
the experience of surviving with dignity in a society that did not recognize
black humanity.

The faith of Macedonia, which my parents imbibed deeply, was a powerful
antidote against the belief that blacks were less than whites. According to this
faith, God created all people equal—as brothers and sisters in the church and in
society. No person or group is better than any other. As evidence for that claim,
preachers and teachers often cited the text from the prophet Malachi: "Have we
not all one father? Hath not one God created us?" (2:10 KJV) They also quoted

Paul, *selectively*—carefully avoiding the ambiguous and problematic texts, especially in *Philemon* where Paul returned the slave Onesimus to his master and in *Ephesians* where servants were told to "be obedient to them who are your masters . . . as unto Christ" (Eph. 6:5 KJV).

Preachers and Sunday school teachers at Macedonia were quite skilled in picking biblical texts that affirmed their humanity. They especially liked Luke's account of Paul's sermon on Mars Hill where he said God made of one blood all nations of men [and women] to dwell on the face of the earth (Acts 17:26 KJV). They also quoted Paul's letter to the Galatians: "There is neither Jew nor Greek . . . neither slave nor free . . . neither male nor female." We are "all one in Christ Jesus" (3:28 KJV)—blacks and whites, as well as other human colors and orientations. When one truly believes that gospel and internalizes it in one's way of life, as I and many black Christians in Bearden did, it is possible to know that you are somebody even though the world treats you like nobody.

From the time I was conscious of being black and Christian, I recognized that I was a problem for America's white politicians and invisible to most of its practitioners of religion. I did not quite understand what made me problematic or invisible since skin color appeared to be a minor difference between human beings. Yet politicians found it difficult to pass laws to protect black humanity. Even those that were passed were rarely enforced. White ministers seemed not to notice the daily white assault on black humanity. They preached sermons about loving God and the neighbor as if the violence that whites committed against blacks did not invalidate their Christian identity.

While struggling to understand how whites reconciled racism with their Christian identity, I also encountered an uncritical faith in many black churches. They not only seemed to tolerate anti-intellectualism as whites tolerated racism; but they, like most whites in relation to racism, often promoted it. It was as if the less one knew and the louder one shouted Jesus' name, the closer one was to God.

I found it hard to believe that the God of Jesus condoned ignorance as if it was a virtue. It contradicted what my parents and teachers taught me about the value of education and a disciplined mind. It also contradicted what I read in history books about black slaves who risked life and limb in order to learn to read and write so they could understand more clearly the meaning of the freedom to which God had called them. I was, therefore, deeply troubled by the anti-intellectualism that permeated many aspects of the ministry in the black church.

How could ministers preach the gospel in a world they did not understand? How could they understand the gospel without disciplined reflection and critical debate? "A religion that won't stand the application of reason and common sense," wrote W. E. B. Du Bois, "is not fit for an intelligent dog."[4]

The search for a reasoned faith in a complex and ever-changing world was the chief motivation that led me to study at Garrett Theological Seminary (now Garrett-Evangelical). It seemed that the more I learned about the gospel through a critical study of the Bible, history, theology, and the practice of ministry, the more I needed and wanted to know about it. I wanted to explore its meanings for different social, political, and cultural contexts, past and present.

Theology quickly became my favorite subject in seminary because it opened the door to explore faith's meaning for the current time and situation in which I was living. I loved the give-and-take of theological debate and eagerly waited for the opportunity during and after classes to engage my professors and fellow students on the burning theological issues of the day. That was why I remained at Garrett and Northwestern University for the Ph.D. in systematic theology. After I completed the doctorate in spring 1965, writing a dissertation on Karl Barth's anthropology, I thought I had enough knowledge of the Christian faith to communicate it to persons anywhere in the world. Who would not feel adequately endowed after reading twelve volumes of Barth's *Church Dogmatics*?

But the Civil Rights and Black Power movements of the 1960s awakened me from my theological slumber. As I became actively involved in the black freedom movement that was exploding in the streets all over America, I soon discovered how limited my seminary education had been. The curriculum at Garrett and Northwestern had not dealt with questions that black people were asking as they searched for the theological meaning of their fight for justice in a white racist society. And as individuals and isolated students within a demanding educational system, neither I nor the token number of black students had the intellectual resources to articulate those questions. I found myself grossly ill-prepared, because I knew deep down that I could not repeat to a struggling black community the doctrines of the faith as they had been reinterpreted by Barth, Bultmann, Niebuhr, and Tillich for European colonizers and white racists in the United States. I knew that before I could say anything worthwhile about God and the black situation of oppression in the United States, I had to discover a theological identity that was accountable to the life, history, and culture of African American people.

In a way, my education had pulled me away from my people. The educational quest had been to master the theological systems of the well-known European theologians of the past and present. As students, we obediently spent most of our time reading books, listening to lectures, and writing papers about their views of God, Jesus, the Holy Spirit, and the church. But recognizing the community to whom I was accountable, I wanted to know more than just what Europeans and white Americans who emulated them thought about sacred reality. I was searching for a way to create a Christian theology out of the black experience of slavery, segregation, and the struggle for a just society. When I asked my professors what theology had to do with the black struggle for racial justice, they seemed surprised and uncomfortable with the question, not knowing what to say, and anxious to move on with the subject matter as they understood it. I was often told that theology and the struggle for racial justice were separate subjects, with the latter belonging properly in the disciplines of sociology and political science. Although I felt a disquieting unease with that response, I did not say much about it to my professors as they skirted around talking about what the gospel had to say to black people in a white society that had defined them as nonpersons.

While reading Martin Luther King, Jr., and Malcolm X, the blackness in my theological consciousness exploded like a volcano after many dormant years. I found my theological voice. Using the cultural and political insights of Malcolm and Martin, I discovered a way of articulating what I wanted to say about theology and race: it not only rejected the need for my professors' approval, but challenged them to exorcise the racism in their theologies. Malcolm taught me how to make theology black and never again to despise my African origin. Martin showed me how to make and keep theology Christian and never allow it to be used to support injustice. I was transformed from a *Negro* theologian to a *Black* theologian, from an understanding of theology as an analysis of God-ideas in books to an understanding of it as a disciplined reflection about God arising out of a commitment to the practice of justice for the poor.

The turn to blackness was an even deeper metanoia-experience than the turn to Jesus. It was spiritual, radically transforming my way of seeing the world and theology. Before I was born again into thinking black, I thought of theology as something remote from my history and culture, something that was primarily defined by Europeans whom I, at best, could only imitate. Blackness gave me new theological spectacles, which enabled me to move beyond the limits of white theology and empowered my mind to think wild, heretical thoughts when evaluated by white academic values. Blackness opened my eyes to see African American history and culture as one of the most insightful sources for knowing about God since the Bible was declared a canon. Blackness whetted my appetite for learning how to do theology with a black signature on it and thereby make it accountable to poor black people and not to the privileged white theological establishment. The revolution that Malcolm X created in my theological consciousness meant that I could no longer make peace with the intellectual mediocrity in which I had been trained. The more I trusted my experience the more new thoughts about God and theology whirled around in my head—so fast I could hardly contain my excitement.

Using the black experience as the starting point of theology raised the theodicy question in a profound and challenging way that was never mentioned in graduate school. It was James Baldwin's *The Fire Next Time* which poignantly defined the problem for me: "If [God's] love was so great, and if He loved all His children, why were we, the blacks, cast down so far?"[5] This was an existential, heart-wrenching question, which challenged the academic way in which the problem of evil was dealt with in graduate school. It forced me to search deep into a wellspring of blackness, not for a theoretical answer that would satisfy the dominant intellectual culture of Europe and the United States, but rather for a new way of doing theology that would empower the suffering black poor to fight for a more liberated existence.

In writing *Black Theology and Black Power* (1969), I suddenly understood what Karl Barth must have felt when he first rejected the liberal theology of his professors in Germany. It was a liberating experience to be free of my liberal and neo-orthodox professors, to be liberated from defining theology using abstract theological jargon that was unrelated to the life-and-death issues of black people. Although separated by nearly fifty years and dealing with completely different theological situations and issues, I felt a spiritual kinship with Barth, especially his writing of *The Epistle to the Romans* (1921) and in his public debate with Adolf Harnack, his former teacher.

As I think back to that time in the late 1960s, when white American theologians were writing and talking about the "death of God theology" as black people were fighting and dying in the streets, the energy swells once again. I was angry and could not keep it to myself. Like Malcolm X, I felt I was the angriest black theologian in America.[6] I had to speak out, as forcefully as I knew how, against the racism I witnessed in theology, the churches, and the broader society. And that was why I began to write.

The anger I felt while writing *Black Theology and Black Power* was fueled by the assassination of Martin Luther King, Jr. Thirty years later as I prepared the Aims of Religion address on the anniversary date of King's death, I am still just as angry, because America, when viewed from the perspective of the black poor, is no closer to King's dream of a just society than when he was killed. While the black middle class has made considerable economic progress, the underclass, despite America's robust economy, is worse off in 1998 than in 1968. While the statistics are well known, they still fail to shock or outrage most Americans. One-third of young black males are involved in the criminal justice system. One-half of black babies are born in poverty, and their life expectancy in the urban ghetto is lower than that of Bangladesh.

America is still two societies: one rich and middle class, the other poor and working class. One-third of the African American population is poor. Predominantly women and children, they are, in the words of William J. Wilson, the truly disadvantaged,[7] with few skills that enable them to compete in this technological, informational age. To recognize the plight of the poor does not require academic dissection. It requires only a drive into the central cities of the nation to see people living in places not fit for human habitation.

What deepens my anger today is the appalling silence of white theologians on racism in the United States and the modern world. Whereas this silence has been partly broken in several secular disciplines, theology remains virtually mute. From Jonathan Edwards to Walter Rauschenbusch and Reinhold Niebuhr and up to the present moment, progressive white theologians, with few exceptions, write and teach as if they do not need to address the radical contradiction that racism creates for Christian theology. They do not write about slavery, colonialism, segregation, and the profound cultural link these horrible crimes created between white supremacy and Christianity. The cultural bond between European values and Christian beliefs is so deeply enmeshed in the American psyche and thought process that their identification is assumed. White images and ideas dominate the religious life of Christians and the intellectual life of theologians, reinforcing the "moral" right of white people to dominate people of color economically and politically. White supremacy is so widespread that it becomes a "natural" way of viewing the world. We must ask therefore: Is racism so deeply embedded in Euro-American history and culture that it is impossible to do theology without being anti-black?

There is historical precedent for such ideological questioning. After the Jewish Holocaust, Christian theologians were forced to ask whether anti-Judaism was so deeply woven into the core of the gospel and Western history that theology was no longer possible without being anti-Semitic? Recently feminists asked an equally radical question regarding whether patriarchy was so deeply rooted in biblical faith and its male theological tradition that one could not do Christian theology without justifying the oppression of women. Gay and lesbian theologians are following the feminist lead and are asking whether homophobia is an inherent part of biblical faith. And finally, Third World theologians, particularly in Latin America, forced many progressive First World theologians to revisit Marx's class critique of religion or run the risk of making Christianity a tool for exploiting the poor.

Race criticism is just as crucial for the integrity of Christian theology as any critique in the modern world. Christianity was blatantly used to justify slavery, colonialism, and segregation for nearly five hundred years. Yet this great contradiction is consistently neglected by the same white male theologians who would never ignore the problem that critical reason poses for faith in a secular world. They still do theology as if white supremacy creates no serious problem for Christian belief. Their silence on race is so conspicuous that I sometimes wonder why they are not greatly embarrassed by it.

How do we account for such a long history of white theological blindness to racism and its brutal impact on the lives of African people? Is it because white theologians do not know about the tortured history of the Atlantic slave trade, which according to British historian Basil Davidson, "cost Africa at least fifty million souls?"[8] Have they forgotten about the unspeakable crimes of colonialism? In the Congo alone, "Reputable estimates suggest that between five and eight million [people] were killed in the course of twenty-three years."[9]

Two hundred forty-four years of slavery and one hundred years of legal segregation, augmented by a reign of white terror that lynched more than five thousand blacks, defined the meaning of America as "white over black."[10] White supremacy shaped the social, political, economic, cultural, and religious ethos in the churches, the academy, and the broader society. Seminary and divinity school professors contributed to America's white nationalist perspective by openly advocating the superiority of the white race over all others. The highly regarded church historian, Philip Schaff of Union Seminary in New York (1870-1893), spoke for most white theologians in the nineteenth century when he said: "The Anglo-Saxon and Anglo-American, of all modern races, possess the strongest national character and the one best fitted for universal dominion."[11]

Present-day white theologians do not express their racist views as blatantly as Philip Schaff. They do not even speak of the "Negro's cultural backwardness," as America's best-known social ethicist Reinhold Niebuhr did as late as 1965.[12] To speak as Schaff and Niebuhr spoke would be politically incorrect in this era of multiculturalism and color blindness. But that does not mean that today's white theologians are less racist. It only means that their racism is concealed or unconscious. As long as religion scholars do not engage racism in their intellectual work, we can be sure that they are as racist as their grandparents, whether they acknowledge it or not. By not engaging America's crimes against black people, white theologians are treating the nation's violent racist past as if it were dead. But as William Faulkner said, "The past is never dead; it is not even past." Racism is so deeply embedded in American history and culture that we cannot get rid of this cancer by simply ignoring it.

There can be no justice without memory—without remembering the horrible crimes committed against humanity and the great human struggles for justice. But oppressors always try to erase the history of their crimes and often portray themselves as the innocent ones. Through their control of the media and religious, political, and academic discourse, "They're able," as Malcolm put it, "to make the victim look like the criminal and the criminal look like the victim."[13]

Even when white theologians reflect on God and suffering, the problem of theodicy, they almost never make racism a central issue in their analysis of the challenge that evil poses for the Christian faith. If they should happen to mention racism, it is usually just a footnote or only a marginal comment. They almost never make racism the subject of a sustained analysis. It is amazing that racism could be so prevalent and violent in American life and yet so absent in white theological discourse.

President Clinton's call for a national dialogue on race has created a context for public debate in the churches, the academy, and the broader society. Where are the white theologians? What guidance are they providing for this debate? Are they creating a theological understanding of racism that enables whites to have a meaningful conversation with blacks and other people of color? Unfortunately, instead of searching for an understanding of the great racial divide, white religion scholars are doing their searching in the form of a third quest for the historical Jesus. I am not opposed to this academic quest. But if we could get a significant number of white theologians to study racism as seriously as they investigate the historical Jesus and other academic topics, they might discover how deep the cancer of racism is embedded not only in the society but also in the narrow way in which the discipline of theology is understood.

Although black liberation theology emerged out of the Civil Rights and Black Power movements of the 1960s, white theologians ignored it as if it was not worthy to be regarded as an academic discipline. It was not until Orbis Books published the translated works of Latin American liberation theologians that white North American male theologians cautiously began to talk and write about liberation theology and God's solidarity with the poor. But they still ignored the black poor in the United States, Africa, and Latin America. Our struggle to make sense out of the fight for racial justice was dismissed as too narrow and divisive. White U.S. theologians used the Latin American focus on class to minimize and even dismiss the black focus on race. African Americans wondered how U.S. whites could take sides with the poor out there in Latin America without first siding with the poor here in North America. It was as if they had forgotten about their own complicity in the suffering of the black poor who were often only a stone's throw from the seminaries and universities where they taught theology.

White theology's amnesia about racism is partly due to the failure of black theologians to mount a persistently radical race critique of Christian theology—one so incisive and enduring that no one could do theology without engaging white supremacy in the modern world. American and European theologians became concerned about anti-Semitism only because Jews did not let them forget the Christian complicity in the Holocaust. Feminists transformed the consciousness of American theologians through persistent, hard-hitting analysis of the evils of patriarchy, refusing to let any man anywhere in the world forget the past and present male assault against women. It is always the organic intellectuals of an exploited group who must take the lead in exposing the hidden crimes of criminals.

While black theologians' initial attack on white religion shocked white theologians, we did not shake the racist foundation of modern white theology.[14] With the assistance of James Forman's "Black Manifesto"[15] and the black caucuses in Protestant denominations, black theological critiques of racism were successful in shaking up the white churches. But white theologians in the seminaries, university departments of religion, divinity schools, and professional societies refused to acknowledge racism as a theological problem and continued their business as usual, as if the lived experience of blacks was theologically vacuous.

One reason why black theologians have not developed an enduring radical race critique stems from our uncritical identification with the dominant Christian and integrationist tradition in African American history. We are the children of the black church and the Civil Rights movement. The spirituals have informed our theology more than the blues, Howard Thurman more than W. E. B. Du Bois, Martin Luther King, Jr., more than Malcolm X, and male preachers more than women writers. We failed to sustain the critical side of the black theological dialectic and opted for acceptance into white Christian America. When whites opened the door to receive a token number of us into the academy, church, and society, the radical edge of our race critique was quickly dropped as we enjoyed our new-found privileges.

Womanist and second-generation black male theologians, biblical scholars, and historians are moving in the right directions. The strength of these new intellectual developments lies in their refusal to simply repeat the ideas of the original advocates of black theology. They are breaking new theological ground, building on, challenging, and moving beyond the founders of black theology. Using the writings of Zora Neale Hurston, Alice Walker, Toni Morrison, and a host of other women writers past and present, womanist theologians broke the monopoly of black male theological discourse. They challenged the male advocates of black theology to broaden their narrow focus on race and liberation and to incorporate gender, class, and sexuality critiques and the themes of survival and quality of life in our theological discourse.[16] Some younger black male critics locate the limits of black theology in its focus on blackness,[17] and others urge a deeper commitment to it, focusing especially on the slave narratives.[18] Still others suggest that the Christian identity of black theology contributes to black passivity in the face of suffering.[19] Biblical scholars and historians are laying exegetical and historical foundations for a critical re-reading of the Bible in the light of the history and culture of black people.[20] All these critiques and proposals make important contributions to the future development of black theology. But what troubles me about all these new theological constructs is the absence of a truly radical race critique.

Malcolm X was the most formidable race critic in the United States during the twentieth century. He was the great master of suspicion in regard to American democracy and the Christian faith. His critique of racism in Christianity and American culture was so forceful that even black Christians were greatly disturbed when they heard his analysis. His contention that "Christianity was a white man's religion" was so persuasive that many black Christians left churches to join the Nation of Islam. The rapid growth of the religion of Islam in the African American community is largely due to the effectiveness of Malcolm's portrayal of Christianity as white nationalism. It was Malcolm via the Black Power movement who forced black theologians to take a critical look at white religion and to develop a hermeneutic of suspicion regarding black Christianity. How can African Americans merge the "double self"—the black and the Christian—"into a better and truer self,"[21] especially since Africa is the object of ridicule in the modern world and Christianity is hardly distinguishable from European culture?

While we black theologians appropriated Malcolm in our initial critique of white religion, we did not wrestle with Malcolm long enough. We quickly turned to Martin King. The mistake was not in moving toward King but rather in leaving Malcolm behind. We need them both as a double-edged sword to slay the dragon of theological racism. Martin and Malcolm represent the yin and yang in the black attack on racism. One without the other misses the target—the affirmation of blackness in the beloved community of humankind.

Malcolm X teaches us that African Americans cannot be free without accepting their blackness, without loving Africa as the place of our origin and meaning. Martin King teaches us that no people can be free except in the beloved community of humankind—not just blacks with blacks or whites with whites but all of us together (including Indians, Asians, Hispanics, gays, lesbians, and bisexuals) in a truly multicultural community. Malcolm alone makes it too easy for blacks to go it alone and for whites to say "Begone!" Martin alone makes it easy for whites to ask for reconciliation without justice and for middle-class blacks to grant it, as long as they are treated specially. Putting Martin and Malcolm together enables us to overcome the limitations of each and to build on the strengths of both and thereby to move blacks, whites, and other Americans toward racial healing and understanding.

There can be no racial healing without dialogue, without ending the white silence on racism. There can be no reconciliation without honest and frank conversation. Racism is still with us in the academy, in the churches, and in every segment of the society because we would rather push this problem under the rug than find a way to deal with its past and present manifestations.

Most whites do not like to talk about racism because it makes them feel guilty, a truly uncomfortable feeling. They would rather forget about the past and think only about the present and future. I understand that. But I only ask whites to consider how uncomfortable the victims of racism must feel, as they try to cope with the attitudes of whites who act as if racism ceased with the passage of the 1964 Civil Rights Bill. At least when people express their racism overtly, there is some public recognition of its existence and a possibility of racial healing. Silence is racism's best friend.

"A time comes when silence is betrayal,"[22] Martin King said. That time has come for white theologians. Racism is one of the great contradictions of the gospel in modern times. White theologians who do not oppose racism publicly and rigorously engage it in their writings are part of the problem and must be exposed as the enemies of justice. No one, therefore, can be neutral or silent in the face of this great evil. We are either for it or against it.

Black theologians must end their silence too. We have opposed racism much too gently. We have permitted white theological silence in exchange for the rewards of being accepted by the white theological establishment. This is a terrible price to pay for the few crumbs that drop from the white master's table. We must replace theological deference with courage, and thereby confront openly and lovingly silent white racists or be condemned as participants in the betrayal of our own people.

In 1903, W. E. B. Du Bois prophesied, "The problem of the twentieth century is the problem of the color-line—the relation of the darker to the lighter races of [people] in Asia and Africa, in America and the islands of the sea."[23] As we stand at the threshold of the next century, that remarkable prophecy is as relevant today as it was when Du Bois uttered it. The challenge for black theology in the twenty-first century is to develop an enduring race critique that is so comprehensively woven into Christian understanding that no one will be able to forget the horrible crimes of white supremacy in the modern world.

Notes

1. James Baldwin, *The Fire Next Time* (New York: Dell, 1964), 61.

2. Ibid., 21.

3. Ibid., 14.

4. Cited in Manning Marable, "The Black Faith of W. E. B. Du Bois: Sociocultural and Political Dimensions of Black Religion," *The Southern Quarterly*, vol. 23, no. 3 (Spring 1985): 21.

5. James Baldwin, *The Fire Next Time*, 46.

6. Many people called Malcolm X "the angriest Negro in America." See his *Autobiography* (New York: Ballentine Books, 1965), 366.

7. See William Julius Wilson, *The Truly Disadvantaged: The Inner City, the Underclass and Public Policy* (Chicago: University of Chicago Press, 1987).

8. Basil Davidson, *The African Slave Trade: Precolonial History 1450-1850* (Boston: Little, Brown, 1961), 80.

9. Louis Turner, *Multinational Companies and the Third World* (New York: Hill and Wang, 1973), 27.

10. See especially Winthrop D. Jordan, *White Over Black: American Attitudes toward the Negro 1550-1812* (Baltimore: Penguin Books, 1969).

11. Cited in Martin E. Marty, *Righteous Empire: The Protestant Experience in America* (New York: Dial Press, 1970), 17.

12. See Reinhold Niebuhr, "Man's Tribalism As One Source of His Inhumanity," in *Man's Nature and His Communities* (New York: Charles Scribner's Sons, 1965), 84-105; and his "Justice to the American Negro from State, Community and Church," in *Pious and Secular America* (New York: Charles Scribner's Sons, 1958), 78-85.

13. *Malcolm X Speaks* (New York: Grove Press, 1965), 165.

14. In addition to *Black Theology and Black Power* (Maryknoll, N.Y.: Orbis Books, 1997; originally 1969), my contribution to black theology's race critique included *A Black Theology of Liberation* (Maryknoll, N.Y.: Orbis Books, 1985; originally 1970) and *God of the Oppressed* (Maryknoll, N.Y.: Orbis Books, 1998; originally 1975). Other critiques were Albert B. Cleage, *The Black Messiah* (New York: Sheed & Ward, 1968); J. Deotis Roberts, *Liberation and Reconciliation: A Black Theology* (Maryknoll, N.Y.: Orbis Books, 1994; originally 1971), *A Black Political Theology* (Philadelphia: Westminster, 1974), and Gayraud S. Wilmore's *Black Religion and Black Radicalism* (Maryknoll, N.Y.: Orbis Books, 1998; originally 1972). Significant essays included Vincent Harding, "Black Power and the American Christ," *Christian Century*, January, 4, 1967, "The Religion of Black Power," in *Religious Situation 1968*, ed. D. R. Cutler (Boston: Beacon, 1968) and Herbert O. Edwards, "Racism and Christian Ethics in America," *Katallagete* (winter 1971).

15. See "The Black Manifesto," in James H. Cone and Gayraud S. Wilmore, eds., *Black Theology: A Documentary History, Vol. One, 1966-1979* (Maryknoll, N.Y.: Orbis Books, 1993), 27-36.

16. See "Womanist Theology," in James H. Cone and Gayraud S. Wilmore, eds., *Black Theology: A Documentary History, Vol. Two, 1980-1992* (Maryknoll, N.Y.: Orbis Books, 1993), 257-351.

17. See Victor Anderson, *Beyond Ontological Blackness: An Essay on African American Religious and Cultural Criticism* (New York: Continuum, 1995).

18. See "The Second Generation," in James H. Cone and Gayraud S. Wilmore, eds., *Black Theology: A Documentary History,Vol. Two*, 15-75; see also Josiah U. Young, *A Pan-African Theology: Providence and the Legacies of the Ancestors* (Trenton, N.J.: Africa World Press, 1992); Dwight N. Hopkins and George Cummings, eds., *Cut Loose Your Stammering Tongue: Black Theology in the Slave Narratives* (Maryknoll, N.Y.: Orbis Books, 1991); Dwight N. Hopkins, *Shoes That Fit Our Feet: Sources for a Constructive Black Theology* (Maryknoll, N.Y.: Orbis Books, 1993); Garth Kasimu Baker-Fletcher, *Xodus: An African American Male Journey* (Minneapolis: Fortress, 1996); Riggins R. Earl, *Dark Symbols, Obscure Signs: God, Self, and Community in the Slave Mind* (Maryknoll, N.Y.: Orbis Books, 1993).

19. See Anthony B. Pinn, *Why, Lord?: Suffering and Evil in Black Theology* (New York: Continuum, 1995). Pinn is building on an earlier critique of black theology by William R. Jones, *Is God a White Racist?: A Preamble to Black Theology* (Boston: Beacon, 1998; originally 1973).

20. See "New Directions in Black Biblical Interpretation" in James H. Cone and Gayraud S. Wilmore, eds., *Black Theology: A Documentary History, Vol. Two*, 177-254; Cain H. Felder, *Troubling Biblical Waters: Race, Class, and Family* (Maryknoll, N.Y.: Orbis Books, 1989); Cain H. Felder, ed., *Stony the Road We Trod: African American Biblical Interpretation* (Minneapolis: Fortress, 1991); Brian K. Blount, *Go*

Preach!: Mark's Kingdom Message and the Black Church Today (Maryknoll, N.Y.: Orbis Books, 1998); Theophus H. Smith, *Conjuring Culture: Biblical Formations of Black America* (New York: Oxford, 1994).

21. W. E. B. Du Bois, *The Souls of Black Folk* (Greenwich, Conn.: Fawcett Publications, 1961), 23.

22. Martin Luther King, Jr., "Beyond Vietnam," a pamphlet of the Clergy and Laymen Concerned about Vietnam, April 4, 1967.

23. W. E. B. Du Bois, *The Souls of Black Folk*, 23.

Contributors

Christopher Beem directs the program Democracy and Community at the Johnson Foundation in Racine, Wisconsin.

Stephen L. Carter is the William Nelson Cromwell Professor of Law at Yale University.

Rebecca S. Chopp is the Charles Howard Candler Professor of Theology and Provost at Emory University, Atlanta, Georgia.

James H. Cone is the Charles A. Briggs Distinguished Professor of Systematic Theology, Union Theological Seminary, New York City.

Jean Bethke Elshtain is the Laura Spelman Rockefeller Professor of Social and Political Ethics, The Divinity School, the Department of Political Science, and the Committee on International Relations; all at the University of Chicago.

Jacquelyn Grant is the Callaway Professor of Systematic Theology and Director of Black Women in Church and Society at the Interdenominational Theological Center, Atlanta, Georgia

Renée Leslie Hill is an independent scholar from Pasadena, California.

Dwight N. Hopkins teaches theology at The Divinity School, the University of Chicago.

Manning Marable is Professor of History and founding Director of the Institute for Research in African American Studies at Columbia University, New York City.

Peter J. Paris is the Elmer G. Homrighausen Professor of Christian Social Ethics at Princeton Theological Seminary.

Jamie T. Phelps, is a Roman Catholic woman religious who has been a member of the Adrian Dominican Congregation since 1959. Currently she is Visiting Professor of Theology at Loyola University, Chicago.

Rosemary Radford Ruether is the Georgia Harkness Professor of Applied Theology at Garrett-Evangelical Theological Seminary in Evanston, Illinois.

Silvia Regina de Lima Silva is a professor at the Latin American Biblical University in San José, Costa Rica.

J. Alfred Smith, Sr., is the senior pastor of the Allen Temple Baptist Church in Oakland, California. Allen Temple is a national leader in both the Progressive National Baptist Convention and in the American Baptist Churches, U.S.A.

Linda E. Thomas teaches theology and anthropology at Garrett-Evangelical Theological Seminary, Evanston, Illinois, and is the director of the Center for the Church and the Black Experience at Garrett.

Emilie M. Townes is Professor of Christian Ethics at Union Theological Seminary, New York City.

David Tracy is the Andrew Thomas Greeley and Grace McNichols Greeley Distinguished Service Professor of Roman Catholic Studies and Professor of Theology; Professor in the Committee on the Analyses of Ideas; and Professor in the Committee on Social Thought; all at the University of Chicago.

Cornel West is the Alphonse Fletcher, Jr., University Professor at Harvard University.

Gayraud S. Wilmore is a scholar in the areas of black religious studies, American religion, and church history. Wilmore co-initiated the first public black religious interpretation of black power, with the publication of a full-page ad in the *New York Times*, July 31, 1966. He is retired from the Interdenominational Theological Center, Atlanta, Georgia.

Jeremiah A. Wright, Jr., is senior pastor of the Trinity United Church of Christ in Chicago. Trinity is the fastest growing and largest church within the U.C.C. denomination.